GROVER CLEVELAND

Portrait of Grover Cleveland (*Courtesy of The New-York Historical Society, New York City*)

Grover Cleveland

Rexford G. Tugwell

The Macmillan Company

Collier-Macmillan Ltd., *London*

The Macmillan Company
Collier-Macmillan Canada Ltd., Toronto, Ontario

Printed in the United States of America

List of Illustrations

viii

Preface

WHEN I was a young man my family lived in a western New York village not far from Buffalo. My father was a member of the Buffalo Club on Delaware Avenue, and I sometimes went there with him. In the reception hall there was a large portrait of an impressive-looking man, dressed in a heavy broadcloth suit and a choker collar, who must have weighed well over two hundred pounds. It was obvious that he had been important, and it was obvious, too, that if the Buffalo Club gave his portrait such prominence its members were proud of him.

I discovered that they were. He was the second President of the United States to have come from Buffalo; before becoming President he had been mayor of the city and governor of the state. The members were proud, too, of Millard Fillmore, who had been their first President; but Fillmore had been nothing like so strong a character as Grover Cleveland. Not emphasized was the fact that Cleveland had not been a regular member. He had been made an honorary one after becoming mayor. Before that he had hardly been acceptable to such respectable company.

I recognized the portrait at once because I had gone to high school in the city and had worked for a time on the Buffalo *Courier* as a reporter. I had naturally heard a good deal about Cleveland. All Buffalonians were proud of him and there were many stories about his career; but by then there were very few persons still alive who could actually recall him. He had left the city to become governor in 1882 and, except for a few visits, had not returned. After he became President he never visited the city at all except for one or two ceremonial occasions. The reason was that, although he had been an outstanding mayor and governor, when he had been a candidate for the presidency, an old scandal had been exhumed and blown up to exaggerated proportions. He felt that the affair had been taken advantage of by some of the clergy who wished to defeat him. He also felt that his friends, who had known the facts, had not taken much trouble in his behalf. And so he carried a bitter feeling about Buffalo until the end of his life.

Later Buffalonians preferred to forget his feeling about their city and adopted him as a heroic civic figure, hence the portrait in the club.

Some of the older newspapermen passed on to me the tales of his life in the neighborhood of the *Courier* plant when Buffalo was a smaller but rapidly growing city. That neighborhood had been rough and tough. It was close to the waterfront and, besides being the commercial center, had fringes of railroad yards, factories, warehouses, and slums. There were saloons on every corner as well as other hangouts for drifting men who worked on the docks or as hands on the wheat, iron-ore, and lumber ships.

Cleveland had become a lawyer by studying with a firm whose offices had been across the street from the *Courier*. And when he had gone into practice he had stayed there. He had lived there, too, in a room close by. He had not married until he was President and as a bachelor had spent his leisure time in the German beer halls and saloons with companions who were quite different from the members of the Buffalo Club.

I was always curious about the twenty years or more he spent in this way. But there was no dependable information, only stories growing less credible—and more sensational—as time passed.

When I tried to establish some facts about this long passage in his life I found very little more to go on. I have quoted here from a book made up of a series of articles written for the *Buffalo Evening News* by Charles Armitage. But Armitage was almost too late; writing in the twenties, forty years after Cleveland's time, he had only faint recollections from very old men or second-hand accounts from their descendants. Allan Nevins, the distinguished historian, wrote a life of Cleveland (*Grover Cleveland: A Study in Courage,* Dodd, Mead and Co., N.Y., 1962), but it was notably lacking any convincing account of his Buffalo years. Denis Tilden Lynch, in another biography (*Grover Cleveland, A Man Four-*

Square, Liveright, N. Y., 1935), offered many more anecdotes about Cleveland's companions and a lively account of his leisure-time activities. But there still remains, and I am afraid there always will remain, a certain mystery. A strong and courageous statesman rose out of most unlikely circumstances to purge American politics of corruption and to establish the principle that public office is a public trust.

His distinguishing characteristic was plain honesty. He made an indispensable contribution to our history. True, he never discovered that this simple virtue was not enough, and that the changes boiling up in American life required much more sophisticated leadership than he was able to offer. But his first impact on politics and government was a shock that was badly needed. The nation would never return to the slack tolerance of corruption he shamed it into rejecting; he made integrity the first virtue of political life.

It remains to thank A. H. Kirchofer, publisher of the *Buffalo Evening News,* for his interest and for the loan of the Charles Armitage account of Cleveland's life in Buffalo, referred to several times in the text. The Buffalo and Erie County Historical Society and the Buffalo and Erie County Public Library regretted that they had no material not already used by historians, but their replies to my inquiries were helpful.

Most of all I wish to thank Richard Marek of The Macmillan Company for his labors with the text and for careful supervision as it was prepared for printing.

R . G . T U G W E L L

Southern Illinois University

An Outline of Cleveland's History

THE CLIMB

(Until Nineteen)

1837 Born in Caldwell, New Jersey, on March 13, son of Richard Falley Cleveland, Congregational-Presbyterian minister.

1841 Moved with his family to Fayetteville, New York, near Syracuse.

1850 Moved again to Clinton, New York, site of Hamilton College, district headquarters of the American Home Missionary Society. His father had been made director.

Visited his uncle, Lewis F. Allen, at Black Rock, just outside Buffalo, during the summer. His uncle was a prominent citizen with many interests, including a large farm on Grand Island in the Niagara River, where he maintained a pioneering herd of shorthorn cattle.

1852 The family had now grown to nine children and his father could not support them on his salary of one thousand dollars a year. Grover had been studying to enter Hamilton College; but at his father's request he went back to Fayetteville, where a position had been arranged for him in the general store of John McVickar at fifty dollars a year and keep. He lived over the store in a bare room without heat and with only a bed for furniture.

1853 His father was unable to keep up the heavy missionary work and he took another pastorate in Holland Patent, New York, but died almost at once, leaving the mother and children destitute. There was no further possibility of more education.

The oldest brother, William, had been appointed to a teaching post in the New York Institution for the Blind, and Grover followed him there to be an assistant teacher for a year.

1854 The school for the blind was an unhappy place to work, and after a year Grover went back to Holland Patent. He looked for work in the neighborhood, and in Utica and Syracuse, but with no success. In the spring he borrowed twenty-five dollars and started for Cleveland, Ohio, to try his fortune there. When he reached Buffalo and visited his uncle, he was persuaded to stay. He was given room, board, and fifty dollars for six months' work on the shorthorn herdbook his uncle was maintaining.

1855 He moved to a room in downtown Buffalo and began apprenticeship to the firm of Rogers, Bowen and Rogers, prominent lawyers. He had no pay at first but presently was allowed four dollars weekly for subsistence.

(Nineteen to Forty-one)

1858 When he was well on his way to becoming a lawyer, he began to do political work; at first, merely as a ward heeler. He helped to line up voters and generally to keep the machine running.

1859 He was admitted to the bar by the Supreme Court on the recommendation of his firm. He continued his political work, lived in bachelor's quarters, and spent much time in neighborhood saloons.

1862 He was made a delegate to the city convention of the party from the second ward—largely German; and was elected supervisor of his ward—his first elective office. Shortly afterward he was appointed assistant district attorney.

1863 The Civil War became something of a problem. His two brothers had enlisted in 1861 and it had been decided that he should take over support of the mother and younger sisters. When he was drafted he bought a substitute, as could be done then, and continued his usual pursuits.

1865 He was nominated for district attorney but was defeated in the election and returned to the practice of law.

1868 He was made a delegate to the Democratic state convention. In this year he formed law partnerships, first with Isaac K. Vanderpoel and then with A. P. Laning and Oscar Folsom.

1870 He had now moved to a suite of rooms in the Weed block and continued to eat and spend his evenings in saloon-restaurants. He seldom saw his uncle's family, although he went fishing occasionally at the farm on Grand Island. As the result of an irregular association with Maria Halpin, an illegitimate son was born.

He was elected sheriff of Erie County, and disappointed his fellow politicians by strict and honest administration of an office they had expected to profit by.

1872 His two brothers died, leaving him responsible for his mother
1878 and sisters, who still lived in Holland Patent.

During the next few years he became a trusted and prominent attorney, a partner in three successive firms: Bass, Cleveland and Bissell; Cleveland and Bissell; and Cleveland, Bissell and Sicard. Their offices were in the same Weed building as Cleveland's apartment. This was at Main and Swan streets, not far from where he had always lived since moving to town. He was now among the leading lawyers of Buffalo.

(Forty-one to Forty-seven)

1881 Nominated by the Democrats and elected mayor of Buffalo at the instance of a group of citizens concerned with the prevailing bipartisan corruption.

1882 By vetoing a street-cleaning contract wanted by grafting politicians, he won a reputation for unassailable honesty. This was followed by other acts as mayor that confirmed his reputation as an incorruptible public official.

Nominated and elected to the governorship of New York for much the same reason as he was chosen to be mayor—because of his reputation for efficiency and integrity.

1883 In a single year he had established himself as an able and independent governor, having no close ties with any political faction but supported by those most interested in good government. This did not include Tammany Hall, and opposition from that source soon became apparent.

His appointments were good, and his veto messages of bills giving favors to individuals and political groups were given wide publicity.

He became identified with the slogan "Public Office Is a Public Trust."

1884 Nominated by the Democrats and elected to the presidency against the Republican, James G. Blaine.

His campaign was directed mostly against the years of Republican power since the Civil War, during which the federal government had fallen into the same habits of corruption as the city and state governments he had just headed. Blaine, his opponent, was a well-known politician who rejected reform and stood for the same policies that had so discredited the party during Grant's presidency.

His worst problems during the campaign were his evasion of service during the war and his illegitimate child.

THE PRESIDENTIAL ADMINISTRATIONS

(first term)

1885 First year; he took office with a cabinet consisting of Thomas F. Bayard as Secretary of State, Daniel Manning as Secretary of the Treasury, William C. Whitney as Secretary of the Navy, William C. Endicott as Secretary of War, Augustus H. Garland as Attorney General, and Lucius Q. C. Lamar as Secretary of the Interior.

Troubles began at once as Democrats demanded government jobs and he refused to comply.

The most serious undertaking was the reform of the executive departments, especially Navy and Interior, where there had been scandalous situations for years.

1886 Second year; after a severe struggle with the Senate, the repeal of the Tenure of Office Act was secured.

Troubles concerning the free coinage of silver began—one phase of the long dispute between the advocates of soft money and supporters of the gold standard. In this year, also, the tariff and labor questions presented themselves in acute form.

On June 2 he married Frances Folsom, daughter of a former law partner, whose guardian he had been.

1887 Third year; he came into the open as an advocate of lowered tariffs. A message to the Congress in December set the issue for the campaign of 1888.

1888 Fourth year; he was defeated for reelection by Benjamin Harrison, Republican, largely on the tariff issue.

INTERVAL BETWEEN PRESIDENTIAL TERMS

1889 Moved to New York City and became an associate of Bangs, Stetson, Tracy and MacVeagh, a firm with a large corporate practice.

x v i

1890– Carried on law practice; established a summer home at Gray
1891 Gables on Buzzards Bay in Massachusetts. Lived quietly on
Madison Avenue in New York City.
1892 Was again candidate for the presidency against Benjamin Harrison and won. It was a dull contest with no new issues.

(second term)

1893 The Cabinet for the second administration included a Republican—Walter Q. Gresham—for Secretary of State, and John G. Carlisle, former Speaker of the House, for the Treasury. Richard Hoke Smith for Interior, Hilary A. Herbert for Navy; J. Sterling Morton for Agriculture and David S. Lamont for War.
Immediately after inauguration, he had to decide what to do about the serious depression just then beginning. In general he refused to intervene. But he had two problems resulting from it. One was depletion of the gold reserve as a result of hoarding and of speculation, and about this he was resolved on its protection. The other problem had to do also with money. More and more members of the Congress were resolved to add silver to the coinage in order to increase the money supply and raise prices. This he was also resolved to oppose. He won on this issue when the Congress repealed a Silver Purchase Act passed several years before.
In this year he had to decide whether he would accept the overturn of the Hawaiian monarchy and the application of the de facto government for United States recognition. His attitude was a firm refusal. This expressed an opposition to the acquisition of overseas territory and a repudiation of imperialism.
There also began a long struggle for the more moderate tariffs foreshadowed in the past campaign.
1894 Predominantly this was the year of prolonged debate about tariffs centering in the Wilson bill. This act passed the House satisfactorily but was so modified in the Senate that Cleveland refused to sign it. He did, however, allow it to become law without his signature.
There were continuing problems about revenue, and bonds had to be issued. The gold standard again was under attack and much time and effort were spent on the problem.
This was the year of the Pullman strike. When riots in the Chicago area threatened public order, the Army was called on;

there were many casualties, and controversy arose concerning the necessity for intervention.

1895 The outstanding event of this year was Cleveland's stand in a dispute with Britain over the Venezuela-British Guiana border. He insisted that the United States should be the arbiter.

The depression was continuing and even deepening. Misery throughout the country, and during the winter especially, was severe; but nothing was done in the way of relief.

Cleveland's worry was mostly about government finance. He was forced to accept a private arrangement with the House of Morgan to purchase government bonds for gold, thus maintaining solvency and bolstering the gold reserve.

1896 By now he had become extremely unpopular and there was no question of his running again in the fall election.

It gave him enormous anxiety to watch the growth of Populist sentiment, centering in attacks on the gold standard, and then to see the Democratic nomination go to William Jennings Bryan, one of the leaders of the silverite group in the Congress.

He was relieved when Bryan was defeated by McKinley, the Republican nominee.

RETIREMENT

1897– The Clevelands moved to Princeton, New Jersey, where the ex-
1908 President made his base until his death on June 24. He had no regular occupation but did consulting and writing. He became a trustee of the university.

The family life in Princeton was a happy one. Altogether, there were four children of his late marriage, one of whom died in Princeton. His wife, Frances, survived him for many years.

x v i i i

GROVER CLEVELAND

I

T H E boy who later became President Grover Cleveland
started his life as Stephen G. Cleveland. His friends in Fayetteville, New York, where most of his boyhood was spent, called
him Steve or *Big* Steve. He *was* big. At twelve, say, he did not yet
promise to be the enormously bulky figure he would become in his
twenties; but he was already large for his years and entitled to the
nickname. It was when he began to think of being a mayor, then
governor—and perhaps to consider how many documents he
would have to sign in future years—that he dropped the Stephen
and became plain Grover.

The preference for plainness shown by the shortening of his
name was a permanent trait. As much when he was a statesman as
when he was a boy, he disliked any sort of showing off. This may
seem somewhat out of character for a politician, but then he was
no ordinary politician. He had an amazingly rapid rise to the
presidency after being mayor of Buffalo, but his success was owed
to other causes than use of the usual political arts.

Of all the Presidents, only one other had in the end a reputation
that rested so wholly and simply on honesty. That, of course, was
Washington. And if Washington is thought of not as a revolutionary general or as the proprietor of an extensive estate but only as
a man, he and Cleveland were a good deal alike. Both were
heavy, somewhat narrow, a little dull, inclined to be conservative;
but both were of a sort to inspire confidence. They were competent for executive duties. Neither was a gifted speaker or writer,
but neither was afraid to say bluntly what was called for—as we
shall see in Cleveland's case. Neither cared to undertake more
than could be accomplished; but when necessary, both would risk

a good deal for a principle. This might be called stubbornness or even stupidity, but it was always respected.

Comparisons of this sort are, however, useful only in a limited way. By Cleveland's time, almost a hundred years after Washington's, the United States had become something very different from the small country Washington knew. The first President's was a seaboard nation. True, he looked to the West, and one of his fixed policies was expansion; but actually, the country beyond the Alleghenies was unexplored, its ownership still in dispute, more French, English or Spanish than American. Cleveland's nation was enormously expanded. It ran to the Pacific; there were transcontinental railroads; Texas had become a state, and the territories of New Mexico and Arizona were preparing their entrance. Its parts were still loosely bound together, but that there would be an indissoluble union was now a settled matter.

The industrial revolution was well under way too; and besides expansion, industrialization was the most important of the movements taking place. The wagon trains moving out across the prairies were now following trails that would soon be additional railway rights-of-way. The California gold rush and the development of Pacific ports had made even the inland Easterners conscious of national greatness.

Cleveland's parents, and he himself, were inland Easterners with no outlook on the sea. Most of the population of the country still lived on farms or in small villages, and most of it still lived within a few hundred miles of the Atlantic coast. When he was a boy, immigration was already changing the character of that population, but not yet noticeably. Most of his neighbors and friends, until he went on to Buffalo in 1855, were of British ancestry as the first colonists had been. They had common customs, common religious beliefs, a common view of government. They lived together without the turbulence that would begin to show itself when other nationals began to arrive. Even the Irish and Germans, although they were northern Europeans, made disturbances in the older settlers' ways of life that no one knew how to deal with. And as the growing factory system called for more laborers, the complications were intensified. This was beginning when Cleveland was a boy, and he grew up with problems of adjustment and accommoda-

Birthplace of Grover Cleveland, Caldwell, New Jersey (*Courtesy of The Firestone Library, Princeton University, Princeton, New Jersey*)

tion all around him. His methods of dealing with them were responsible for his election to successive public offices.

He lived until he was seventeen in villages little disturbed by the events of the greater world. And the household he lived in was similarly untouched. When he did come out into the larger world, he had a sturdy frame, a well-developed character, and the self-reliance of his ancestry. But he had no preparation, no schooling that would help or guide him in making his way.

He came to Buffalo in 1854, a boy disappointed in his hope for a college education, disappointed even in the hope of finding some opportunity for profitable work in central New York. It was in the city at the foot of Lake Erie that he made his way into the career that ended in the White House.

2

THE Clevelands were good people—always had been; they belonged to a sort of American elite. There never had been a wealthy Cleveland, although some had had a certain local prominence, and one had been so much a friend of Ben Franklin's that he had died in Franklin's house. But ever since Moses Cleveland had come from England in 1635, they had been merchants, landowners, artisans, and—especially—clergymen. It was characteristic of those equalitarian times that men of this sort should be poor. No one thought it a matter for comment. Something else counted most—that a family should be well regarded in its community. However close to the poverty line a man lived, he could still be a prominent citizen; and the Clevelands had always been.

The grandparents and parents of the future President lived in places that were typically American in their time. Besides the city of Buffalo, Grover is usually associated with three central New York villages—Fayetteville, Clinton, and Holland Patent. He was born in Caldwell, New Jersey, now a suburb of New York City; but since his parents moved to Fayetteville when he was four, his earliest recollections were of that small town of a thousand people. His father was a Presbyterian minister there and continued to be for nine years.

Life in a minister's home had its own customs, some of them confining. The puritan Sunday lasted from sundown on Saturday until sundown on Sunday, and during that twenty-four hours, all activities of most interest to young people were forbidden. Since the Cleveland household now had nine children—Grover being the fifth—the restraints were sometimes only restlessly observed. On Sunday, there were two long services, morning and evening, besides

Sunday school. It was usual for the sermon itself to last for two hours or more. It is still a matter for wonder how these earnest ministers could find the materials for such long discourses; and it is certain that the sermons must have grown very dull, loaded as they were with biblical references and involved theological argument. No wonder young people were restless!

Other village children might have been excused regular attendance at these services and the midweek prayer meetings as well, but not those of the minister's family. If Grover seldom went to church after he left home—although he kept his religious faith—it is understandable. Otherwise, also, the family had to recognize Father's need for seclusion and quiet in order to prepare those formidable sermons.

Then there was the economic situation. During these years, Richard Cleveland, Grover's father, was never paid more than six hundred dollars a year, and some of the time less than that. If it is considered that this had to feed, clothe, and provide for the future of all those growing children, the feat seems miraculous. It was not accomplished without much scrimping and some hardship. There could be no luxuries and not too many comforts. Even clothing was hard to come by, and in a climate of severe winters this was serious.

Six hundred dollars in the 1840s had the buying power of several times that a hundred years later—for inflation went on intermittently as the country grew; but still the restrictions were severe. This was the more true because a minister's family was regarded as belonging to the intelligentsia and was expected to go on to an education beyond that provided by the village schools. The ministry was the most likely career for them; and actually the eldest son, William, followed the family tradition. The educational opportunity most sought in that neighborhood was at Hamilton College in nearby Clinton, and Richard Cleveland hoped all his sons might go there. Before he moved to Clinton in 1850—Grover then being thirteen—William was nearly finished at Hamilton and looking forward to theological school. Anna, the oldest girl, was already teaching in the Fayetteville Academy, but she was the only one of the children who was helping the family financially.

There was something wrong about this situation. A minister was

6

supposed to be the spiritual leader of his flock, to instruct them not only in theological matters—although the appetite for long and involved discourses on biblical matters was apparently immense—but in morals as well. A man could hardly do this without a library of commentaries and prolonged and thoughtful contemplation. But there were those numerous children overrunning the small house and there was the problem of caring for them! Richard Cleveland met his responsibilities as best he could, sometimes complaining but never shirking. He was dedicated, but he was not creative. By the time he reached his thirties it was already evident that he would always be a laborer in the vineyard, never a noted divine.

There were, however, compensations in big-family life that the children of smaller families never know. The intimacies, the shared troubles, the lessons learned from each other, and, above all, the necessity of living together in peace and helpfulness were lessons Grover could have learned in no other way. From the older children he inherited not only clothes, but manners and a certain discipline, and for the younger ones he felt a responsibility he did not shirk.

The last child of the family, Rose, was born in Fayetteville, and one of the anecdotes of that life, told later by his older sister, was of Grover, set to mind baby Rose when his companions were playing noisily outside, and of his despair because she refused to fall asleep and free him from duty. That same baby many years later would be hostess for him in the White House before his belated marriage.

Another evidence of his sense of responsibility was that he carried most of the burden of family expense for many years after Father's death. Even when he had no more than a few dollars at the end of the month, he folded some of them into an envelope and mailed them to his mother.

Fayetteville was a village of a thousand people. But like many such communities at that time in American history, it expected to become much larger. And it was a busy place. The country around was a grain-growing region with pasture land supporting cattle and with self-sufficient farmsteads. Such New York State homes were thought ordinary then; later, their serene adaptation to the landscape would be more appreciated. The barns were big; they had to

7

be to hold the hay for feeding work horses and a dairy herd through the winter. And the village houses were of the same pattern as those on the farms except that the barns were smaller. Almost all did have barns, however, because horses and buggies were depended on for getting around.

There were only dirt streets in Fayetteville and dirt roads in the country round about; but there were several other villages nearby; and Syracuse was not too far for a day's excursion when the weather was favorable. The minister had few occasions for such expeditions, and the family did not keep a horse. So Grover and the other children were pretty much confined to the village. Everyone knew everyone else; when mischances occurred, neighbors helped; and when boys misbehaved, they had a hard time concealing it. There were some tolerances. Cleveland, returning to the village when he was President, said that if anyone still recalled the 1840s, he could tell them who had removed their gates and done other mischief on the Halloweens of those years.

The best times for the boys were the summers. Then they could escape to fishing and swimming in the streams and lakes. That part of New York has many creeks and ponds, and Grover knew them all. He was especially proud of his expertness as a fisherman— something that stayed with him all his life, for as an elderly man, retired from the presidency, he wrote a whimsical little book about fishing. It was an interest that began on the shores of Green Lake and along Limestone Creek before he was thirteen.

It was when he was thirteen that the family moved to Clinton. His father had been rescued from the hopeless poverty of a village pastorate and made district secretary of the New York agency of the Home Missionary Society. This was the agency that started new churches and helped them to become independent. It was a promotion, even if not an important one—and it carried a salary of one thousand dollars a year. But this was still not much for a family of such size, and presently Grover's plans to enter Hamilton College, as his older brother William had done, had to be given up. When he was fifteen, he would go back to Fayetteville to work for his board and fifty dollars a year in a general store.

8

3

ONE of the influences in Grover's early life was the Erie
Canal. This waterway was not important for very long—
not much more than a generation—because when it was at the
height of its usefulness, a railway across the state began to parallel
it. The railway service was faster and more flexible, and the canal
lost its position as the chief transportation facility from the seaboard
to the Great Lakes. While it was being dug, however, the cities
and towns along it called themselves ports and looked forward to a
commercial importance that began to develop but then was arrested. The names Spencerport, Brockport, Lockport, and many
others still perpetuate these canal-side expectations.

Immigrant Irish labor was used for the digging, and when it was
completed in 1825, many of the diggers sent for their families and
settled down in towns along the finished ditch. This served to dilute
the exclusively British and Protestant character of the older society.

The immigrants had a bad name among the old families. When
they had been living in gangs they had been drunken and rowdy,
especially on Sundays when they had a day off. During the following years, their numbers continued to increase until they were a
significant force in politics and business, often opposed to those of
English ancestry who were in positions of power.

Grover began his acquaintance with the canal and its peculiar
folk while he was a boy in Fayetteville. Some of the bargemen were
independent, offering their boats for hire anywhere along the way.
Fayetteville was a mile from the canal; but it had limestone quar-
ries, whose product was useful in larger towns where iron was made
—the limestone made a flux with the ore in the crude smelters then
in use—and it had a small harbor for this commerce.

9

The limestone shippers often needed space they had not contracted for in advance from passing barges; and one of the sources of revenue for the village boys was going down to the main canal and intercepting boats that might take loads of stone. Oldsters telling about this a half century later recalled young Grover as one of the most energetic of the boys. The pay for a successful interception was ten cents. It was said that Grover often got down to the canal while it was still dark, before the other boys were up, and earned his dime before time for school. The story may well be true. It would be characteristic.

If a dime seems poor pay for several hours of effort in a chilly dawn, it does tell a good deal both about Grover and about the town where he spent his growing years. A boy of ten or twelve was not yet able to do a man's work or even to be trusted with the odd jobs that bigger boys could do. He had to pick up what he could. Ten cents was indeed not much; but the men who worked at the hardest jobs then seldom earned that much an hour. To the Cleveland family, a dime was a pair of stockings, two dozen eggs, meat for dinner, or perhaps admission money for a traveling circus.

Grover recalled in later years how much small contributions to the family income had been needed, but he also recalled days of another sort. Like many boys in small towns, he always had a dog, a succession of them. They gave him the same uncritical affection dogs always have to give, and when he went fishing or when he ventured into the brush his dog went with him. It was not only a companion, but also protection against the resident tiger his generation of boys believed to lurk in that neighborhood.

When Grover was thirteen and there came the interruption in the Cleveland family life of the move to Clinton, the situation was not so much improved as the nearly doubled salary would seem to suggest. Richard Cleveland had more expenses. He had to travel a good deal, and there was a good deal of entertaining to do. This was especially true at graduation time in spring, but all during the year there were church visitors and especially young ministers to be entertained.

Before Grover went back to Fayetteville for his first job, he had made an adventurous journey. He had no idea that it might, as it did, change the whole course of his life; it was merely an exciting trip for a boy of fourteen. During the summer of 1850, he rode a canal boat to Black Rock, the canal terminal near Buffalo, and stayed there with the family of his uncle, Lewis F. Allen. For the first time, on this summer visit, he lived in a relaxed, almost luxurious, environment. His uncle was a prosperous and prominent citizen, and the home overlooking the Niagara River was commodious. It seemed almost empty after the smaller houses of a minister with nine children.

Black Rock was a sort of suburb. It had a busy port; but otherwise it had only the usual appearance of an outlying town that would sometime be part of the city. It was two miles from Buffalo itself and could be reached by walking out Niagara Street or by taking the horsecars. Grover, on his first visit, came by canal and landed in Black Rock itself, so he did not have to take the walk; but many times later on he would take it when he was so tired it seemed endless.

The passenger services on the canal were mostly on barges that carried freight as well as people. Such a trip could be tedious, but if there was no hurry it had its own fascination. The canal was only forty feet wide, and the barges glided along at the pace of the horses or mules used for towing. If the weather was good, passengers could sit on shaded decks and watch the passing countryside.

The canal traversed the most beautiful and productive counties of New York, a country of meadows and fields with frequent small towns. For added interest, there were the locks, with gates that were worked by hand. The water began to be let in when the barge entered and the rise to another level took some time. In a few places like Lockport, the rise required several locks, and there was often a delay while preceding barges made their slow way through the whole series. It was spoken of as a water-level route across the state; but it was not quite that; there were sometimes rises or falls amounting to a hundred feet or more.

Grover can be pictured making this first journey away from home, excited by getting ready and setting out, then watching as the mules were headed toward Buffalo along the path. He carried a bundle with clothing and food for several days. He would sleep in a bunk if one happened to be available. He would go ashore at the lock stops and perhaps help to work the gates. He would be one of a dozen passengers, some of them families, perhaps immigrants who had landed in New York from Europe and were surrounded by their luggage. Others would be men on business, making their way from one town to another. He might find a boy or two of his own age and be able to make temporary friends.

He had almost no money in his pocket—only what he could have saved up from the few jobs he had managed to find in Fayetteville, but he had no real need of more. While he was at his uncle's, he wrote home that his funds were almost gone, but that he was quite all right. He could buy passage back for two dollars, he said, and, otherwise, he could get along.

The vacation of summer in 1850 was partly spent in and around the Black Rock house with its acres of yard, and partly on Grand Island a few miles down the Niagara River toward the falls—a large and fertile island where Lewis Allen owned a six-hundred-acre farm. There he kept a herd of shorthorn cattle which were his chief pride. He had imported the basic stock some years before from England and had opened the herdbook that served to register the cattle in his own, and in others', herds. He meant to establish the breed as a contribution to American agriculture.

This avocation of his uncle was of some importance to Grover because, when he returned a few years later, the keeping of the herdbook would be his first job in Buffalo and would see him on his way to becoming a lawyer. During the summer of 1850, however, the shorthorns were merely part of an interesting life. His cousins, Cleveland and Gertrude, were real companions, and he was taken into the family circle as one entitled to all its privileges.

He had a chance to learn, although it was evident to him as a boy only through the comparative luxury of the Allens' life, that his uncle was an important citizen in the vicinity of Buffalo. He was not only a partner in many enterprises and the owner of much real estate, but was prominent in all sorts of civic affairs. He was of an enterprising and adventurous temperament, the sort who is apt to be on boards of trustees and directors. He had even been a member of the state legislature. He was always seeing new things to do or ways to do old things better. He was prominent in church affairs too, and was altogether a leading and most respected citizen.

His temperament and interests would contrast sharply with Grover's rather stolid attitude and narrow ambitions as a man. But at this time, of course, differences that would be so marked later were not discernible. For Grover, his stay was a real vacation. The house faced Niagara Street and only its back porches looked toward the river. But it was surrounded by lawns and by the orchards his uncle was also experimenting with. The river there was just funneling out of Lake Erie and beginning its confined rush toward its spectacular plunge over the Niagara Escarpment twenty miles away. It boiled and eddied and, except in inlets and small harbors, could only be navigated by a craft able to overcome its swift current. The children spent a good deal of time on the water or at the Grand Island farm in and around the stables and fields, inventing games and making excursions. They fished often, and because of the turbulence of the water, it was much more exciting than the fishing on Green Lake at home.

When the summer came to an end, Grover went back to Clinton where the family was now established and where he was to enter a new school at the foot of the hill where Hamilton College was situated. His parting from his cousins was reluctant, but for him worse because he was leaving a friend he had grown even more attached to: a neighbor boy named Timothy Mahoney. Tim would play a much larger part in his later life than his cousins, for both he and Tim were to be Buffalo politicians and lifelong allies. Notice that Mahoney was an Irish name. This was Grover's first real contact with the immigrant families he was to have so much to do with in future years. Tim was no more like Grover than the Allen cousins; but he had an Irish quality of friendliness that overcame Grover's shyness. He would not allow differences of temperament to keep them apart, and Grover's rejections were overcome by the warmth of the Irish boy.

Grover was back in Clinton by September. The following year—1850–51—was the last one the Richard Cleveland family would be together. It was always recalled by its members as the best year they had ever had. William, the oldest brother, was finishing at

Hamilton, and Grover was studying Latin and mathematics with three other students at the Clinton Liberal Institute. There was a little more money, although it soon proved not nearly enough; but all were hopeful and generally optimistic. There was, however, something wrong with their father now that the medical arts of the 1850s could not cope with. The tensions and overwork of his years in the ministry had finally resulted in chronic illness. He was developing gastric ulcers.

He could barely endure the horse and buggy journeys to towns that were hours and even days away, over roads that were dusty or muddy seven months of the year and buried in snow the other five. When he got where he was going, he lived in the homes of other ministers, usually the poorest ones. Worst of all, his work was never done. There was always more than he could do, and, being conscientious, he could never be content with what he had accomplished. His was a missionary post, and he worried about the new ministers and their work, a worry that had no end.

It became clear two years later that he could no longer continue, and in a kind of desperation, he took another pastorate in a town even smaller than Fayetteville called Holland Patent. But even before this, poverty had forced him to make the arrangement for Grover that we have mentioned. Deacon McVickar of the church Richard had left in Fayetteville was the proprietor of a general store, and he offered to take Grover as one of his two assistants. So Grover really spent only one school year at Clinton. By the next he was back in Fayetteville as an apprentice merchant.

Whether he thought at any time that he was learning an occupation there we do not know. Probably not. To be in trade was quite outside the family tradition. None of the children, in their parents' view, was destined to anything but some sort of profession. It did not turn out that way. Both Fred and Cecil, Grover's brothers, later became businessmen; but they were in somewhat higher reaches of business than general storekeeping.

There can be no doubt that Grover got some useful knowledge from his tedious employment. He learned about all sorts of goods and how they got into people's possession. He also watched McVickar practice the art of trading at a time when people brought to the store eggs, butter, bacon, sausage, cheese, and maple syrup and exchanged them for the sugar, salt, cloth, shoes, and other goods they needed. The merchant then sent farm products on to larger city markets. These dealings went on all the time and sometimes Grover had to manage them. True there was more physical work to do than trade to be managed. The store had to be kept in order, the stock replenished, the boxes and barrels handled, the floors swept, the fires tended, and the customers waited on.

Deacon McVickar was kept busy much of the time in his small and cluttered office where the smells of vinegar, molasses, and kerosene from the barrels by the back door were strongest. Grover and his colleague, a boy of his own age named Tippett (who later became the village dentist), had most of the chores to do and most of the customers to wait on. From morning until night they seldom had a moment to themselves, and by closing time they were exhausted.

The contract to furnish room and board was kept by McVickar, but not in any lavish fashion. The boys ate at the family table and no complaints seem to have been registered about this; but their room was a small one in an unheated second floor above the store, and their furniture was only a cord bed with a cornhusk mattress. They slept there together. They washed, when they did wash, in a horse trough by the curb, and their toilet was a privy out back. Considering the harsh New York State winters, these arrangements seem to us now cruel ones; but at the time, no one seemed to regard them as unusual, and the boys endured them as a matter of course. They had to haul themselves out of bed long before daylight so that the store could be put in order for the day's business, fires built, sweeping done, and goods replenished and displayed by opening time at seven when the proprietor arrived for his early inspection.

Grover's sturdiness and good health enabled him to withstand the hardships and even to grow rapidly. It was an experience he afterward considered, on the whole, to have been valuable.

4

T W O years at McVickar's store fulfilled Grover's contract, and it was enough. There was no future in it that he could see. The business was not growing; and McVickar wanted boys for help, not young men who would want more pay. So Grover went back to Clinton and renewed his study for entrance to Hamilton.

The family was together again, but only briefly. Richard Cleveland had already found that he could no longer carry the duties of district secretary and was planning to move his family to Holland Patent, where he would resume his ministry. Yet the family was hardly settled in the new parsonage and Richard had preached only one sermon when he died suddenly of peritonitis.

This tragedy happened so unexpectedly that Grover was actually in Utica with his sister Mary when the news came to him. Mary expected to be married soon and was making some last purchases for her wedding. They had driven the ten miles from Holland Patent through woods gorgeous with October foliage and past farmsteads getting ready for the siege of winter. Now they drove back to a household deep in sorrow, lost without its head.

Grover, just emerging from boyhood, had now to consider what to do. For one thing, his plans for college could not be carried out. He would have to earn his own living; but also he would have to bear part of the responsibility for his mother and the younger children. There were four of these who were still to be prepared for going into the world.

What could he do? Only one opportunity offered itself at once. His older brother William had taken a job in New York City at the Institution for the Blind. He could take his younger brother along as an assistant teacher. Grover went with him.

He stayed there, working with William, for a year. That too was enough, as his two years as an apprentice merchant had been. The reason was not obscure. The Institution was more of an asylum than a school; it was managed as economically as possible, and the children led lives of strict discipline. They were wards of the state and it was intended that they should keep that in mind. There was no gaiety, and every attempt at self-expression was repressed. To be blind and, besides, to live in such an institution amounted to daily punishment.

William and Grover were in charge of what was called the Literary Department. They were teachers from early morning until late afternoon. The rest of the time they were in charge of the boys' dormitory. As always, in such a place, there were some sympathetic and capable teachers; but in this one, there were not many. The superintendent had no affection for his charges. There were severe punishments for minor mischief and whipping for infringements of rules. The food was execrable and the halls were cold and damp. The building itself was of a style known as Victorian Gothic. This meant that it was a gloomy pile, scantily windowed, and looked more like a prison than a home for children. Such confinement for youngsters so handicapped is the sort of thing later generations find hard to understand. Grover was revolted and said so on occasion—something that did not endear him to higher authority. But the children had been selected by overseers of the poor in the various counties of the state. They were charity wards and economy was an important consideration in the management of the place.

This experience contributed something more to Grover's education. He was not an expressive lad; but then, as later, his sense of justice was shaped by a sympathy that sometimes became sentimentality. There were occasions when his indignation overcame the constant sense of family responsibility that reminded him of the need for his salary. There were several rebellious scenes. And when his year had been served, he was glad to leave—as his brother William also did. William now had found a way to go on with his theological training. Grover went back to Holland Patent without much notion of what came next except that he must find some sort of work.

It seems strange that he did not try for a start in New York

City, but instead began looking for a job in Syracuse or Utica. For New York was in the full rush of becoming a metropolis. The Institution, when it had been built in 1831 on the block bounded by Thirty-third and Thirty-fourth streets, and Eighth and Ninth avenues, had been well outside the city. Now, a quarter of a century later, expansion northward had surrounded it with solidly occupied streets. New York was obviously destined to be the nation's largest city; there were many opportunities for young and ambitious men, and they were coming in large numbers. We do not know why Cleveland did not stay to grow with the city; but certainly he left it without regret, and the only guess we can make is that he was so embittered by his experience in the Institution that he wanted to get as far away as he could.

His arrival in Buffalo some months later and his decision to make his career there are not so hard to explain; still there are elements of chance involved that cannot be said to have been in any way planned. This is the more curious because, looking back to the end of his stay there twenty-seven years later, it can be seen how perfectly his temperament, his talents, and his ambitions fitted the circumstances rather than those he might have encountered in New York.

His search for an opening in central New York, the country he knew so well, had had no result at all; and this seems strange because the towns there were in an expanding stage too. As he wrote to his sister Mary in 1853–54:

I am kind of fooling away my time here, I think. . . . I have used all the rules in *my* arithmetic, and I have not solved the problem yet, viz., How is a man going to spend four years in getting an education with nothing to start on and no prospect of anything to pay his way with. Until I see how I am going to get through, you don't catch me inside of College walls. . . .

Having found another young man in smiliar difficulties, he resolved to make his way with him westward to Cleveland. It is not known why his choice was for Cleveland, Ohio, and not at once for Buffalo where he had relatives and friends. The only thing he ever said about his choice was that the name attracted him. A distant

Buffalo from Lake Erie 1836. (*Courtesy of The New-York Historical Society, New York City*)

member of the family had given the city its name; and perhaps some notion of luck in such a concurrence influenced him.

His resolve to go west was strong enough so that he brought himself to do something that he disliked intensely: he went to a well-off friend of his father and asked for a loan. He did not need a large one, only twenty-five dollars, but he calculated that it would cover the journey and give him support for the short time he would need to find a job. He rejected an alternative offer of support while he went to college if he would engage himself to become a minister as his father had been. He had already determined that somehow he would become a lawyer. How he arrived at this, we do not know. There were no relatives or close family friends who were lawyers; but he had told his brother William, when the two parted in New York, that this was what he had in mind. This was not such a formidable ambition as it would seem at a later time. Most young men went into the profession by way of apprenticeship to an older man or an established firm. It was not necessary to have law school training.

When the journey began, Grover was in a frame of mind to take anything he could get in the way of work; and to begin in some Cleveland law office when and if he could. It cannot have been a very real hope just then, since he had gone into debt and still had to help out if possible with the support of his mother and the younger children. No apprentice could hope to earn anything at first, and not much for some time after. He had no connections in Cleveland, where he was headed; it was a venture into the blue.

There were trains to travel on now instead of canal boats, and the boys got off the cars at Buffalo, disheveled from the dusty trip. They would change there to another line that went on to Cleveland. Grover left his friend at the station while he went out to call on his relatives in Black Rock. It was a walk he had taken before and one he would take many times in the next few years. When he got to the Allen home, he went directly to his uncle's small basement office. The Allens had had no notice of his coming and his uncle was surprised. At the moment, he was working at the papers that would become the herdbook of the American Shorthorn Association.

He naturally asked at once where Grover had come from. When

Buffalo Harbor showing Michigan Ave. bridge, canal barges and sail-steam vessel 1888. (*Courtesy of The Buffalo and Erie County Historical Society*)

the boy said he was on his way to Cleveland, his practical uncle asked what he expected to find there. He had no reasonable answer. His uncle, who was genuinely fond of the nephew who was so well liked by his own children, offered him an alternative. Why not stay in Buffalo? If, as Grover said, he hoped to find an opening in some law office, it would be easier where he had an older relative with many connections. Besides, the older man said, pointing to the litter of papers he had been working on, there was something useful Grover could do in the meantime—and could legitimately get paid for. He could take charge of the herdbook. The shorthorns were his favorite avocation, but tracing out and recording the blood lines was beginning to need more attention to detail than a man of his many interests could spare.

Grover already knew about the shorthorns and his uncle's interest in establishing the breed as an accepted line; he knew about the big farm on Grand Island; and especially he knew about the big house in Black Rock with its agreeable relatives. His uncle was more than cordial. Grover could have a home with the family, he said, as long as he cared to stay. How could Grover say no? But he had his companion to deal with. Their compact to start out together for Cleveland could hardly be ignored. What Grover did was to walk the two miles back to the station, tell his friend of his new opportunity, and ask whether he might be released from their mutual undertaking. His friend consented and went on alone. Grover went back to Allens, grateful for the refuge.

It was thus simply that the decision for Buffalo was made. He would have a place to live and fifty dollars for six months' work; but also his uncle would do his best to find some law office where a young man could help with chores and at the same time study. There was no definite prospect of such an opening, since his uncle, not knowing Grover was coming, had not looked into it; but Lewis Allen's dealings with members of the Buffalo bar were frequent, and he promised to see what he could do. This suggestion Grover accepted gratefully. He must have wondered why he had not thought of it before, instead of starting on a hunt for work in a city quite strange to him. Not every boy has an influential relative more than willing to help him get a start. Grover may have hesi-

Hon. Henry W. Rogers (*Courtesy of The New-York Historical Society, New York City*)

tated because of his instinct for independence. If he did, his reluctance was overcome by the older man's cordiality.

Grover at once went to work on the herdbook, and his uncle looked around for a lawyer willing to have him as a helper and student. His first attempt ended badly. A lawyer friend in Black Rock consented to interview the young man; but his questions were so offensive that Grover simply walked out. A little later his uncle reached higher in the scale and approached one of the leading firms in the city: Rogers, Bowen and Rogers. None of the partners really wanted to be bothered with an inexperienced—and under-educated—young man, but because Lewis Allen asked it, they consented to allow him an unoccupied table in an outer room and access to their collection of books.

The senior Rogers, Grover afterward said, threw a copy of Blackstone on the table before him and abandoned him to it. He was given no stated duties, and was pretty much ignored. It was some time before his natural industriousness impressed itself on the busy lawyers. He was timid about asking questions and even afraid to volunteer for office-boy duties. He was so quiet and unnoticed that on one occasion he was left in the office when the others had gone, and had the door locked on him. He spent the night sleeping on the floor.

At length, however, his unusual industriousness *was* noticed. Once begun, he mined the books he found on the shelves and gradually began to put in order for himself a course in the law. It certainly would not have been approved in any professional school, but it served the practical purpose of advancing him toward membership in the Buffalo bar.

In October 1855, he wrote to Mary:

I have laid aside Blackstone for a few minutes, for I don't feel like study this afternoon. . . . Aunt and Uncle have gone West, but we expect them back in a few days. . . . I am trying to find a place to board in the city, but I am so far unsuccessful. I have to work pretty hard at present, as the senior clerk is absent. But it is better for me, as the more I do, the more I learn. As you say, I find oftentimes "Jordan a hard road to travel," but for the most part, I feel pretty well encouraged. I think and hope I shall have no trouble, that is any more than is the unavoidable concomitant of poverty.

2 4

He watched the partners and clerks prepare documents and briefs; and when appearances were made in Court, he followed the argument. With unflagging persistence, he related what he saw and heard to what he could find in the books. It came slowly and with discouraging gaps, but when he had a year of digging behind him, he began to feel that he had made a start. He was now being watched by the real lawyers and given small jobs to do—looking up precedents, preparing parts of briefs, and drafting instruments. This was the thankless work of any large office; but for him, it was a way to favor and learning.

There could be no doubt that he was going to be a lawyer; and almost from the first no one doubted it. His ability to outstay any of his fellow clerks in the tiresome pursuit of answers to troublesome questions was especially noticed by his elders, who noted too that he seemed to have no other interests. He continued to live for a few months with the Allens; then he moved to a room in town near the office so that he could work evenings without interruption.

He made few friends, and, particularly, he made no effort to become a member of the Allen circle. They belonged to Buffalo's upper crust; the houses of their friends would have been open to him, but he never followed up any suggestion of the sort. He began rather to find his recreation in a different way. The office and his room were in a part of Buffalo almost exclusively occupied by business offices. There were some rooming houses; but people of good family did not live there. The only places of recreation were saloons, eating places, and hangouts of various sorts, some patronized by homeless men like himself, some of a more regrettable kind, only to be described as dives. Grover had only to go around the corner or down the street to find a place where there was company, where he could sit at a table, for hours if he liked, drinking beer and playing cards or checkers or just talking. It was all he asked.

The Allens found this growing tendency regrettable; but Grover found it agreeable, and after a year his visits to his relations had almost stopped. He occasionally took a little time off and brought the herdbook up to date, incidentally earning a few urgently needed dollars. His pay at Rogers, Bowen and Rogers, after a few payless months, seems to have been calculated with the cost of room and board in mind and with nothing left over. This was about four dollars a week. Along with his brothers, he was trying to find a little money every month to send back to his mother, but this often meant going without necessities.

The young man, now reaching twenty, was set in a way of life he would not depart from very much during his whole quarter century in Buffalo. He would make progress in the law, become a capable attorney, find his way into politics and then out again, affiliate with old friends in a series of partnerships, become quite wealthy and much respected. But he would still not have made contact with Buffalo's elite on the social level. He would still live in downtown bachelor quarters, and would still prefer evenings in saloons with careless companions to any other sort of recreation. True, he occasionally went fishing; this, indeed, was his only outdoor interest—had been, as we have seen, since Fayetteville days.

He was becoming what his character, his temperament, and his capabilities determined—what he wanted to be. It was a tough discipline; but he was a tough boy, and he was getting ahead.

5

D U R I N G the next few years, Grover gradually became proficient in the law; but he also began an involvement in politics that would ultimately be more important than his profession. As to the issues that were splitting the whole country and would lead to the Civil War—slavery and secession—he avoided public commitment. He was single-mindedly concerned with getting ahead.

He was admitted to the Bar in the spring of 1859. He had been studying and working in the Rogers, Bowen and Rogers office for three-and-one-half years and had already got to be managing clerk with a salary of one thousand dollars a year (somewhat enlarged by fees for extra work). This was no spectacular performance. Others achieved their admission in much shorter times. All that was needed was the recommendation of several seniors and the concurrence of the Court. Why it took so long we can only guess, as we have to guess about so much during his Buffalo years.

The reputation he was earning was that of a hard and thorough worker. He was never brilliant. He preferred working on briefs and references to appearances in Court. In fact, then and later, he always tried to arrange some sort of accommodation for clients without arguing an action at all. A lawyer of this sort wins his appreciation more slowly than the showier advocate. But this kind of counselor founds firms and attracts permanent clients. Usually, too, he prefers civil practice, the handling of property, and advice for corporate clients. He takes criminal cases with reluctance, or, if he can afford it, not at all. This was the way Grover was going.

Rogers, Bowen and Rogers were a conservative firm. At this time they did accept different sorts of clients, but they were already selective and becoming more so as time went on. This gave Grover

Wilson Shannon Bissell, LL.D. (*Courtesy of The New-York Historical Society, New York City*)

a varied experience during his apprenticeship. There was no area of the law he did not have something to do with, so that when he was admitted to the Bar, he might have established himself in an independent office at once if he had liked. For the time, however, he stayed on with the firm; and when he did leave, it was to take a position they advised him to take.

The job was that of assistant district attorney. This was an appointment earned only partly by his work as a lawyer. Partly it was offered because of the political work he had begun even before his admission to practice.

When he had come of age (in 1858) he had immediately volunteered for work in the Democratic organization. He was given a list of voters who ought to show up at the polls but who might need reminding at election time. Those in the second ward, where he was assigned, were mostly German immigrants, and Grover had no difficulty in making friends. He tramped the streets, found the voters on the list, and saw that they got to the polls. This was ward heelers' work—necessary, but the lowliest of political tasks. A young man undertook it to earn credit with the political bosses; and if he was a lawyer, it was recognized as the preliminary to some office, either elective or appointive. Grover was looking to the future. Even if he got no office, much of his lawyer's work had to do with politics and politicians. He was merely being thorough in the preliminaries of practice.

His approach to work for the organization was not so very different from that for the members of his firm. He was a plodder. He did carefully what he was supposed to do. Long hours meant nothing to him. The young man who had studied Blackstone or worked at the preparation of briefs for many hours and days, sometimes sitting over his papers all night, was the same young man when he had a political job to do. There is something about this kind of person that everyone recognizes. He is the one who has studied and worked; he can answer questions; he can be depended on.

Grover's introduction to politics by Dennis Bowen, one of the partners, was quite natural. Bowen was a prominent Democrat, just now alderman for the tenth ward. He was so effective as Grover's sponsor that in 1862 Grover was elected to the Democratic city convention as a delegate from the second ward. In the following year, he was nominated to be ward supervisor. He was now twenty-five, the right age to make a real start. Almost at once the man who had been elected district attorney of Erie County at the same election asked him to be his assistant and he accepted.

The influence of Bowen can be seen in this, but Grover's decision to accept needs some explaining. He was leaving the firm where his salary was now assured and taking a job that paid only half as much, and this was a time when he badly needed money. The reason, of course, was that in his public position he could have expectations. And if he was to be an office holder, he must start at the bottom. District Attorney Torrance was an elderly and infirm lawyer from Gowanda, a county town some distance from Buffalo. Grover might reasonably expect to succeed him soon, and then perhaps to go to the state legislature or to the Congress. Bowen thought it an opportunity the young man ought not to turn down, and Grover took his advice.

But there is more explaining to be done. Why had Grover become a Democrat instead of a Republican? He was a conservative and business-minded young man. His uncle Lewis Allen had been a lifelong Whig who had turned Republican as the new party had succeeded the old in recent years. And the better people of Buffalo —the merchants, the bankers, the owners of wheat elevators, the iron masters and machinery makers—were largely Republican. Grover's affiliation with the Democrats grieved his uncle and would have a good deal to do with his separation from the family.

There were involved in his decision attitudes toward issues that were agitating everyone, even if he did not make any public declaration. Lewis Allen, like so many prominent Northerners, was a Free-Soiler; that is to say, he thought the new Western territories now becoming states ought to come into the Union without the taint of slavery. Also, he was an abolitionist. He had been outraged by the operation of the Fugitive Slave Law of 1850; to see escaped slaves being captured and returned to the South seemed to him a crime sheltered by a law that ought never to have been passed. He was so active in antislavery politics that he had presided over the first Republican convention in Erie County when that party was just replacing the old Whigs.

3 0

Buffalo City and County Hall in 1871 (*Courtesy of The Buffalo and Erie County Historical Society*)

It grieved him to have his nephew align himself with and work actively for a party that he regarded as involved with slavery, and, even more outrageous, seemed to tolerate secessionist proposals. Nevertheless, Grover went his own way, and all through the years of approach to war and then the war itself, he remained an active Democrat. Why? Grover himself said nothing about it until many years later when he remarked to Richard Watson Gilder, a New York friend, that he had been repelled by the Republican presidental candidate, Frémont, who had been "flamboyant and theatrical." This seems an inadequate explanation, and there is a more likely one even if it is no more than a guess.

The members of his firm, especially Dennis Bowen, but also both the Rogerses, in a less active way, were Democrats. The elder Rogers was a Jacksonian of the old breed, and often spoke pridefully of having been appointed collector of the Port of Buffalo by President Polk. Then, too, there were Grover's other associations. He was deeply involved by the time he reached his twenties with the barroom set he spent so much of his leisure time with; and many of these were Democratic ward workers as he was. It was understandable that he should go on as he had started.

But there was, as well, the war itself and all its ramifying issues. He opposed its beginning, apparently, as he had opposed Lincoln's election, although conclusions about his convictions are mostly inferences. He wrote nothing and said nothing that was recorded. But he may well have resented the extremism of the abolitionists. His father had, and there were more Northerners who felt that way than is often realized. The agitators in New England, it was felt by conservative citizens, were stirring up troubles that could better be settled in quieter negotiation.

He may well have felt that the split now advancing so rapidly to its acute stage was more the fault of demanding Northerners than of the Southerners who were mostly merely defensive. This was essentially the attitude of Pierce and Buchanan, the last two Presidents, both Democrats and both Northerners, before the Civil War. Cleveland had only to accept the party attitude; it was natural that he should, even if it offended his uncle and his prominent friends.

Lincoln, in this view, was a dangerous agitator whose election would make it impossible for North and South to live in peace. The Republican victory in 1860 would make actual war inevitable, and this seemed both unnecessary and horribly dangerous. These views of most Democrats in the North were considerably modified as the conflict came on and hostilities began. There were some, called Copperheads, who wanted the South to win; but there were not many in upper New York, and there is no reason to think Cleveland was one of them. The Democratic party itself in the state was firmly Unionist and active in working for victory. But it could not escape its history; and Democrats were to be labeled for a generation as the party of slaveholders, and of disloyalty to the Union.

Grover did not advance to the district attorneyship he had hoped for. Actually, he would not be an office holder again until, in 1870, he was elected sheriff of Erie County. He tried. In 1865 he ran for the district attorneyship but was defeated. His opponent on that occasion was Lyman K. Bass, a close friend—in fact, at that time, his roommate—and a later law partner.

Actually, his defeat probably worked out well for him in the long run. He went on rising in his profession, and although he continued to work in the Democratic organization, he was no longer looking for office. He was beginning to make a name for himself as a lawyer, and in his private practice he was making influential friends.

Having already left his original employers, he now went into partnership first with a former state treasurer, Major Isaac K. Vanderpoel, and then, when Vanderpoel became a magistrate, with Albert P. Laning and Oscar Folsom. Laning was the senior of these and brought to the firm a large practice that included important business firms. He was one of the most important Democratic leaders and had been a member of both branches of the state legislature. Folsom was a very different sort, a popular and brilliant young man. Cleveland was soon bound to him by more than partnership ties. He was closer to him than to any other of his Buffalo friends.

The firm prospered and Cleveland's reputation for industry and dependability grew. There are records of several of his cases and they are wholly creditable. What he really thought or felt about

33

the war as it progressed, no one really knew, or, if anyone did, left no record. How a young man, a politician, and a lawyer could have passed through the excitements of those years without having become more involved, it is very hard to understand. But it seems to have been so.

We do know what happened when he was confronted with the necessity of answering the draft call in 1863. The Conscription Act had clauses allowing a draftee to buy himself out for three hundred dollars, or to make his own bargain with a substitute who would serve for him. Grover was one of those whose name was drawn on the first day. He could not find three hundred dollars at once, but a friend put him in touch with a man who would become a substitute for one hundred and fifty dollars and the bargain was made.

It is an axiom among politicians that in a postwar period, any candidate for office must have served in the armed forces. Veterans' organizations are always politically powerful, and anyone not eligible to be a member is looked on with suspicion. He is certain to be called a shirker or worse, and advancement in elective offices is practically closed. Perhaps Grover chose to ignore this; perhaps he did not foresee the veterans' strength and cohesiveness. Then again, he may have felt—there were those who *did* feel in 1863—that the war was a mistake and that there would be no disapproval for not having served.

There was another reason, made much of by his later defenders. Both his brothers, Fred and Cecil, had enlisted almost at once. They had agreed among themselves that Grover should be the one to stay at home and provide for their mother. But this argument is fallacious. By the time Grover was drafted, Fred had served the period of his enlistment and had been mustered out and Cecil would be getting out soon afterward.

When Grover was drafted, Fred, hearing about it and being unemployed still, offered to be his substitute, but Grover rejected the offer. Fred, he said, had done enough. Whether it was altogether for this family reason, or whether he was not affected by the patriotic fervor that moved so many western New Yorkers, he did buy a substitute; and he had as little connection with any of the climactic affairs of those years as anyone could possibly have had.

3 4

So far as he personally was concerned, the war might not have happened at all.

Possibly this was why he was beaten by his friend Bass for the district attorneyship in 1865. It was no time for Democrats, even in local politics. They would not regain favor for a long time to come.

Still, by 1870, when he was thirty-three and had developed into fair prominence, he ran for sheriff in a fairly nonpartisan way and was elected.

Why he should have wanted the office, which usually went to a political hack and required no real ability, is another matter that needs explaining. The reason is quite clear: money. The fees were very high, and although Grover had a good practice, he had not been able to accumulate much wealth. He earned several times as much during his term as he had ever earned before.

He was defeated for re-election in two years, and he went back to the practice of law. His excursion into political life seems not to have counted much against him as a responsible counselor, perhaps because the partners in the new firm he joined were so respectable.

One of the curious facts about his service as sheriff is that he paid little attention to his duties. He had an able undersheriff and he left much of the work to him. He had never spent so much time fishing—and with companions in the saloons—as during this time. It seems quite out of character, but ample testimony leaves no doubt that it was so.

It is interesting, too, in view of his later career, that this interval was not used for education. He had missed college and he had taken no interest in public affairs, at least national ones. During his thirties, he might have realized his limitations and tried to catch up. He did nothing of the sort.

When he had made sure that the office was being run honestly and had made a few changes to insure that this would continue, he pretty much allowed his subordinate to carry on by himself. He fished and played cards. If he read further in the law, no one knew it; but then he was not communicative. And if he read anything else it does not appear in his later history. He never became a cultivated man.

6

I F Grover looked back when he left the sheriff's office, he must have done so with mixed feelings about his accomplishments so far in life. For he had made several serious mistakes; and they went far to offset his considerable progress in the law. General recognition of his ability was enabling him at the moment to set up partnership with substantial and highly respected colleagues; and his income, when added to the sums he had accumulated while sheriff, at last freed him from the financial distress he had endured during his apprenticeship. But his mistakes were serious, and it is probable that he regretted them.

He had failed to get the start in politics he had calculated on, largely because he had drifted into the Democratic party in Republican times. He had been indifferent to the ordeal of his country as it passed through civil war, and because he was not a veteran, any renewed hope of public office, except perhaps in his local area, had disappeared. Also his term as sheriff had been a waste of time.

In a city filled with corruption and graft, he had taken no part in the reform movement started by some of Buffalo's leading citizens. Reform *was* needed—not only in Buffalo, but throughout the state. The corruption of both municipal and county governments was notorious; it had become so much a part of political practice that public life was avoided by respectable citizens. Officials reached office through the support of bosses, such as one John C. Sheehan, who was representative of the whole complex of graft and favor in the Democratic organization; or a certain Jack White, who was his counterpart among the Republicans.

These two, and their allies, were able to trade votes with each other all during the sixties and seventies. Between them, they controlled the first ward, passing majorities back and forth as seemed most profitable. This was possible because there was so close a balance between the parties—the closest in all of Erie County. Only a few votes need be bought to swing elections either way. In the aftermath of civil war, the normally Democratic city gave General Grant, running for the presidency, a small majority over his opponent, Governor Seymour of New York. This was in 1868; but in 1867 the Democrats had carried the county in local elections and, in 1864, had given McClellan, the Democrat, a majority over Lincoln.

This close division between the parties gave the bosses the opportunity they knew how to make use of. Again and again they elected councilmen who would vote as they were told. All the time this was going on, Grover was a member of the political organization. He worked to deliver Democratic votes in elections he knew to be manipulated, but he was reported by his intimates to have denounced the individuals involved, using the picturesque language learned in the saloons he frequented. They knew he despised the crooks, but no one else knew it. He made no public protest and joined in no effort for reforms, which would have made Sheehan's and White's bargaining impossible.

One story, illustrating both his honesty and his unwillingness to make trouble, became generally known while he was sheriff. Being custodian of the County Jail, he had to make many purchases of food, fuel, maintenance materials, and transportation facilities. The bookkeeping for these transactions was quite in order, but Grover knew quite well that graft was involved—and he knew how. It was characteristic of him that he said nothing about his knowledge.

The suppliers had a regular arrangement with the bosses in power and regarded themselves as privileged. It was understood that they would deliver short weights and measures. Profits from this graft were enormous and were regularly shared among the politicians who were in on the deal. Grover, to the consternation of all, appeared when the wagons bringing coal, flour, and meat arrived and, with the help of a trusty prisoner, used the scales and yardsticks himself. He certified the delivery of real weights and measures and no more. He made no effort to punish the grafters. But after that, he was able to leave to a subordinate most of the actual management. It was understood that cheating was finished.

Such sources of party funds and of profit for the politicians of all grades were quite usual. There was a curious tolerance of graft on public contracts that existed for many years. The politicians had learned how to exploit democratic institutions. The very word "politics" came to mean something dirty to most people. And they felt themselves helpless. Nothing much was gained by voting one party out and another in; each was equally dishonest.

The trouble went very deep. The politicians controlled the machines that ran conventions, nominated candidates, and got voters to the polling places at election time. Occasionally, in most American cities, there were reform movements, sponsored by outraged citizens. These organizations appeared when grafting just got too bad to tolerate. If the reformers succeeded in ousting the worst crooks and electing decent officials, as they sometimes did, the reforms never seemed to last long. The good citizens went back to their own occupations—they were lawyers or businessmen, not politicians—and when their vigilance was relaxed the bosses quietly took control again. They were always on the job. It was a business with them.

Buffalo was typical of other cities, both in having bosses who ran the city most of the time and in having sporadic temporary reforms. But graft was worse here than elsewhere because of the city's fantastic population growth through several decades and because of the nature of that growth. When Grover arrived in Buffalo in 1855, it was a city of forty thousand; when he was elected sheriff fifteen years later, it had reached nearly one hundred thousand. Much of this increase was immigrant: the Irish, in quest of better economic conditions, who dug the canal and built the railroads; the Germans, forced by the suppression of civil liberties to leave their homeland; and the Poles; the Italians; and others soon followed.

Many of these immigrants were laborers who came without their families to do contract labor. Many were illiterate, and most were from farms and villages, so that they had no skills. They were the manpower for the fast-growing industries of Buffalo—the machinery, soap, flour, and other factories, the port facilities, the railway yards, the enormous grain elevators and processing plants.

The sailors and roustabouts from the Great Lakes ships, the dockworkers and the railway and elevator employees made up a further floating population of homeless men who lived in cheap boardinghouses and patronized the saloons and honky-tonks along and near the waterfront. There were nearly seven hundred saloons in Buffalo at this time, selling Monongahela rot gut, a famous spirit distilled, often, by moonshiners in the Pennsylvania mountains and delivered to the saloons in barrels. It sold for a few cents a drink; whiskey, it was said, was the cheapest thing in town. But it had a competitor in German-American beer, made by brewers who brought the art with them from the old country. A "schooner" could be bought for a nickel, and often a free-lunch counter was open to customers. The Germans ran the respectable beer halls and, mostly, frequented them. The other immigrants patronized the waterfront saloons. Few, if any, cared about the corruption in Buffalo—and many were Grover's friends. He himself was incorruptible. But his public record shows no attempt to rebuke the dishonesty of his political leaders or the public officials with whom he worked.

Grover may have had regrets about his public record. Yet his private life, later to be an issue in his public career, seems not to have troubled him at all.

He happily cultivated the company of the characters who hung around clubrooms and nearby saloons, and this preference kept him away from the decent citizens of Buffalo, separated him from his uncle's family, and prevented him from having any social life with people of standing.

It wasn't as though he had been a merely interested observer of barroom life: he took full part in it. In his biography of Cleveland, Charles Armitage quotes a Mr. Level, a livery stable proprietor, on Cleveland as a barroom brawler:

"What it started over, I don't remember . . . but it grew out of Democratic politics. Whatever the start may have been, the finish began when Falvey called Cleveland a liar. Cleveland banged

39

him into the gutter near Seneca Street. John Meyer and I followed along the sidewalk, watching the battle." [1]

And another biographer, Denis Tilden Lynch, told of the effects of the barroom atmosphere on the young lawyer:

> One of the beer gardens sold a cigar that Cleveland liked above all others. So he had some of these made up and sent to his room. He lighted one. But it did not taste the same. He smoked another. But that one also seemed to lack something. At last he hit upon what was lacking—it was the sanded floor of the beer garden. He missed the crunching of the sand underfoot and all that went with it—the gas lights, the gay laughter, the foaming steins, the joyous songs, the pretty women.[2]

True, many of his evening companions who drank beer with him and played pinochle at The Shades or at Louis Goetz's just behind City Hall were young lawyers like himself. They were not yet married, and if they enjoyed poker sessions in Level's Livery Stable, in one of the many German beer gardens, or in the back room of one of the saloons, it was a temporary amusement until they could find wives. But what for them was temporary, for Cleveland was permanent. He stayed, until he grew middle-aged, with the same sort of loafers, at the same sort of diversionary occupations. It was seedy company, but it was what he liked.

The part of town where Grover lived all the time he remained in Buffalo was either on the edge or in the midst of a sort of frontier civilization. It was not his habit to spend his evenings in the places maintained for the entertainment of the rowdy Irish and Poles; he preferred others, run by the very different Germans who carried over from Bavaria the tradition of the beer garden and the family restaurant. A man could go there with friends, occupy a table in the rear, and stay on for hours over checkers or cards. If the place was a garden, it would have music and there would be singing, and everyone was welcome to join in the choruses.

In Grover's neighborhood there were many such places. And

---

[1] Charles Armitage, *Grover Cleveland as Buffalo Knew Him*, p. 34. These recollections gathered in the 1920s made up a series of articles later published as a book by *The Buffalo Evening News*.

[2] *Grover Cleveland: A Man Four-Square*, p. 48.

it would have been thought he was as typically German as the big-bellied workers and merchants to be found there. He sang choruses lustily with the others; he drank stein after stein of beer; and he loved the hearty food—the sausages and sauerkraut, the thick stews, and the immense cuts of meat. Since he worked over a desk and spent much of his leisure with law books and briefs, this sort of recreation was certain to have results. In the fifteen years between his arrival in Buffalo and his becoming sheriff, he had gained a good deal more than a hundred pounds. The nieces and nephews he was beginning to see on those few occasions when he visited his family in Holland Patent began to call him "Uncle Jumbo."

He was not only a hulking figure with hanging jowls when he reached his late thirties, but he had grown what was called a "walrus" mustache. Since he made little effort to appear attractive to women, had no social aspirations, and seldom even made an appearance before a jury, this ungainliness was no handicap—or at least not enough of one so that he did anything about it. On the contrary, for the sort of clients he had, for appearances in judicial proceedings, and for the duties of the sheriff's office, his bulk gave him a ponderous dignity. No one could look at him without having the impression of enormous solidity. This was easily translated into trustworthiness.

Having no family ties, and having no cultural interests outside the law, it was almost inevitable that Grover should make an even more serious mistake. He found himself attracted by an un-attached widow, visited her from time to time, and presently dis-covered, after their intimacy, that she was to have a child. Instead of marrying the lady and giving the boy a father, he met his obligation by providing for her confinement and providing ample support. She was not the sort of woman he would want for a wife.

Mrs. Maria Crofts Halpin was thirty-five when her relationship with Grover began; she was tall, graceful, attractive and amusing. She lived with her two children not far from Grover's apartment, and earned a living for them and for herself by working in a department store. His unwillingness to marry her may have arisen from a suspicion that he was not her only friend, perhaps not even the father of her child; but about this he never made any comment.

Obviously he might have been the father, and he was not one to shirk an obligation.

During the next few years, Mrs. Halpin, still supported by Grover but no longer visited by him, fell into dissolute ways and began to neglect the child. Grover's paternal sentiment was satisfied by persuading one of his cronies, who was an official, to sign an order taking the boy away from his mother and placing him temporarily in an orphanage; afterward Grover arranged a home in the family of a friend and the boy grew up quite happily. Ultimately, under the name of his adopted parents, he became a prominent physician.

As might be expected, Mrs. Halpin resented the legalized separation from her son and brought suit for the boy's return. She lost, and presently she dropped out of sight, or, at least, out of Grover's life. She would make a ghostly return when the story, well known to Buffalonians, was revived in 1884 during the presidential campaign, with what effect we shall see.

Those who have written about Grover, and have had to confront the apparently contradictory facts of his career, have been apt to speak in despair of "the two Clevelands": one a roisterer, a sort of legal bum, a consorter with low comrades, a participant in the prevalent practices of the political life he loved, and the other an enormously industrious and capable lawyer who labored over his cases and was always the master of the situations he was involved in. But the two Clevelands, however contradictory the facts make him appear, were the same fellow.

He was no drunkard, although he often drank quantities of Buffalo's favorite pale German lager; he was never dissolute, although he often spent his evenings in beer gardens or playing cards in saloons. He simply preferred these amusements and these companions. His sturdy constitution allowed for both work and the strain of overeating and copious drinking. Besides, when it was looked into, it could be seen that he was joined in these recreations, as in his occasional fishing expeditions, by other young fellows who also became in time the most dignified and affluent members of the Erie County bar. True, they resigned from the saloon crowd sooner than he and took to family life. But others came along; and he always had company in his favorite resorts.

When he finished his term as sheriff and formed the partnership with Lyman K. Bass and Wilson S. Bissell, he was almost at once recognized as a capable and trustworthy attorney. Political job holding was not long held against him. Besides, he had a good deal of useful knowledge. That is to say, he knew all about the city, from top to bottom. He knew its virtues, its vices, its men of integrity, and its crooks and grafters. He knew how to get done whatever had to be done. Such a counselor, it was evidently thought, was preferable to one who knew only the law to be found in books and had had no such experiences. It was known that he had associates of doubtful character, but it was also known that he never shared in any dishonest deals. Perhaps his term as sheriff, usually the end of usefulness for any man of integrity, had even added to his reputation for honesty and dependability.

It could be summed up in this way: his mistakes were behind him, and if he meant only to be a lawyer and to remain a private person, they would remain buried. His child was adopted into a good family; his war record was seldom mentioned; and since he had remained an honest man in crooked company and everyone knew it, his political history counted rather for than against him. He need explain to no one why he preferred to be with those who hung out in the saloons—many of his clients, the wealthy corporate executives, the merchants and men of property probably understood this well enough. Their great houses on Delaware Avenue were, many of them, wasteful burdens and sources of boredom, rather than places of enjoyment and satisfaction. They may well have envied Grover his carefree existence and his common associates. At any rate, they were glad to have him as their lawyer. His practice was as profitable and respectable as any in the city of Buffalo.

7

THE years after Grover left the sheriff's office to become again a practicing lawyer were on the whole uneventful. He matured in his profession, he modified his roistering habits somewhat, as would be expected of a man grown out of his twenties. He now lived in a suite of well-furnished rooms and frequented more respectable restaurants and higher class saloons. But his apartment and the eating and drinking places were in the same old neighborhood he knew so well, or, at least were no farther away than a few blocks.

Many of his meals of this period were taken in Gerot's French restaurant, or in the Tifft House, Buffalo's best hotel. He was one of the organizers of the City Club, too, and went there often. The more sedate Buffalo Club he did not join—or perhaps was not asked to join. He would be made an honorary member when he became mayor and his portrait would be hung in the lounge, but its heavy solemnity was not the sort of atmosphere he liked.

The offices of Bass, Cleveland and Bissell were on the second floor of the Weed building, an ugly utilitarian structure at the corner of Main and Swan Streets, and were reached by an outside staircase. Their furnishings were much in the style of the building. There were plain tables and desks, together with shelves of law books; and heat was furnished by a fat-bellied coal stove sitting on a zinc mat.

Grover's living quarters were in a sort of addition at the rear. A few of his friends lived nearby, but usually only temporarily. One of these was Powers Fillmore, son of the old President, now dead. Powers was eccentric and never amounted to much, but was tolerated by Grover's circle. Oscar Folsom, an original partner

Cleveland thought so highly of as a friend, lived nearby for a time too. But Folsom soon married and moved to a house on the west side. In due time he had a daughter named Frances. Cleveland went to see the baby a number of times—she was called Frankie—and when Folsom was killed in an accident in 1874, Grover became the executor of the family estate and guardian of the child. He watched her grow with developing affection. Once he told an inquiring sister who complained of his continued bachelorhood that he was "waiting for his wife to grow up." Perhaps he was.

A tragedy during those years saddened him. His brothers Cecil and Fred were lost together in the burning and sinking of the steamship *Missouri* off the Bahama Island of Great Abaco on October 22, 1872. Fred left a small estate, but Grover, after his death, was more than ever responsible for his mother and sisters. William, the eldest brother, was much the same sort of impecunious minister his father had been and could hardly support his own dependents. There was no one else.

Cecil and Fred had emerged from their military service to follow business careers. Of the two, Fred had prospered more; and he had eventually taken Cecil into partnership. He was a speculator and hotel proprietor, his largest property being a hotel in Fairfield, Connecticut. But he had also acquired a lease of the Royal Victoria in Nassau, and went there in winter to operate it, with Cecil to assist him. It was on a journey to open the hotel for the season that they were lost at sea.

Not for many years had all the brothers lived near one another; but there were strong affections among the members of the family. When Grover was away from Buffalo, his friends there could guess that he was in Holland Patent where his mother continued to live. There the brothers and sisters gathered when they could and recaptured something of the family fondness they had had when they were young and their father was still alive.

Before he died, Fred had bought the Holland Patent house for his mother; and he had now left some property to Louise, the sister who had remained unmarried and was caring for their mother. The Connecticut hotel was soon disposed of, but the Royal Victoria was more of a problem. The depression of 1873 was a severe one and to get rid of a resort hotel at such a time

45

was not easy. For some years Grover supervised its management. There is no real record of it, but he is said to have gone there once or twice to assure himself about the management. If he did, it was the only time in his whole life except for a few excursions across the border into Canada, and a trip to Bermuda after retirement, that he traveled outside the United States.

The Halpin affair must have been a worry. Providing for a child he only half acknowledged, and whose mother he did not respect, was certainly not an easy matter for a leading member of the Bar. But once the boy was adopted and had a good home, he could be easier about his future. The boy's first names, by the way, were Oscar Folsom. This was a way of acknowledging paternity; and a gesture of affection for his closest friend; but it did lead later to rumors that Folsom rather than Grover was the father, something Grover indignantly denied.

He continued to add poundage. His friends testified that he was no voracious eater, although he did prefer hearty German food; it was immoderate quantities of beer that made him so unwieldy. Now that he no longer visited the Allen family and no longer spent days or weekends at Grand Island, he was more than ever sedentary. His favorite recreation was still fishing, although he was now able to afford the considerable expense involved in hunting ducks. This, however, was so seasonal a sport that it did not rank in his estimation with fishing in the lake or in the river. He now went farther for the sport, often as far as the lower Niagara in the Youngstown or Lewiston area, and with parties of friends hired a boat for a day or two. The cronies also formed a club and built a retreat for themselves on a small island in the upper Niagara—the Beaver Island Club, they called it. They kept it well stocked with beer and food, and it was often a weekend rendezvous.

The firm of Bass, Cleveland and Bissell, with its extensive affairs, now had young men in training as Grover had trained with Rogers, Bowen and Rogers. In 1877, Bass was found to have incipient tuberculosis and moved to Colorado Springs where, when he was able, he went into practice, leaving Grover in virtually sole command of the Buffalo office. Bass came back to Buffalo occasionally, but in 1880 the firm changed its name to Cleveland,

Bissell and Sicard—the Sicard who joined being already a well-known lawyer. Wilson S. Bissell, familiarly called "Shan," gradually became Cleveland's best friend; especially after Folsom died they drew closer together. But Bissell was quite different from Grover. He was gay and gregarious, much given to going in for society; and he was a family man. They had deep respect for each other, and even after he had left Buffalo, Grover would depend on Bissell for many services only a close friend could provide. Bissell would be a name well known in Buffalo for generations to come.

Grover and Bissell did have one difference that could later be seen to have influenced Grover's career in an important way. Bissell wanted to accept an offer that came to them from the New York Central Railroad to act as the corporation's attorneys in western New York. This was a signal recognition of the status attained by the firm, and Bissell could see no reason for not accepting. It meant taking into the partnership two lawyers who had recently been acting for the Central, and it was urged by Chauncey M. Depew himself, who was president of the railroad.

Bissell could not understand why Grover was hesitant, and he was even more surprised when Grover finally told him he must refuse. Grover gave as his reason that if they accepted they would have to enlarge their offices and staff, thus taking on more responsibility; but, even worse, they would practically be at the disposal of the railroad with its many interests and its large volume of work —acquiring land, defending damage suits, representing it in all its dealings with the city and, of course, with the other cities and towns of western New York.

Grover's view prevailed. If he had consented to have the firm represent the railroad, he would certainly not have run for mayor and would not have gone on from there to the governorship.

He had not the slightest intention of going back into politics; only a week or two before he consented to be nominated for the mayoralty, nothing could have seemed to him less likely. We can see why. He was now a man of some property, head of a respected firm having custody of many estates, and attorney for banks and industrial firms of the highest standing. He could imagine himself going on to only one further post—that of a judgeship, prefer-

4 7

ably a federal one, if there should ever again be a Democratic President to appoint him.

He was keeping in touch with the Democratic organization, not so much with a judgeship in mind, since he was quite satisfied with things as they were, as because of old associations and the same sense of loyalty that was always important in his scheme of things. He had a strong feeling that the party stood for the right principles, but he resented its sponsorship and support of bosses like John C. Sheehan.

Sheehan had by now developed a "ring" of corrupt politicians, and its members had grown bolder and bolder. They bought votes to place their henchmen in the Common Council, then got the council to approve contracts for favored contractors. The contractors, in turn, kicked back part of their profits.

Another source of income for the politicians was the waterfront district where the saloonkeepers exploited the sailors and roustabouts and paid the politicians to see that they were left alone. The politicians also shared pay-offs from brothelkeepers. All in all, it was corrupt in a way that was all too common at that time. The city machinery, indeed the processes of democracy, were used for personal profit. The degradation of the city was complete.

Just recently the notorious Tweed ring in New York had been exposed and ousted. The Buffalo ring was the same sort, and it operated in the same way. The organization used part of its profits to do small favors for the poor—take care of a widow's rent, buy a few buckets of coal for a family whose father was out of a job, arrange for offenders to be kept out of jail, protect illegal gambling places—and in these ways buy support. They actually had to pay very little for votes; but, whatever the going price, the loot was worth it.

The participants in the Buffalo ring were mostly Irish; but there were Germans in it too. It was something to be expected, really; the voters were immigrants inexperienced in democracy, living in extreme poverty, continually insecure, and without other defenses against a hostile world than the friendly boss who could be depended on "to take care of them."

There were many even among the Irish and German politicians who resented what was being done to the city and to government in general, and refused to participate. But the ring was powerful. Its allies operated at every level. Corruption infected the government at Albany, and the Republican regime in Washington seemed a reflection of what was happening in the cities.

Cleveland, even if he had no desire to be known as a reformer, was revolted by Sheehan's system. He had many friends in the Democratic organization who were also dismayed by the bosses' excesses. Why, Sheehan was actually comptroller of the city—an instance of putting a wolf to guard the sheep if there ever was one!

Among the Irishmen who not only were honest, but had grown more and more outraged, was Grover's boyhood friend, Timothy Mahoney, who had occupied various offices in the police force and the city government. Mahoney—"Captain Tim" he was called, since he had been a captain of detectives—had been chairman of the Erie County Democratic Committee in 1881 and was succeeded by Peter Doyle. Both were Roman Catholics, something that would prove to be important; both were firm friends of Grover's; and both were ashamed of the organization's involvement in corruption.

By 1881, they had had all they could stand. They and their friends—for there were others—resolved on a cleanup. And it was for this reason that Cleveland was urged to run for mayor. It was partly accidental, as most such occurrences are. Mahoney, Doyle, and the others did not at first think of Grover. They hoped to find a prominent businessman who would take on the job of heading a reform ticket. Past experience should have told them that this was not a very good idea. The last two mayors had been "prominent businessmen." One of these had been Solomon Scheu, a wealthy brewer, the other a manufacturer, Alexander Brush. These two had been as ineffective in office as they had been effective in business. They had accepted the honor, occupied the office, and allowed the ring to go on with its operations without the slightest interference.

Still Mahoney and his friends, set on ousting Sheehan, could think of no other way to get outside the circle of politics altogether, as they felt they must do. They formed a group to call on several respectable men whose prestige would have been unquestioned, but all refused. They were sitting in the back of Billy Drainger's saloon one evening, after a day spent in this effort. They were consoling themselves as best they could after their rebuffs when Grover walked in, and having gotten himself a full stein at the bar, sat down and asked them why they looked so doleful. They told him. Then, as the story goes, they looked at each other and said, "Why not Grover?" True, he was a lawyer, not a business-man; true, also, he had been "mixed up in politics." But everyone knew his reputation for absolute honesty, and he was well known to detest Sheehan and his crowd. Finally, there was his practice as counselor for the most respectable of Buffalo's citizens.

Perhaps to their surprise, Cleveland did not hesitate. He accepted. But there was one condition—he must be allowed to name the other candidates on his ticket. His companions knew that this meant ousting Sheehan as candidate for comptroller. They were willing, but how could it be done and Cleveland's nomination still brought about? They went over and over it; it looked almost impossible. But they would try. They were again surprised when Sheehan agreed to Cleveland's candidates without argument. He may have thought his time had come; he may have thought he could go on with his machinations as well out of office as in—the behavior of the Common Council right after the election would seem to indicate that Grover was thought to be another Scheu or Brush, who would sit at the mayor's desk without knowing what went on in the city's offices. At any rate, Cleveland was allowed to have Tim Mahoney as his substitute for Sheehan on the ticket as comptroller. It was arranged in the convention of 1881. Charles Armitage tells how it was accomplished:

. . . the convention was called to order by James Muldoon, Chairman of the city committee. Cleveland's name was presented for Mayor and promptly withdrawn by his friend, Warren F. Miller. Mr. Miller contented himself with merely saying that Mr. Cleveland wouldn't accept. He didn't tell why, but that wasn't necessary. Everybody present knew that Cleveland had insisted on knowing the identity of the nominee for Comptroller before giving an answer . . .

So, passing the Mayoralty for the time being, the convention took up the nomination for Comptroller and promptly handed it over to Sheehan. And Michael Shannon as promptly announced Sheehan's declination. Sheehan had scored the point. . . . He had made it known to the world that he could be nominated if he wanted to be, all the "Big Steves" [supporters of Grover] in it notwithstanding. Then he yielded to pressure and most unwillingly effaced himself . . .

While the convention was storm-tossed between those who insisted on the nomination of Cleveland and the elimination of Sheehan and others who bitterly resented Cleveland's attitude . . . a committee of three sought Cleveland in a last effort to bring about harmony. They found him in the Supreme Court, engaged in a trial before Judge Haight . . .

"The Committee," the judge afterward said, "came into court and attracted the attention of Cleveland, who stepped aside and held a brief conference. Then he came up to my desk, leaning his elbows on it, and talking across in low tones.

" 'This,' he said, indicating the committee with a nod, 'is a committee from the Democratic convention, and they want to nominate me for Mayor. They've come over to see if I'll accept. What shall I do about it?'

" 'I think you had better accept,' " was Judge Haight's reply . . .

" 'But I'm practicing law and I don't want it interfered with,' " objected Cleveland.

" 'The Mayoralty is an honorable position,' " urged Judge Haight. " 'We are all interested in having a good city government. You're an old "bach." You haven't any family to take care of. I'd advise you to accept.' " " 'May I have a little time?' " asked Cleveland.

" 'How much time do you want?'

" 'Half an hour.'

" 'Court stands in recess for half an hour,' " announced Judge Haight.

"He was back on the minute," Judge Haight recalled. "He came up to the bench again and said in an undertone, 'John Sheehan has got enough delegates to nominate him for Comptroller. I won't go on the ticket with him and told the committee so . . . If they get rid of him, I'll take the nomination!' "

Within an hour the convention got rid of Sheehan and Cleveland became its nominee.[1]

[1] This account by Judge Haight was recalled from forty years in the past but seems to have been vivid in the judge's mind. The face-saving for the Irish boss who had to be got rid of is characteristic of political processes of any day and age. And the account of Cleveland's start on the amazingly quick climb to the White House is at least a ray of light to illumine that mystery.

The complete ticket was as follows:

For Mayor
GROVER CLEVELAND

For Comptroller
TIMOTHY J. MAHONEY

For Attorney
GILES E. STILWELL

For Engineer
THOMAS J. ROGERS

For Treasurer
GERHARD LANG

For Street Commissioner
JOHN MAHONY

For Superintendent of Education
JAMES F. CROOKER

For Overseer of the Poor
JOHN R. WALTER

For Assessor
JOHN H. LUDWIG

Grover made numerous campaign speeches, mostly in the districts he was familiar with but some in other parts of the city. He called on the Democrats to stand by. He urged the respectable citizens to accept his promise of honest administration. And that was his whole plea. He said nothing about reform, nothing about reorganization. He merely promised to be a businesslike mayor.

It was enough. He defeated his Republican opponent by a striking majority, and in a year when the Democratic candidates for state office all ran behind their Republican opponents in Erie County.

8

GROVER Cleveland, now mayor (and Big Steve only to old friends), proceeded at once to behave as he had promised the voters he would behave. He was able to display his methods dramatically because the Common Council of the city, or a majority of them, conspicuously lacked the virtues he himself exemplified. They regarded public office as a way of profiting at the public expense and they had no scruples about the means used either for getting into office or using it for their own purposes when they had arrived. Cleveland meant to stop this. It seems to have been his only reason for running, that and perhaps a more personal determination to show Sheehan and White that he could get the best of them. Certainly he had no thought, at first, that the mayoralty might lead on to the governorship.

The malefactors had plenty of warning. In almost every one of his campaign talks, he had said that the business of government ought to be carried out "on the same principles" as any private business, "competently and economically." If he was elected, he had said, he intended to see that things were run in just that way. The following excerpt from a speech in Tivoli Hall is typical:

There is, or there should be, no reason why the affairs of our city should not be managed with the same care and economy as private interests. And when we consider that public officials are trustees of the people, and hold their places and exercise their powers for the benefit of the people, there should be no higher inducement to a faithful and honest discharge of public duty.

The members of the ring must have thought this mere campaign talk. The last two mayors had talked this way too before

5 3

Mayor Cleveland (*Courtesy of The Firestone Library, Princeton University, Princeton, New Jersey*)

they were elected; and the councilmen probably thought that Cleveland was another of the same sort. Once in office he would be "reasonable." True, he had a reputation for honesty, and his supporters had certainly been out to get rid of Sheehan. But he had never been a reformer, and he had in the past been a faithful party worker. He had been a troublesome and uncooperative sheriff, but memories are short and that was some time in the past. Mainly, they relied on his being a "regular fellow," "one of the boys."

It was really most fortunate for Cleveland that he had a corrupt council to deal with. A look back over the careers of many political leaders who have risen to the top makes it quite apparent that some of their worst trials contributed effectively to their advancement. A leader needs an enemy as a foil. He needs something the voters can be made indignant about—in fairy-tale terms, he needs dragons to slay, ones breathing smoke and fire, readily identifiable, easily made to seem evil. When he overcomes them, he demonstrates his fidelity and his toughness. He becomes a hero.

Cleveland had enemies and they soon became bitter ones. They were members of the old ring. With unalloyed stupidity, they offered him all the chances any champion could desire. It was not a role that Cleveland would have cast himself in. By temperament he was stolid and reticent, not a knight in shining armor. He was better at composing lawyerlike vetoes than stirring political pronunciamentos, and he had no gift for oratory. He kept closely to simple issues, but when he had an open-and-shut case, what he said had pile-driver force.

He was as well aware as anyone that very few mayors had advanced beyond mayoralties. Somehow the job always seemed to be terminal. Even city reformers who had been notable people's defenders seldom became governors; and only one President had ever served as chief executive of a city.[1]

No, when Cleveland consented to run for mayor in Buffalo, he could not have had it in mind to strike for a higher elective office. His political ambitions had been dead for years. To be a

[1] This was Andrew Johnson who had been mayor of Greeneville, Tennessee.

judge, however, was different; this he may still have hoped for. But when he castigated and defeated the ring in the spring of 1882, he was merely doing something that needed to be done. He had long known about the misfeasances of the politicians and had often expressed his indignation. He was now in a position to do something about it, and it was indeed stupid of his opponents to conclude that he had not meant it and to provide him with such rich opportunities.

The council members, if they had not listened when he made his campaign speeches, might have taken warning from his inaugural address. This was no inspiring call for reform. He simply denounced the neglect apparent in the care of the streets and said plainly that the bills for repairing and furnishing schools had been extravagant. He pointed out that the city auditor had a duty to do more than add up columns of figures to see that totals were correct; he ought, he said, to examine the merits of the claims he allowed to be paid. This was clear enough, and he used no high-flown language. There was plenty of reference to the worst practices he intended to stop, but still he apparently was not believed.

The spoilsmen should have recalled that they were dealing with a man who had been assistant district attorney, the investigating agency of the county. He could not have served in this office without knowing exactly how the city was being robbed and who was doing it. Nevertheless, within a few weeks, as though they neither knew his record nor believed his statement of intentions, the council members were back at their old tricks.

This gave Cleveland the chance to veto a large number of small bills handing out favors, and he was soon able to demonstrate in two particularly notorious instances what he had meant by honesty in office. Both of these attracted so much publicity that they became unmistakable lessons in citizenship. They also distinguished him once and for all as a determined defender of the public interest. What many politicians have to do by speechifying and making wordy defenses was done for him by the newspapers. His own prose might be dull and awkward, but reporters could turn it into startling pronunciamentos; and they did.

The first opportunity with dramatic possibilities was his veto of a street-cleaning contract approved by the council. This contract was awarded to one George Talbot for $422,000. There had been five other bids, all lower, and some more than $100,000 lower. It was apparent to everyone when Cleveland pointed out the facts that the added sum was going to be divided among the council members who had voted for it. This can have surprised no one. It was cynically recognized as a regular thing. But when Cleveland, for once almost eloquent in his indignation, wrote his veto message, and the newspapers underlined its phrases, it rang like an alarm bell in Buffalo's streets: "I withhold my consent . . . because I regard it as the culmination of a most barefaced, impudent, and shameless scheme to betray the interests of the people, and to worse than squander the public money."

He did give the council members a way out. Many of them must have voted for this contract, he said, not knowing what it meant. They hastily backed down. They had approved the resolution 13 to 11; they rescinded it by a vote of 23 to 2. But they were too late. They were labeled—and so was the vetoing mayor. They were foxes caught in the chicken yard. He was the faithful watchdog.

The vetoing mayor—that was the way he was known now. It was a strange way to become a famous figure; it was purely negative. It did not state any new or progressive intentions. Honesty was not a radical principle, but it was strange in city affairs. When thieves and grafters were denounced everyone woke up to their prevalence in public life—in nation and state as well as the cities. It was as startling as a cry of fire in the night. And it carried far. The news of a sturdy honest man in public life could not long be confined to Buffalo alone. It was first heard outside of Buffalo, even if faintly, in the state capital, Albany, where the ring had allies and where graft was rampant too. In June, the suggestion had been made that Cleveland was just the sort of person needed in the governorship, and the thought was being repeated outside the city. This was the beginning of something that rapidly developed into a cause.

But between the veto of the street-cleaning contract and the proposal that he be a candidate for governor, there were other performances only slightly less disturbing in a city used to the sale of favors and promotions. The one that had most impact was the usually unexciting matter of the city's sewers. There was a somewhat complicated situation because of Buffalo's nearness to Lake Erie and the existence of the Erie Canal. Because a branch of the canal crossed the line of sewage flow to the lake, the water filled with filth simply stayed there and became a noisome mess, not only one that stank, but one that bred disease.

These were not enlightened times in matters of public health. Most cities simply allowed their sewers to empty into the nearest streams, and if they were stagnant ones, the resultant conditions were much like those in Buffalo. But this particular nuisance was in a thickly populated district and was getting worse from year to year. There had been many proposals for abatement, all of them needing expert engineering and all of them costly. The most sensible called for an intercepting sewer, but this was also the most complicated and expensive. If not engineered with the best advice and with close management, it would neither serve the purpose nor be financially feasible.

To meet the situation, Cleveland proposed that the state legislature create a Citizens' Commission to make final studies and take responsibility for construction. He had already pointed out that epidemic disease rates of frightening proportions could be traced to the stewing sewage. The work would take some years to be completed—longer than the terms of city officials—and it ought to have continuing supervision.

In ordinary circumstances, experts in city government would oppose a proposal for outside management. The public works of a city ought to be planned and built by its own engineers. This one had been contemplated for a long time; and if the city's departments could not carry it out, some employees who could ought to be found. This might be true in theory, but Cleveland was confronted with a fact. This was that the city's engineering department was under the control of the ring. Its employees owed their jobs to favor and not to competence. He did not exactly say so, but it was plainly implied that this most expensive public work in Buffalo's history would be more a source of profit to grafters than a relief for the city if it should be left to the department.

The proposal for outside help caused a furor. The profits in works of this size were immense; moreover, there would be many

5 8

jobs to be distributed among the faithful. Advertisements had been put out for bids, and one had been received for more than a million and a half dollars. The city engineer declared that his staff was entirely capable of doing the job and in anticipation proceeded to hire a number of new employees. The council refused to back Cleveland's plan.

Their defiance provoked a message from Cleveland pointing out that the city had already displayed its incompetence by allowing the situation to grow into a crisis: several years ago the city had been cited in a grand jury presentment for maintaining a nuisance. Moreover the engineer had been directed at that time to prepare plans. He now said the job would be easy, but the fact was that the plans were yet to be made. He had done nothing.

The councilmen did not give up easily. A bill in the legislature creating the commission asked for by Cleveland was opposed by a council resolution; then, when they saw how little support they had —all the newspapers were pillorying them—they offered a substitute bill that would have set up a commission, but one with no real powers of oversight. But when in June the legislature passed Cleveland's bill, not theirs, they were whipped.

They still tried to interfere by rejecting Cleveland's nominations for the commission. With newspaper support firmly on his side, he simply sent the same names back, saying in his message that he was sure the members had not looked closely enough into the matter. The names were indeed those of honest and capable citizens. Finally, having brought upon themselves all the disgrace they could well have contrived, and having given Cleveland the opportunity to appear as a rigorous reformer, his enemies gave up. It remains to be said of this incident that the project was built and the nuisance abated at about half the cost of the bid received and endorsed by the council.

These were two of the issues that got notoriety beyond the city's limits. But there were others, and taken together they represented so formidable a record that Cleveland as a potential governor became a familiar idea, at least in the western part of the state; and his reputation was well known as far east as Syracuse and Albany. New York City had still not heard of him; but New York was a provincial place. Nothing that went on upstate was much noticed;

if it did not affect the city directly, it could not be important. Especially was this true of Tammany, the powerful political organization in the city. They took care of their own, did what they could in Albany, and went on with their system of graft and corruption. They knew very well how to manage this, and their constant effort was to bulwark their domain against interference from Albany and Washington. Sometimes they went further and tried to use state and national officials for their own purposes. Cleveland would have some experience of this. But it was so much like the operations of the ring in Buffalo that he was always ahead of the grafters and always able to frustrate their plans.

9

CLEVELAND may have grown fat and even lethargic, but it suddenly appeared that his old political aspirations were merely latent; they had not been extinguished. It was now 1882 and his defeats for office years ago had seemed to end his ambition for public office. Comfortable settlement into practice apparently indicated complete satisfaction with the law as a career. As time passed he could expect to become even more well off; he would have more and more respectable clients; and presently he would stand among a few fellow lawyers at the very head of the Buffalo bar. But now, having made something of a sacrifice to become mayor, and having seen how well he did the job, his old desires were relit.

It did not take so old and experienced a hand as Cleveland long to figure out the advantage he had gained by his successive victories over the ring. His present ambition may have run more to a judgeship than to elective office; but these were Republican days and a federal appointment was unlikely. He could only hope for a place in the state judiciary; and this was a minor honor. If he were to pursue his new career of public service instead of going back again to the law, the best way to do it was by way of Albany —by being elected governor. It was just possible that the way was open. We must briefly inquire why this was so.

The office was indeed an important one; New York was the largest of the states and all its governors were eligible to nomination for the presidency. The parties usually selected as governor, for this reason, a man who had already become an important figure —a senator or a congressman. In 1882 there were two contenders who were considered to be in the lead. One was Roswell P.

Flower of Watertown, and the other was General Henry W. Slocum of Brooklyn. Flower was a wealthy financier as well as a lawyer, an attractive youngish man who had already been a member of the Congress and was extremely ambitious. Slocum, an older man, had been one of Sherman's generals in his march to the sea and carried the glamour of having been an authentic fighter for his country.

The political leaders who would have the real say about the nomination were, as usual, maneuvering for advantage, and, as usual, were divided into Tammany and anti-Tammany cliques. Tammany had not yet wholly shaken free of the odium accumulated during the regime of the infamous Tweed and his ring ten years earlier. The present leader was John Kelly, a much cleverer man than Tweed, but not much more inclined to check the grafting of minor leaders, who, as always, were more interested in maintaining local power than in serving the party. If it meant throwing votes to Republicans, they were willing to do so. In state conventions, Tammany sought to commit the selected candidate to its interests, and if it could not accomplish this it knifed him. In national politics, in 1876, it had treated Hancock, the Democratic candidate, in this way and had helped to elect the Republican, Garfield. This betrayal had stimulated the organization of a group of reformers who called themselves the "County Democracy." Its most prominent members were Abram S. Hewitt, Hubert O. Thompson and William C. Whitney. They were formidable citizens; and their organization, having won elections in 1881 for state offices, might be more important in the state Democratic convention of that summer than Tammany itself.

Another influential figure was Daniel Manning of Albany, whose regional organization was expected to unite with the County Democracy against Tammany.

Cleveland's strength lay in the fact that none of the factions—Tammany, the County Democracy or Manning's organization in Albany—had a candidate they were really satisfied with. And Cleveland's supporters had a qualified man, although he was still little known outside of western New York and hardly at all in the city.

Cleveland himself saw soon enough that he might very well be a convenient candidate for all to agree on. The Flower and Slocum supporters were likely to reach a stalemate, each more willing to turn to a third person than to give in to the other. By early September—the state convention was to open on September 21— Cleveland's friends were hard at work, and his name was becoming familiar farther and farther to the east. One candidate from Elmira, David B. Hill, who would later be governor, saw the possibilities and indicated his willingness to withdraw in favor of Cleveland.

Even more important, one of Daniel Manning's lieutenants, Edgar K. Apgar of Albany, had suggested to Cleveland that he visit Manning. This was actually something of a trap, but Cleveland was too shrewd and far-sighted to fall into it. He answered Apgar that a visit would be unwise, since he wanted his name, if it was to be presented to the convention, to be that of a man who had no alliances and was free from entanglements. At the same time he realized well enough how important Manning's support was. The Albany leader was the inheritor of the organization that had formerly supported both Tilden and Seymour, the one a candidate who had *almost* become President, and the other the governor who had been nominated for the presidency but had lost the subsequent election to Grant. So his answer was very carefully worded, and evidently did not offend the Albany leader. When Apgar then began to work in Cleveland's interest, it showed where Manning stood. This, combined with other Cleveland support, made him a very strong contender when the convention opened.

He made his first real move when he came back from visiting his mother in Holland Patent during her last illness. He sent for Mahoney and surprised his old friend by asking if he was a good Catholic. Mahoney could see what was coming; and sure enough, the next question was whether he was a member of the Catholic Mutual Benefit Association. This was the only hint Mahoney needed. The Irish by now had nearly a monopoly of second-rank political jobs everywhere in upper New York. They were not casual laborers and homeless men as their fathers had been; they were the second generation and full citizens. Their treatment as inferiors in earlier days had kept them in a close association that still held. Word passed among them was certain to have concerted results.

Cleveland's accord with the Germans, begun when he had worked in the second ward, together with Mahoney's standing with the Irish, similarly begun in the eleventh ward, made a strong combination. But that was only for Buffalo, and the nomination was not going to be won in that city alone; so Mahoney went on tour. All the cities along the canal had Catholic political bosses; and the Irish had spread into valleys to the south as well. Mahoney found allies as far east as Syracuse and even down on the Pennsylvania border in Wellsville and Jamestown, and in total lined up some sixty delegates.

The Buffalo delegation itself had a whole series of stories to tell besides the ones concerning the street-cleaning and sewer contracts. A favorite one was how Cleveland, to save money, had cut off some lucrative printing contracts given by custom to German- and Polish-language newspapers. And it pleased the delegates to brag that he had also refused an appropriation for the annual celebration of the Grand Army of the Republic. He wasn't even afraid of the old soldiers! And he had cleverly combined this rejection with a personal gift to the entertainment fund, so that the veterans could hardly express their anger in public. It was not the city's business, he had said, to provide a picnic for the boys.

Taken altogether, by July the Cleveland reputation as a careful and courageous public servant was not only solidly established in Buffalo and its surrounding counties, but was talked of in Albany. Even his old friends in the demi-world where he had lived so long were proud of him—not only because he was mayor, but because he was so impregnably honest. It sort of made them feel respectable too.

It was evident that Cleveland, sitting through the summer nights with his dying mother and walking in the village streets, had come to some conclusions. His present life, comfortable as it was, did not satisfy his sense of duty. He had lived without protest among the corrupters of public life for twenty years; he had even benefited from the degenerate system. He had discovered as mayor that a man who steadfastly refused to benefit further, or to allow the

Brooklyn's welcome to Governor Cleveland, 1884 (*Courtesy of The New-York Historical Society, New York City*)

corruption he knew of to go on, could prevail. Moreover, it might just be that a candidate, by displaying a record of integrity and making that his only claim as a candidate, would find the voters responsive.

But first he had to be nominated. And that might not be easy. No candidate for governor, much less any higher office, had come from Buffalo in a long time. Yet the situation was such that there might be a chance for a western man if the Slocum and Flower forces refused to give way to each other and looked for a compromise candidate. Honesty in office would not appeal to the professionals. It might even turn them against him. But in their desire to win, they might overlook his virtues.

There were some complications and some tense moments, but that was the way things did work out.

The state convention at Syracuse began on September 21. It was not notably different from others before and after. Three factions came prepared to put forward their choices, much maneuvering and trading having gone on for some time, and all knew quite well that there might be need to maneuver and trade some more.

In this instance the Flower and Slocum supporters each could count on about one hundred delegates. Since the whole number was 385, nearly a hundred more had to be coralled if either was to be nominated. Cleveland's lively Irish and German supporters had collected fewer delegate promises, but they had more enthusiasm and were prepared to work harder.

Two factors were important. One was the split in the New York City delegation. The other was Manning's interest in Cleveland. In the bargaining to come there were many possibilities, and Tim Mahoney was alert to all of them.

Then, on the day the convention met, word came that the Republican convention, meeting the day before in Saratoga, had nominated a candidate who might be easier to beat than the Democrats had calculated. This needs a word of explanation.

The national Republican party had as its leader President Chester A. Arthur. Arthur, for most of his life, had worked in the interest of Senator Roscoe Conkling of New York; and together they had dominated Republican politics in New York for many years. They were allied with Jay Gould, the financial speculator who had been a notorious suborner of New York politicians for almost as long. This group had now exerted its combined influence and decided to name a more pliable candidate than the present governor, Alonzo B. Cornell, who had balked at some of their demands. They had named Charles J. Folger, a submissive politician; and it could now be seen that they had been getting ready to nominate him all along. In fact, President Arthur had recently made him Secretary of the Treasury, obviously to give him a prestige he would not otherwise have had. The ditching of Cornell in favor of Folger could be easily exposed as a trick of the worst element in the party.

Those who had already had quite enough of Gould's continued influence in government and were tired of the recurrent scandals in both Washington and Albany were ready to abandon the party. The meaning of this for the Democrats was that if they picked an appealing candidate they would have a good chance of winning.

This made Cleveland's chances much better. He was being offered as a scrupulously honest man in contrast with the Republican offering of Folger. He had no entanglements with any of the factions; he came from the western end of the state, quite outside the reach of the New York City machine. Then there was his record as mayor, not widely known until now, but enthusiastically being publicized by his supporters.

It was Cleveland's reputation for integrity and efficiency that impressed the political factions most at this moment. He was the man they needed. Even Tammany agreed that this was so and the sachem, John Kelly, may have thought that if he gave his support, Cleveland would be submissive when in office. Complete independence was inconceivable to Kelly. At any rate, when it came to actual voting, the Tammany delegates swung into the Cleveland column.

On the night before the voting began, Cleveland made a mysterious trip to Syracuse and had a long talk with Daniel Manning, the Albany boss. No one knows what was said, but it can be imagined that what he emphasized was the favorable reception his acts as mayor had had in Buffalo and the likelihood that the state's voters would be attracted by the promise of a similar regime for the state.

It was not until the third roll call that Cleveland was nominated. In the earlier votes, there was the expected deadlock between Flower and Slocum; but Hewitt and Whitney, of the County Democracy, broke it when they abandoned Slocum and went to Cleveland. There were then enough votes to give him a majority.

When the news came to Buffalo with the returning delegates, there was a grand celebration. Cleveland had to make a speech to his old friends. He spoke from the balcony of Billy Drainger's saloon. Whereupon all present filed past the bar, took full schooners and made the street ring with the chorus of "Drink 'er Down."

Sure enough, it was largely because of Cleveland's record as mayor that the election was won. After the usual formal notification an answer was made by the candidate. This constituted very nearly his whole campaign. It was not a document calculated to stir emotions; but then nothing Cleveland said or did had that effect. It kept in focus the picture of a solid, determined advocate of probity in office.

He did not make speeches; but Manning and his old associate Bissell deployed combined troops and Cleveland's margin of victory turned out to be nearly two hundred thousand. It was obvious that this was more than a mere Democratic victory. The people had spoken for reform.

For one thing, there was a definite movement of independent Republicans into Cleveland's camp, something that would be of importance for some time to come. Many influential Republicans in New York, Philadelphia, Boston and elsewhere were alienated from their party by the behavior of its inner circle—the senatorial clique of Reconstruction days, including Roscoe Conkling, who had now disappeared from politics. This had continued throughout the scandalous Grant administrations for eight years. The Hayes administration had been better, but no permanent reforms had been made; and the favoritism, the peddling of votes and the selling of privileges had soon returned. Folger, the Republican candidate, represented these very interests in the party. Decent Republicans were not inclined to stand for it any longer. They were not yet called by the name that would characterize them in our history—mugwumps—but they were already identifiable.[1]

The country-wide movement of protest against the continued control of the Republican party by such men as Conkling, Blaine and Arthur was similar to the smaller movement in Buffalo itself. The mugwumps were often only amateurs as politicians, but they were substantial; they possessed wealth and influence; and their approval could be valuable. They were delighted with Cleveland. He was a politician, true; but he was also a corporation lawyer, conservative and trustworthy. They hoped he would use his office for the benefit of legitimate business, keeping the grafters at arm's length. They knew he would not surprise them by any wild schemes such as they had begun to hear of in the West where the wild demands of the Populists were already audible. He would not favor cheap money, for instance, or drastic regulations that would affect banking and finance. Of course, a governor would not actually have much to do with such issues; but it was comforting to know that he was safe as well as competent and honest.

The support of the mugwumps had been good for perhaps two hundred thousand votes in the state. With such backing, Cleveland was sure that he could conduct himself independently, and this he meant to do. Even Manning had accepted his condition of no favoritism, and he was an old experienced professional. Cleveland felt now that he was not only being lifted by a movement, but that the movement had expert guidance.

[1] Mugwump—A name taken out of Eliot's Indian Bible in 1872 and revived at this time by Charles A. Dana's New York *Sun*.

The mugwumps were sufficiently strong to decide the election of 1884 and had considerable effect on two later ones. Some of the most prestigious names during Cleveland's presidency were associated with the movement; among the most influential were Carl Schurz, Henry Ward Beecher, George Haven Putnam and former Secretary of the Treasury Benjamin H. Bristow. From Massachusetts, the Cleveland committee included such members as Charles Francis Adams, Leverett Saltonstall, William Everett, John C. Dodge, Richard H. Dana, Josiah Quincy, T. W. Higginson and Frederic J. Stimson. From Harvard, there was Charles Eliot Norton.

The name *mugwump* meant Indian chief in Algonquin, and the *Sun* meant it to be derisive. It proved to be a serious matter for the Republican party.

10

CLEVELAND, as we have seen, had an extremely demanding conscience; and as he approached the duties of the governorship he began to be bothered by the thought that perhaps he had offered himself for a job he was not well prepared to do. He wrote of his concern to his brother William—now in charge of a church in the village of Forestport, New York:

I have just voted. I sit here in the mayor's office alone. . . . I have been for some time in the atmosphere of certain success, so that I have been sure that I should assume the duties of the high office for which I have been named. I have tried hard in the light of this fact to properly appreciate the responsibilities that will rest upon me . . . the thought that has troubled me is, can I well perform my duties, and in such a manner as to do some good to the people of the state? I know there is room for it, and I know that I am honest and sincere in that desire to do well, but the question is whether I know enough to accomplish what I desire. . . . Do you know that if mother were alive I should feel so much safer? I have always thought her prayers had much to do with my success. I shall expect you to help me in that way.

He had wanted the office and worked strenuously to capture it; but it was true that he was quite ignorant about its demands. He had been a good mayor of Buffalo because he knew the city; his duties were definite and practical; the ring could not fool him; and he had found a simple way to prevail. Besides, he had felt that he was more competent than any rival. But now, in Albany, he would have to fend off lobbyists for the biggest businesses in the country and would have to deal with financiers like Jay Gould who were notorious for corrupting legislators—and governors as well—when they could. Then too, there was the certainty that a New York governor would be a logical candidate for the presidency. He would have to contend with all the pressures such a position implied.

Still, he was not a humble man. He knew his capabilities, especially his capacity for intense and sustained labor. He felt that if he refused to be moved by any interest but that of the public, and if he worked as hard at his problems as he had when he had been mayor, he would succeed. He said so to Bissell.

He began his term as governor by going to his office at the capitol early and staying late, coming home only for lunch and dinner. The Executive Mansion, a commodious old house on Eagle Street within walking distance of the capitol, was without library or study; so when there was evening work to do, as there usually was, he walked back to his office after dinner and often worked until after midnight.

It cannot have been easy to have been secretary to so industrious a governor, but Cleveland found one who was devoted and willing to work almost as hard as himself. Daniel Lamont and he were inseparable all through that crucial spring when his governorship was taking shape.

When the legislative session that began in January ended in May, Cleveland had become for the state of New York almost exactly what he had been for the city of Buffalo: a symbol of integrity. He had again earned a reputation for industry and honesty. He had rebuffed those who would have used the government for their own purposes; his split with the spoilsmen became state-wide rather than city-wide. It was clear that he had mastered the job he had been so uncertain about. It was also clear that the people of the state knew they could trust their governor.

"Leader" would not be the right word to describe him. He was never that in the usual sense. He made no flourishes, he promised nothing except close attention to the dullest business, and he more often vetoed bills than suggested them. He kept the politicians away from the treasury, he appointed only people he had investigated thoroughly, and he refused absolutely to do favors at the public expense. But he offered no startling reforms and suggested no innovations; he merely stood firmly against graft and by working long hours and attending closely to detail made sure that the state's business was well conducted.

One of his faults appeared almost at once. He tried to do everything himself. He had no talent for delegation. He would have done better to have picked a few helpers he could trust and then acted on their recommendations; but he did not, and perhaps could not, because of his own drive for work. It had been the capacity for such grinding effort that had earned him his Buffalo reputation as a lawyer and as mayor; but it began, after a few months in Albany, to show in obvious exhaustion. He was described by visitors, during the spring, as a pale, tired, irascible man, facing a stack of papers he could not diminish, impatient with visitors, and inclined to harass those around him. His weight had now become a burden. It had increased to more than three hundred pounds and he was uncomfortable in his heavy formal clothes. With his huge bulk, his walrus mustache and his pasty complexion he was not a very attractive figure. But he was always at his desk, he was vigilant, he knew everything that went on and everyone knew that the government's affairs were entrusted to an incorruptible servant.

By the end of the legislative session—as had happened in Buffalo—he had found his supporters and his enemies.

His friends were the honest men in the legislature and those few who could be found among the Tammany politicians or in the upstate machines. One young man in the Assembly was Theodore Roosevelt, just beginning his political career and already voicing his indignation at what he saw around him, but since he was a Republican, he was not inclined to support the new governor. The. man Cleveland depended on most for advice and contacts among the politicians was Manning, who had managed the campaign and worked tirelessly to gain and keep the support of the politicians.

His enemies were the seekers for favors, the buyers of legislators' votes and many of the legislators themselves, who quickly discovered that Cleveland could not be fooled and could not be influenced. They had begun by regarding him as just another Buffalo politician, and they had expected no difficulty in carrying on as they always had. The business interests wanted special legislation that would save them money or yield them profits at consumers' expense, and the legislators expected appointments for friends and bribes for voting as they were told. Reporters had a name for these members. They were called the Black Horse Cavalry. They had a difficult time with Cleveland.

But Cleveland's most effective enemies were the powerful men led by "Honest John" Kelly who made up Tammany Hall. Almost as soon as he came into office, he was challenged by them.

Tammanyites lived by the usual machine methods. They were able to offer favors and immunities to those who would pay for them—usually business men—and, after taking their percentage, used the rest to keep their hold on the voters. They could deliver the majorities needed to pass laws, and often they could determine elections. They kept a certain number of legislators in their debt. This was, in the seventies and eighties, a recognized practice. It could go on because in the cities there were so many people living in poverty who depended on the occasional help they got from the bosses and in return voted as they were told on election day. This was the system Cleveland had broken up in Buffalo— at least for as long as he was there. (It did not stay that way. Manning's brother had succeeded Cleveland as mayor. But he was no reformer, and the old conditions were returning.) Cleveland broke it up again in Albany. He would not sign bills Tammany had bargained to have passed, and he would not appoint their candidates to offices. Moreover, he said exactly why, when it came to a showdown; and this naturally enraged those he denounced.

He first offended the organization Democrats by appointing as members of the Board of Railroad Commissioners the very men the railroad officials had maneuvered hard to defeat. An even worse offense followed: he appointed a professional engineer, with no political backing, to be superintendent of public works. There was even fiercer indignation when he appointed, as superintendent of insurance, a deputy who had refused to favor the companies he was supposed to regulate. These were both positions of immense importance as sources of graft and the politicians' rage was unbounded. These were costly losses for them. The railways just then were under fire for maintaining excessively high fares and for refusing to adopt improvements that would have prevented the many accidents on their lines. Financiers were making fortunes in railway securities, but passengers were paying for them. And Tammany did not want the situation changed.

There had been insurance scandals too. Investigations had shown that officials were using the funds in their charge for speculative purposes, and laws had been passed regulating them; but if regulation could be kept under control, it would have very little effect. These were instances of the prevalent favor buying of these years. If regulation could not be prevented altogether, the regulatory laws could be amended so that they would not be hurtful. Then if amenable officials could be appointed, things could go on pretty much as they always had.

The superintendency of public works was a matter quite similar to the issue Cleveland had faced in Buffalo when the city engineer had tried to keep control of the large sewer construction job. The work would be done by politicians' favorites, and the cost would be far more than it need be. These were customary sources of political patronage. A worker on a construction job might give very little time to the work he was paid to do, spending most of it in work for the political machine.

These infuriating appointments made by Cleveland were widely publicized. The politicians mobilized behind their own choices and tried their best to force Cleveland's acceptance; he paid no attention, merely trying with immense care to find the best man for each job and then appointing him. The wrath of Tammany was finally too fierce to contain, and when, in May, the end of the session approached, the remaining appointments were refused confirmation by the Tammany-controlled legislature. The bosses hoped to make a bargain. But what they got was a message so devastating that it amounted to a declaration of war.

The issue Cleveland used for his denunciation was the appointment of a harbor master in New York. This office had customarily yielded some three hundred jobs for Tammany, since the master was responsible for hiring the men under him. The legislators' objection to his appointee, Cleveland said, was not based on any estimate of the man's fitness, but originated in the politicians' "overweening greed for patronage." And when the session ended with numerous appointees unconfirmed, the unsettled issue between

Cleveland and Tammany was a matter of talk everywhere in the state.

These nonpolitical appointments, together with Grover's equal intractability when he was asked to approve legislation he believed to be bargained for by private interests, placed him in much the same situation before the voters of the whole state as he had been in a year earlier before the Buffalo electorate.

The most publicized of the legislative incidents were the veto of the Five-Cent Fare bill and another that would have reorganized the Buffalo fire department in such a way that its control would be transferred to the ring. The first of these gave him an opportunity to rebuke the legislators for violating a contract made in good faith and now about to be abrogated for political convenience. The second was notice to all that he would not be party to the many attempts of a similar sort that were familiar business with the legislators—getting control of patronage and of profitable contracts.

The fare bill had to do with the rapid transit system in New York City. The issue was delicate because the system was owned mostly by Jay Gould, the financier who had already made a fortune by watering the system's securities. By contract, there existed an arrangement for ten-cent fares at certain times of the day; but it was well known that Gould was getting a high profit on inflated capital and that he did not need higher fares. The proposal was to reduce all fares to five cents. Naturally Gould did his best to prevent its passage, but he had been so greedy and had caused such resentment that the legislators in this instance did not dare take his side—or not enough of them—and the bill was passed. Cleveland studied the situation with his usual care and made up his mind that however reprehensible Gould might be, and however unjust his contract, it *was* still a contract and could not be abrogated without compromising the honor of the state.

Knowing that he would be castigated for his decision, he still felt he must veto the bill, and he did. There was an immediate outburst of indignation, just as he had expected, from all the reform groups. But when some time had passed, it came to be admitted that he had been right, and he got more credit for holding to principle than he would have had for giving in to his critics.

It is interesting that young Theodore Roosevelt, who had voted for the bill, rose to say that, after studying the veto message, he was convinced the governor had been right and he wished to acknowledge it. He had voted, he said, in a moment of wrath, against the infernal thieves of the elevated railway. They had bought the legislature, corrupted the judiciary and hired newspapers. Jay Gould and his friends should be sent to jail. This, however, was not a question of feeling toward them, but "of justice to ourselves." This is exactly the way Cleveland had felt, and Roosevelt's was the sort of approval that in the long run would be more valuable than any he could have gained by violating principle and making a show of punishing a wicked corporation and saving money for the public.

Even when the legislature adjourned after the trying session, Cleveland had to stay at his desk for a month. In that time he produced many more of the now familiar vetoes, occasionally pointing out in his comments that the bill in question was merely to give some privilege or grant a favor not in the public interest, but sometimes caustically calling attention to faulty draftsmanship, or probing for hidden clauses that would be of special use to plunderers.

In June, however, he got away for a short vacation, and, after visiting his sister and brother, went on to Buffalo. His old cronies absorbed him then, and there were more nights in the old saloons, exchanging reminiscences and singing the old favorites. When it came to "There's a hole in the bottom of the sea," he joined in with full stein held high and, with the rest, shouted the last line, "Fill 'er up, fill 'er up!"

But he went fishing, too, down again on the lower river at Lewiston. He hired a boat for the day that would accommodate his bulk and that of Bissell and perhaps Louis Goetz or other familiars. He also discovered the Adirondacks, the wild forested country he had lived so close to all his life and never had visited. He fished happily in the lakes, but he never rode and seldom hiked. There were few roads, so he visited only the best-known spots.

Anyway, his conscience would not let him rest for long, and he was soon back in Albany seeing to it that the vast state machinery ran efficiently. He looked carefully into the management of all its institutions—prisons, asylums, schools, the canal, the ports. When the next legislative session came, he was better prepared than he had been for the first and was able to make some constructive proposals.

The state's charitable institutions were put in the way of being reorganized. New York's water supply was enlarged, and he took special pride in signing a bill to create a state park at Niagara Falls.

But the action of most importance to his later political career was his definite break with Tammany.

The issue was the renomination of a man named Thomas F. Grady, who had been boss Kelly's front in the legislature. Grady was dissolute and dishonest, and Kelly was mistaken to trust him as his representative in Albany. But crooks come to have such close associations, and can make such damaging revelations about each other, that their mutual commitments are often final. It was that way with Kelly and Grady.

In October 1883, just before the election for members of the legislature, Cleveland wrote the following letter to Kelly:

It is not without hesitation that I write this. I am determined to do so, however, because I see no reason why I should not be entirely frank with you. I am anxious that Mr. Grady should not be returned to the next Senate. I do not wish to conceal the fact that my personal comfort and satisfaction are involved on the matter. But I know that good legislation, based upon a pure desire to promote the interests of the people, and the improvement of legislative methods are also involved. I forbear to write in detail of the other considerations having relation to the welfare of the party and the approval to be secured by a change for the better in the character of its representatives. These things will occur to you without suggestion from me.

Grady was furious. He pointed out that his ouster would be self-defeating for Cleveland, since voters always seem to resent interferences of this sort with their free choices. In a way Grady was right. Governors and Presidents are reluctant to take such chances, preferring to work under cover to get the results they want. Yet Cleveland was adamant in his stand.

The letter, when made public, probably had something to do with the victory of the Republicans that year in elections for members of the legislature. They captured a majority, and Cleveland then had the experience of working with a presumably hostile

7 7

House and Senate. In the circumstances it made little difference since the Tammany-backed legislators had been equally hostile; and it had the odd result of collaboration between Cleveland and Theodore Roosevelt, who was now chairman of an influential committee of the House.

Cleveland did not need to be told that the Republican success had been contributed to by Tammany. Its weight was thrown where it would do the organization the most good, and if that was to Republican candidates, this did not deter the machine. But Grady was not in the legislature now; Cleveland had won that point.

Much more important for what was about to happen, he had won the implacable hatred of Tammany, paradoxically something any Democratic leader needs if he is to have the respect of party members elsewhere in the country. Democrats generally knew that Tammanyites had no more loyalty to the party than they had to the state. They thought only of their own local interests. That Cleveland was hated by the whole Tammany crowd was his best credential for future success.

I I

TALK of Cleveland as a potential presidential candidate began soon after his inauguration as governor. By June of 1884, the talk had become widespread speculation.

It had begun to look in the nation, as it had in New York State, as though the climate was right for reform. There was the same resentment against continued Republican indifference to the public interest as there had been in New York, and a state executive with a record of honesty had an excellent chance to become the Democratic nominee.

Cleveland, from the first, was well aware of the possibility; but he realized, too, that the nomination was more likely to come to him if he continued with the business of governor, than if he neglected the state's affairs and worked to be chosen. Politics could wait until a groundwork had been laid in solid achievement.

The New York legislative session ran rather late in the spring of 1884, and he kept busy with his governmental duties almost until the opening of the Democratic state convention in June. By that time it was apparent that he had a good chance for the presidential nomination; by that time, too, he had made up his mind that he would try for it.

Several moves had yet to be made, however, before he could be assured of consideration, and Manning was the person to manage these. Cleveland needed the support of his own state. Since Tammany was hopelessly alienated, a majority for this purpose in the state convention (where the delegates to the national convention to be held in Chicago early in July would be selected) would have to be put together from other sources. There were the anti-Tammany Democrats in New York City, his old friends in Buffalo and Manning's following in Albany. Whether these, in cooperation, could produce a majority was not certain.

There were two other vitally needed sources of support: approval by the party's elder statesman, Samuel J. Tilden, and backing from the disillusioned Republicans who had been so helpful to Cleveland during the gubernatorial election—the mugwumps. Tilden was still the party's most respected leader. He had at one time been governor of New York (among other posts in a long public career), and had been the party's presidential candidate in 1876, running against the Republican, Rutherford B. Hayes. He had actually received a greater popular vote than Hayes, but the electoral vote had gone to the Republican—amid Democratic protests and an ensuing delay before Hayes was declared the winner.

Tilden, with commendable concern for tranquillity, had refused to contest the election. His decision was that of one more concerned with national harmony than with his party's political advantage. His patriotism was generally recognized, but he had refused to run again in 1880 and by 1884 was living in retirement. He was now seventy-four, infirm and withdrawn, but nearly every Democrat would gladly have yielded him the nomination if he would accept. He gently declined all such suggestions and, after a talk with Manning, said publicly that in Cleveland the party had a most worthy candidate whom he gladly endorsed.

As for the disillusioned Republicans—who were to be ridiculed as mugwumps during the campaign—they met in New York City and, after some debate, announced that they would support a Democratic candidate if the Democrats nominated a man worthy of their approval. And they made it clear that Grover Cleveland would suit them very well.

They did this because it was practically certain that the Republicans would nominate James G. Blaine. To them Blaine represented all that was deplorable in political behavior during the postwar period. He had been involved in several doubtful deals, especially one yielding considerable profit from railway securities after he had sponsored a bill in the Congress granting the railway valuable rights. All along he had obviously regarded his offices as sources of gain. He was no more guilty than many public men

James G. Blaine (*Courtesy of The New-York Historical Society, New York City*)

of his generation who lacked any sense of public trust, but it was exactly this sort of behavior that the mugwumps resented.

They were glad to endorse Cleveland because in his one term as mayor and one term as governor, he had been generally accepted as the most formidable opponent of the spoilsmen. He had, in fact, said something in his rather awkward way about trustworthiness in office that a clever publicity man had made into a slogan that would be his identifying phrase throughout his career and would go down in political history as epitomizing his peculiar contribution to American Life. It would be hard for later generations to conceive that PUBLIC OFFICE IS A PUBLIC TRUST could distinguish one man from a whole generation of contemporaries; but it was so. And Blaine, in 1884, represented careless morality. In contrast Cleveland stood for stern adherence to honest public service.

The anticipations of the mugwumps were, of course, borne out. Blaine was nominated by the Republicans and then Cleveland was set against him by the Democrats. Grover's nomination was decided by the second week in July. There had been some anxiety, some fast work by Manning and some of the customary bargaining; but the success was impressive.

The alternative Democratic candidates most spoken of before the national convention were Senator Bayard of Delaware, Allen G. Thurman and several other favorite sons: Hendricks and McDonald of Indiana, Randall of Pennsylvania and Morrison of Illinois. Hendricks' followers actually made the most trouble, and, after Cleveland's nomination for the presidency, he was made the vice-presidential candidate. This followed an old political custom: the coming together of the factions, even if only temporarily, to close the breaches opened in struggles for the nomination. It had, on occasion, been violated, but violations had always resulted in political defeat. Much as the leaders hated to swallow their pride, they usually did. In this instance, the election was made easier by the Hendricks' nomination, not particularly to Cleveland's liking; but he did not actually object to Manning's arrangement of Hendricks as second man. He was a politician too.

One question that bothered Manning was whether Cleveland would finally have the votes of the New York delegation. Violent and unscrupulous Tammany attacks on Cleveland by Tammany members of the legislature and in party meetings had had some effect, and Manning had not dared try for an endorsement at the state convention in Saratoga. On the first day of the national convention, however, he sent emissaries to the doubtful New York delegates and finally called a caucus. By then he had rounded up enough votes to defeat Tammany, and he got the endorsement he wanted.

This was important. The Democrats had a long-standing national convention rule that the votes of the entire state delegation would be cast for the candidate who had a majority of delegate support. New York, governed by this unit rule, would give Cleveland seventy-two votes, the largest number from any state. It would also disenfranchise his Tammany opponents.

What sort of promises Manning made that won over the doubtful delegates is not known; but, after the usual practice, he must have offered favors of some sort—jobs, perhaps, if Cleveland should win. The New York commitment was encouraging, but there were still obstacles to overcome. The most bothersome of these was a second rule—that to be nominated a candidate must have a two thirds majority. Cleveland would need to have 547 votes, since there were, altogether, 820 delegates. New York's seventy-two were a start, but hardly more than that.

The worst of his troubles was the frantic opposition of Tammany, begun when the first delegates had appeared in Chicago and continued with increasingly malicious vigor. John Kelly and his man Grady, and now another and very active opponent, the lawyer Bourke Cochran, had been encouraged by Manning's failure at the New York convention to demand an endorsement resolution. They had immediately transferred their activities to Chicago. There they agitated among the delegates and the local Chicago bosses. Cochran was a rousing speaker, and his efforts had more effect than those of Kelly and Grady. These were reflected in the press, and the calumnies he invented had been spread widely by the time the convention was called to order.

The allegations were varied and some were imaginary, mostly calculated to appeal to religious prejudice and race hatred. Cleveland, they said, was an enemy of the Irish and a puritan who would destroy Catholic influence. Since the Democratic party was heavily dependent on the Irish vote, especially in the larger states of New York and Pennsylvania, what they were saying was that he could not win for the Democrats if he should be nominated; the Irish voters would support his opponent, Blaine, who, it seemed, although he was from Maine and a Protestant himself, had a Catholic mother. This gave him at least some standing with the Irish immigrants.

Most of the Cleveland indictment was invented, but some of his official actions could be interpreted to support the Tammany stories. They were not easy to combat. For one thing, the attack came late in the proceedings and this made the lies hard to catch up with. For another, it was certainly true that Cleveland had never been favorably disposed toward political machines of any sort, predominantly Catholic or otherwise. That he had loyal Irish friends in Buffalo, like Tim Mahoney, was left out of the stories; and it was not mentioned that Mahoney when comptroller, had forced Sheehan to make restitution of several thousands of dollars he had appropriated from the city funds. The Tammanyites simply said that Cleveland had called Sheehan "that damned Irishman," as he certainly had; but they did not say why. The sensitive Irish were only too ready to believe that all of them were damned in his mind.

William C. Hudson, the publicity man who had invented the slogan "A Public Office Is a Public Trust," was Manning's advance agent and he worked mightily to convince the most important leaders of delegations that the stories were completely false. Since Tammany was regarded as traitorous to the party whenever it was convenient, most delegates were ready to accept Hudson's explanation. But there were other tricks in Tammany's bag. At one stage in the proceedings, when the decisive vote was to be taken, Kelly, Grady and Cochran got together with their friends in Chicago and packed the galleries. This involved printing a whole set of counterfeit tickets, superseding those issued by the national committee, and distributing them among a crowd of rough characters dragged from neighboring flophouses and dives. They were to make disturbances at command, shouting down speakers for Cleveland and cheering his rivals.

It succeeded. That is to say, the galleries were occupied and

"WE LOVE HIM MOST FOR THE ENEMIES THAT HE HAS MADE."

Thomas Nast cartoon of Cleveland as "clean" candidate in *Harper's Weekly*, July 19, 1884 (*Courtesy of The New-York Historical Society, New York City*)

the legitimate ticket holders shut out; and when it was decided that the most likely substitute for Cleveland was Hendricks of Indiana, the shouting and cheering for him interrupted proceedings for some time. But by then, Tammany's tactics had provoked the inevitable repercussions. Delegates from other states—Wisconsin, Michigan, the South—were sophisticated politicians too. They recognized what was up. And the Hendricks movement died almost before it began. The galleries shouted to no avail.

Kelly also made a speech quite out of order, trying to convince the delegates that if Cleveland should be nominated, he could not carry New York, and if he could not carry New York, he could not be elected; but that too had little effect. The first vote had shown that Cleveland's rivals really had little strength. He received 392 votes and his nearest opponent, Bayard, only 170, This was a formidable lead. But more work had to be done.

It is at this stage in any convention that the leaders of various factions withdraw to make their final deals. Manning and his aides met with the heads of other delegations, and offers were made and accepted, involving mostly positions in the new administration if the election should be won. In this case, the Indianans had forty-five votes to trade with and the several Southern delegations were disposed to abandon Bayard for the promise of positions.

When the second ballot began the success of Manning's efforts was apparent. Cleveland quickly amassed 500 votes; then delegates from other states began to switch. At the end he had 683, with Bayard and Hendricks trailing far behind. The proceedings then ended quickly. The Cleveland forces agreed to Hendricks for vice-president, thus showing shrewd judgment. Indiana was a close state, and Hendricks on the ticket could make the difference between victory and defeat.

Cleveland, in Albany, was working in his office at the capitol when the faint sound of cannons began to be heard. Lamont, working with him, exclaimed, "That means you are the nominee." Cleveland is reported to have said, "Do you think so? Well, anyway, we have to finish up this work."

12

POLITICAL campaigns in the American style are apt to show democratic processes at their roughest. The appeals tend to concentrate on the voters most easily influenced by gossip and falsehood. There had been notorious ones in the past, Jackson's frontiersmen had ousted John Quincy Adams (1828) by using the most unscrupulous lies. When the newly organized Whigs were presenting General William Henry Harrison as a "common man" (1840), it amounted to a monumental hoax. This was called the "log cabin and hard cider" campaign. But the whispered lies and false charges used by the Republicans in the campaign of 1884 were quite as bad as any that had gone before. For a while it seemed that the scandal and innuendo might defeat Cleveland and elect Blaine.

The attacks were peculiarly vicious because they came not only from the Republicans and their candidate, but from Democratic Tammany as well. In spite of having been beaten in Chicago, Kelly and his forces refused to follow custom and accept the decision of the convention.

Tammany had behaved in this maverick way so often that politicians throughout the country distrusted them profoundly, so much so that it was considered an advantage to any candidate of the party to be opposed by Tammany. For this reason Cleveland and Manning were not as worried as they might otherwise have been.

In New York, Tammany had a hard-core following that was estimated at several hundred thousand votes. Since in the whole state there were not many more than a million votes, it was a serious matter to have so large a percentage lost before the campaign had begun; but the Clevelandites hoped to win upstate what they lost in the city. It was true that Tammany kept mostly under cover, but everyone knew that "the word was being passed." Blaine was to be supported no matter what appeared on the surface. As the campaign began it was not at all certain what the outcome might be.

No more unscrupulous politician than Blaine had ever appeared in the upper levels of American politics. In the campaigns that had raised him to his present eminence, he had resorted to every device known to the oldest practitioners, and it was to be expected that this present effort would be a desperate one. One difficulty he would have in making charges against Cleveland was that he himself was so vulnerable. He had been denied the nomination in 1880 largely because of what was known about his relations with railroad financiers, and there were other passages in his life that would not bear examination. He, therefore, had to rely on others to do his dirty work.

He could, however, depend on the Republican inner circle as well as on Tammany to do the hatchet job on Cleveland. He had been among those of the Senate cabal who had made Grant president and then had controlled his administration. The period had become notorious because of its many scandals, and the scandals had reappeared when, after the relatively reputable Hayes administration, Garfield had been elected in 1880 and Blaine had become his Secretary of State. From that exalted position Blaine had carried out negotiations with foreign governments that favored his friends, and they were generally supposed to have shared their profits with him. Nevertheless, the regular Republican party members responsible for his nomination worked hard for Blaine's election in 1884. Their own fortunes were involved as well as his.

During the campaign, of course, Chester A. Arthur was still President, having succeeded to office when Garfield was assassinated. He had been backed by the Conkling faction of the Republican party and, in 1884, the Blaine supporters having gained control, he had been refused the chance to run again. The quarrel between his group and Blaine's made a split likely to lose as many votes as would be lost in the defection of the mugwumps. Just what the loss would be was hard to estimate, but it undoubtedly made Blaine a much weaker candidate than the Republicans might have chosen. When the campaign began, it looked as though he might be on the defensive throughout; and this made his managers more determined than ever to besmirch Cleveland's reputation. They were driven to reaching for any advantage, however mean.

There was much else to be thought of by the Republicans. The year 1884 was a year of economic troubles. There was unemployment everywhere, and this was long before the time when anything was done by the federal government to ease distresses of this sort, and the misery in the slums of the cities was almost unendurable. Businessmen were uneasy about the future. They were normally staunch Republicans, but their faith was shaken. In fact, some of them were bringing their money and prestige to the Cleveland side by way of the mugwumps. Then, too, there were the Southern states. They were solidly Democratic; their votes could be counted in advance for Cleveland.

On the whole it was a doubtful outlook for the Republicans. They had a candidate likely to be attacked as dishonest; a depression they were certain to be blamed for; and, besides, there were at least two minor parties, likely to take more votes from them than from the Democrats. True, this effect was balanced by the Prohibitionists who would draw from the Democrats. It was hard to guess which party would lose the most. The Republicans *could* count on the support of the old soldier vote, the principal strength of the party ever since the Civil War. The veterans were not so numerous any more; the years were thinning their ranks; but there were still many and they could be made to believe that the Democrats would endanger their pensions. Also Cleveland could be called a draft-dodger. The veterans' organization and the businessmen, plus the conservative farmers—these were supporters counted on by the Republican managers.

As the campaign opened, it could be seen how valuable the support of the mugwumps was. This group was nominally nonpartisan and had an organization of its own; but its prominent members were exactly suited by Cleveland. There could be no doubt about his integrity, but also he was conservative; and even if they were reformers, they had no wish to encourage the radicals then beginning to show themselves in both city and country. The depression had unsettled labor to the point of threatening violence; and there were rising voices in the West wanting favors for debtors. The farmers owed huge debts to the banks they were learning to identify with "Wall Street" and mutters about Money Barons could be heard.

Both these—the labor movement and the Populist farmer movement—were to loom large in the future. Now they were just beginning to make themselves heard; but the solid citizens who made up the mugwump membership had no intention of joining or supporting radicals of any sort. And they had ample assurance that Cleveland was of the same mind as they. He stood for good government, but not for a debtor's government or one that favored radical labor.

It might have been thought that Cleveland's failure to understand what forces were beginning to move in the depths of American life would have made him ineligible as President. But really the circumstances of 1884, as the politically aware citizens understood them, did not call for an imaginative leader. They called for an executive who would purge the government of rascals. The campaign was to be one that turned on personalities. The national issues of the Civil War had now receded from acute controversy, and candidates would not be symbols of attitude. They would be themselves. It would either be the Republican Blaine with a long history in federal government but a reputation that could not be defended; or it would be Cleveland, the man of iron honesty. He would promise only probity in the public service after years of laxity. Blaine would have to explain where the lost probity had gone.

Unfortunately, Cleveland was vulnerable too—not in the same way, but in others, nevertheless, that had always swayed voters. His years among the Buffalo riffraff were now certain to come under scrutiny. There had already been hints of this in whisperings at Chicago. The question was how far the exposures would go and what the voters' reaction would be.

Sure enough, the sensational charges involving Mrs. Halpin and her child broke into the open even before the end of July. They were headlined in a Buffalo newspaper—the *Telegraph*—and naturally, they reached every corner of the country with terrific impact:

HEADLINE
FROM THE BUFFALO TELEGRAPH
July 21, 1884

A *TERRIBLE* TALE
A DARK CHAPTER IN A PUBLIC
MAN'S HISTORY

THE PITIFUL STORY OF MARIA
HALPIN AND GOVERNOR
CLEVELAND'S SON

A PROMINENT CITIZEN STATES THE RESULT
OF HIS INVESTIGATION OF CHARGES
AGAINST THE GOVERNOR—
INTERVIEWS TOUCHING
THE CASE

Other newspapers were somewhat cautious, not knowing whether the facts cited were to be depended on; but the Democratic press was at once defensive. Such a story was too sensational to be smothered, and Cleveland knew at once that he would have to meet it.

Without hesitation, he made one of the most courageous decisions any candidate ever made. He telegraphed his Buffalo friends: "Above all, tell the truth," thus risking his career, but in the end gaining rather than losing by his frankness.

"Telling the truth" was not simple. The affair was now some years in the past. It had not been aired either in his mayoralty campaign or in that for the governorship. The boy was now growing up with the parents who had adopted him, and Mrs. Halpin had disappeared from notice after making some frustrated efforts at blackmail. She was now living in another city and had married again. There were investigations by reporters and attempts on both sides to get statements from her. She did not respond, but still respected reporters wrote damagingly of the whole affair in words like these from Charles A. Dana of the New York *Sun*:

> We do not believe that the American people will knowingly elect to the Presidency a coarse debauchee who would bring his harlots with him to Washington and hire lodgings for them convenient to the White House.

The most difficult phase of the matter for Cleveland and Manning was the talkativeness of the clergymen who felt called on to intervene. A certain Reverend Ball, a demagogic minister of small reputation in Buffalo, saw a chance in the affair for the sort of notoriety evangelical exhorters can use in their business. He made the charges in the *Telegraph* his own and enlarged on them, using the few facts he had as the basis for general insinuations about Cleveland's private life since the time of his involvement with the attractive widow. The Republicans naturally seized the opportunity to enlarge rumors and spread suggestive stories. It was even being said that as governor, as well as mayor, Cleveland had led a profligate life. The variations on this theme could be endless; but since there was no truth in them they had to be muted. No facts were found for publication.

There is no doubt that Cleveland was anguished by the notoriety; he said so in many of his private letters. But it soon became apparent, especially after more responsible clergymen had looked into the matter and taken up his defense, that the issue would not have the impact that had at first been feared. It was fortunate that the attack had come so early. If it had been saved for the last days of the campaign when there was no time left for defense and for the sensation to die down, it might have turned the election. But, given time, Cleveland had the benefit of defenses such as the following, from the highly respected Reverend Kinsley Twining:

STATEMENT OF THE REVEREND KINSLEY
TWINING, A REPUTABLE DIVINE,
ABOUT THE HALPIN ISSUE

The kernel of truth in the various charges against Mr. Cleveland is this, that when he was younger than he is now, he was guilty of an illicit connection; but the charge, as brought against him, lacks the elements of truth in these substantial points; there was no seduction, no adultery, no breach of promise, no obligation of marriage; but there was at that time a culpable irregularity of life, living as he was, a bachelor, for which it was proper, and is proper, that he should suffer. After the primary offense, which is not to be palliated in the circle for which I write, his conduct was singularly honorable, showing no attempt to evade responsibility, and doing all he could to meet the duties involved, of which marriage was certainly not one . . .

It was apparent before the campaign had gone on long that the election would be a close one. And gradually it also became apparent that it might well turn on the result in the state of New York. The balance in the rest of the country, as the professionals saw it, was very close indeed. Hendricks could be counted on to carry Indiana for Cleveland; but the rest of the Midwest was still dominated by the veterans' organization and these were populous states with large representations in the Electoral College.

The election for state officials in Maine in September gave the Republicans an even larger majority than was usual. It seemed that the whole of New England might be hostile. Then in October, Ohio, too, elected Republican state officials, although not so decisively as in 1880. And this made that whole area doubtful.

The New York situation seemed to be weakening; so did that in New Jersey and Connecticut. It was one of the first campaigns to draw the candidates into repeated speechmaking and extensive traveling—or rather one of the candidates; for Cleveland only made a few speeches in nearby states. Blaine was a noted spellbinder, and he could not contain his energies. Meetings where he could appear were organized all over the Midwest, and tremendous showings of enthusiasm were stimulated by Republican bosses. It is doubtful whether this actually made much difference, since the Midwest was Republican territory anyway. But Blaine was followed and amply reported; the apparent enthusiasm yielded valuable publicity in the East.

Heretofore it had been the custom, seldom violated, for presidential candidates to remain sedately at home, leaving the active campaigning to their supporters. The image of the President as a statesman rather than a partisan was regarded as too important in people's minds to be risked by frantic appeals and degrading exposures. Cleveland honored this tradition. But since Blaine did not, it was a question whether the times had not changed sufficiently so that Cleveland's decision was mistaken. Manning thought so.

In the last weeks and days Cleveland and his managers despairingly concluded that they had lost. Then, at almost the last moment, an incident occurred that gave them a new lift. It is not yet fully accepted as the incident that actually turned the campaign in Cleveland's favor, but at the time it seemed to do so. And it did give a new fillip to Democratic hopes.

It happened in this way: Blaine, returning from his barnstorming in the West, headed for New York; he had been excited and encouraged by the crowds, and as candidates do, he forgot that the enthusiasm had been synthetic. Suddenly he felt that he could turn the tide in the East by similar appearances there. He was met at Jamestown in western New York by the chairman of the state Republican committee who believed that as much had been done in New York as was possible—he relied mostly on Tammany's treason, which he did not want brought into the open. He told Blaine that if he must make speeches, it ought to be in the upstate cities—such as Syracuse. Preferably, however, he ought just to go home to Maine and wait there for the election.

Blaine refused. He had convinced himself that his personality was irresistible, and he went on to New York City. He was at first encouraged by the crowds assembled as they had been in the Midwest. But then disaster occurred. On the morning of October 29, an advertisement invited clergymen to meet him at the Fifth Avenue Hotel. This was obviously an attempt to recall to people's minds the Halpin affair, now no longer of much interest. No minister of reputation came to the meeting, but there were a number of minor ones. They selected the Reverend S. D. Burchard of the Murray Hill Presbyterian Church to act as spokesman.

It had been arranged that Burchard would address Blaine and assure him that the clergy were on his side, the inference being that his opponent was morally unworthy. In his remarks, Burchard used a phrase that proved to be disastrous. He and his colleagues, he said, would not support any candidate put forward by the party of "rum, Romanism, and rebellion." This was meant to call up Cleveland's old saloon associations, but it also slurred the Catholics and furnished a reminder that the Democrats had been on the

9 4

wrong side in the Civil War. All this had been said many times by the Republican orators, but this time it was said in Blaine's presence and in New York where Irish Catholics were numerous.

Democratic campaign managers had had the foresight to have a shorthand reporter present, and, although the newspaper men there missed the opportunity completely, the politicians saw at once that their enemy had delivered himself into their power. Overnight they printed thousands of handbills with "Rum, Romanism, and Rebellion" in bold type and scattered them throughout New York immigrant neighborhoods. The Irish, including their clergy, were furious. And, although they had been secretly instructed by Tammany to vote for Blaine, they resented the insult so fiercely that Tammany's instructions were ignored.

Blaine made another mistake in the city. On the evening of the Burchard greeting, he was persuaded to be present at a dinner given by a company of New York's wealthiest men. The dinner was held at New York's most lavish restaurant—Delmonico's— and among the guests were many well-known millionaires: Russell Sage, John Roach, Henry Clews, Levi P. Morton, D. O. Mills, C. L. Tiffany, C. N. Bliss, Whitelaw Reid, and many others, all of the same standing. But most famous—and infamous—of all was Jay Gould, who had first tried to buy Cleveland's favor and then, when he failed, set out to defeat him. The dinner was the theme of a half-page cartoon next day in the New York *World,* carrying the title: "Belshazzar Blaine and the Money Kings."

The reaction was instantaneous. It tied the Republicans to the wealthy businessmen who had profited so much from the administrations since the Civil War and who were still affluent while the rest of the country suffered from hard times. The papers had lately been filled with accounts of increasing misery; factories were closed, unemployment was increasing and nothing was being done to make matters better. And here was the Republican who wanted to be the next President showing himself as the wealthy men's puppet—another Grant.

Cleveland on election day voted in Buffalo and then went back to Albany by train. It was cold and rainy, and he was quite convinced that he would not win. When with his close associates he began the evening wait for returns, there was at first some reason

The Republican dinner satirized by Thomas Nast in *Harper's Weekly,*
November 15, 1884 (*Courtesy of Historical Pictures Service, Chicago*)

for encouragement. New York City seemed to have given him a majority. But that was before the slum wards began to be heard from. When they did, it was at once apparent that "rum, Romanism, and rebellion" had not had the effect his managers had led him to expect. There might be some difference, but it could hardly be enough to carry the state. The company sat up late but they had no better news, and finally they dispersed without much hope.

It was three days before the issue was decided, even in New York. There were charges of stuffed ballot boxes and loud protests that one side or the other had rigged the count. And when all the excitement had died down and the additions were finally made, Cleveland had carried the state by less than 1200 votes. But that made all the difference. He had won New Jersey narrowly too, as well as neighboring Connecticut; and Hendricks had brought in Indiana. The South remained solidly Democratic, but the Midwest outside of Indiana was lost—the old soldier vote had gone to Blaine.

There was tremendous elation among Democrats all over the country. After twenty-four years, they were to occupy the presidency and all the positions of power. It would be an upheaval in Washington not seen since Jackson had come to the White House from the wilds of Tennessee in 1828.

But whether it would make as much real difference as it seemed to do on the surface was not clear. Cleveland owed no political debts except those Manning had cautiously incurred at Chicago. He had stood for no reforms other than the same ones he had promised when he had become governor—he would give the nation a careful, honest, conservative administration. That was all.

But the country was changing. It was becoming industrialized; it was linked together by new railroads and communication facilities; it occupied an important place in the world because of its growing riches and power. Was simple honesty enough? It remained to be seen.

The mugwumps were almost as elated as the Democrats. They meant to insist that the victory could not have been won without them—and this was true—but what sort of demands would they make? Cleveland knew that at heart he was one of them—much more, perhaps, than he was a Democrat. They were respectable, earnest and principled, very different from the unruly masses that made up the bulk of Democratic voters. The bosses would certainly want their representatives to take over the government and run it as the cities were being run. It would be a struggle; and Cleveland, the new President, would be in the middle.

When he had come to Albany, he had been quite ignorant of a governor's duties. Now he was to be President; and he was even more ignorant of a President's responsibilities. If he was appalled at the prospect, it is no wonder. And if he was not, he should have been.

13

WHEN the campaigning was over and the excitment had died down, Cleveland could at last consider the duties he had obligated himself to assume. When he did this he was aghast at his own ignorance. Moreover he had little time for preparation —even if he had known what to study. He was still governor and would be until Lieutenant Governor Hill took over. He stayed at his duties in Albany, even preparing with his usual care the annual address to the legislature in January. Presently, however, he did move out of the Executive Mansion to a small house nearby and gradually free himself for learning something of his new duties. The climb to the presidency is often rapid, but none had been more rapid than this one and no transition had caught a new President with so little knowledge of national problems, or even with so little foundation for what he must learn.

Even in the minor matter of White House management he would have unusual difficulty. Since he was a bachelor, he would have to depend on his sister Rose, who was a spinster. She was a formidable lady, large and aggressive, who had been a school-teacher and lecturer. But he meant to have the same sort of simple menage in Washington that he had had in Albany, so this seemed an adequate arrangement. Besides, Rose could be assisted, when necessary, by another sister, Mary—Mrs. Hoyt.

He had never even been in Washington and had only heard of White House customs, so he could only project his Albany experience into his new situation. It is no wonder if he was appalled by the prospect.

It was immediately necessary that he should choose his Cabinet, and not only the Cabinet itself, but many other appointees. In

1885 there were about 125,000 federal employees. Only about 16,000 of these were in the classified service; most of the rest were appointed by the Chief Executive. Incoming Presidents had long complained that the demands of office seekers gave rise to rivalries and maneuverings that monopolized their time and left hard feelings. Even during the Civil War, when life-and-death issues had to be decided, Lincoln had had to deal with long lines of applicants whose claims he had no way of judging. The situation had not improved much since then; and when there was a change in party control, as now, the turnover was immense. The departments were filled with Republicans, and Democrats wanted all their jobs.

Cleveland had no intention of allowing the wholesale replacements demanded by the politicians, but he would have to find some rule to go by unless he allowed them to have their way. Even then, some people would have to be favored over others. Then there was the added complication that his good-government friends expected him to reform the public service. They pointed out that their efforts to correct past abuses had led to the passage of the Pendleton Act in 1883, setting up the beginnings of a merit system, and that it would be his duty to extend it. Meanwhile, he must keep the politicians from filling offices with their incompetent hangers-on.

He accepted his friends' advice and arranged for a letter to be written by the Civil Service Reform League asking his intentions. He answered it by formulating these rules: he would keep efficient employees in their jobs unless they were in policy positions, and he would not appoint Democrats merely because they had done party work. This warning to the politicians of his party was received with anguished protests. This was the first Democratic takeover since the Civil War, and they thought it their right to make the most of it. Cleveland meant what he said, but anyone with experience could have told him that some compromise would have to be found.

He set for himself very early one accomplishment to be made at any cost—the government must be rescued from its reputation for looseness and inefficiency. He considered that his capacity for hard work would suffice for this. It was what he had been elected

President Cleveland's office in the White House (*Courtesy of The New-York Historical Society, New York City*)

to do, and he meant to do it. The more he found out about it, however, the more he understood that custom as well as slackness was involved. Every department was overstaffed; there were many employees who were expected to do political chores and not much else. As a result, federal operations were disgracefully inefficient, but it was a trouble that democratic politics had created. No one wanted to dispense with democracy; the question was whether such an inherent defect could be cured.

The physical establishment of the government had run down; everything was neglected; and even the post office was incapable of performing its elementary task of delivering the mails. There were even worse situations—that of the Navy, for instance. Even nineteen years after the Civil War, there were nothing but wooden-hulled ships with antique smooth-bore cannon, the same ships, many of them, that had seen service then. No plans had been made for modernization, an intolerable situation for a nation becoming a world power.

There were urgent deficiencies elsewhere too. Government agents were giving away vast areas of the eleven Western territories to the railroads or other corporations; lumbermen were slaughtering the forests and stockmen were fencing in the public domain. There was disorder and neglect everywhere that must be put right, and it could be guessed that more than neglect was involved. Plunderers of public resources would fight for their privileges.

All of this was the result of years of careless management, of regarding office as a reward for political services and of cynical refusal to take seriously any sort of public duty. It had been this way in Buffalo and in Albany; it was no surprise to find it this way on a huge scale in Washington. That was why Cleveland's dictum that a public office was a public trust had sounded so revolutionary and why so many people had been slow to believe he really meant to carry out his stated intention. They were taking him more seriously now. The reformers among the mugwumps were watching him closely to see whether he would weaken, and the politicians were preparing to test his courage. His letter to the Civil Service Reform League thus caused a rebellion among the politicians equaled by the satisfaction of the agitators for good government.

But all these problems were ones he felt himself competent to solve. He had only to be as stubborn and unyielding as he had been in the mayoralty and the governorship. He had an ineradicable conviction that application and plain dealing would see him through. There were, however, troubles of quite another order in immediate prospect. They were infinitely more complex and they were ones he had had no experience with.

There was already an almost revolutionary labor movement reacting to the harsh conditions of work imposed by employers in the nation's fast-growing industrial system. There was a boiling indignation in the West over the rapacity of moneylenders in the East; and this was leading not only to demands for relief from oppressive debt, but to proposals for stricter federal regulation of the railroads, whose high rates and arbitrary services made the marketing of farm products costly. These were matters that neither a mayor nor a governor had to consider. He would have to consider them now, ready or not. They would not wait.

Then there was a long-standing and nation-wide controversy about tariffs—should there be free trade with other nations or should customs regulations be used to protect industries at home? Tariff battles in the past had been heated; others to come promised to be equally fierce. Democrats had traditionally been for free trade, or at least for lowered tariffs; and the Republicans, being the party of business, had stood for protection. The Democratic legislators were no longer so forthright about this issue as they once had been. The platform Cleveland had run on had been a straddle that suited no one. The trouble was that only a small minority in the party really wanted any drastic lowering of duties. Yet several of Cleveland's early appointees were known to be low-tariff advocates, and this was taken to define his position. There was apprehension among businessmen, who feared drastic change in the tariff laws. They adopted a wait-and-see attitude, determined to fight if, after the inauguration, their fears began to seem justified.

There was an isolationist mood, natural, perhaps, for an expanding nation, and anything foreign was regarded with hostility. Even industrial workers were inclined to the view that their jobs depended on protection from cheap labor in other countries. Cleveland could thus see that there were issues pending that he would have to understand better than he now did, and ones that might require bouts of concentration as well as new reserves of courage. He was reduced to an unaccustomed humility as he surveyed these controversies he did not understand; and the first onslaught of the job seekers was so massive that even he was unnerved. In December 1884 he wrote to Bissell:

I am sick at heart and perplexed in brain during most of my working hours. I almost think that the professions of most of my pretended friends are but the means they employ to accomplish personal and selfish ends . . . I wonder if I must for the third time face the difficulties of a new official almost *alone?*

Loneliness became something hard to support. The Mrs. Halpin scandal made public during the campaign made him feel that he had been betrayed in Buffalo and that his friends had done far from enough to protect him. This alienation when he was facing the stupendous duties of the presidency gave him a sick feeling quite new to so self-sufficient and sturdy a man. As he put it to Bissell:

I shall not come to Buffalo—just yet at all events. As I feel at this moment I would never go there again if I could avoid it. Elected President of the United States, I have no home at my home.

He resigned his governorship in January. Until then he worked night and day to finish his commitments. Even on Christmas Day he stopped only for the dinner his faithful steward William prepared. But when his annual message was written and he had moved to his temporary house, he could turn to the preliminaries of the presidency.

First, there was the choosing of the Cabinet. This is a delicate task for any President; but for Cleveland it was unusually so. Professionals among the Democrats were anxious to have the party organization represented so that it could be kept together for the future. He was less concerned about this than about support for his intended reforms; but certainly the party's leaders would have to have places, even at the cost of offending the reformers who had been strong allies.

Then there were the inevitable territorial considerations. The

South, for instance, would have to be recognized with the appointment of Southerners to public office, and it was not clear how far he could go in trusting former Confederates with vital national concerns. Southern Cabinet members had defected and had caused infinite trouble as the Civil War had started; and there was certain to be suspicion of anyone from the states so recently readmitted to the Union.

Then, too, he would have to concede something to the West even though he had had little success there. And the East, where his own base had been and whose men he knew, would have to be repaid for faithful support.

Through many days and weeks he struggled with the problem. Finally he determined on the three most important posts; the Secretaries of State, Treasury and Navy. For all these he had had favorite choices from the first, and he at length decided to follow his instinct without consulting anyone. Senator Thomas F. Bayard was a member of an old Delaware family, important for many years in party affairs, who had had a long career in the Senate. He was well suited to be Secretary of State, the post whose affairs Cleveland would need most help in managing.

Manning, for the Treasury, was a more meritorious appointment than was at once apparent. He was known mostly for being boss of the Albany organization, but Cleveland knew of his extensive financial and business experience. He was a wealthy man who was conservative but not selfish. Besides he had been a close confidant all during the governorship. William C. Whitney had been a leader of the County Democracy, Tammany's most troublesome opponent in New York City and faithful throughout to Cleveland. He was vigorous and fearless. He would shake up the lethargic Navy bureaucracy and begin its necessary modernization.

The list was completed by the selection in February of William C. Endicott to be Secretary of War, Senator Lucius Quintus Cincinnatus Lamar of Mississippi to be Secretary of the Interior, William F. Vilas of Wisconsin to be Postmaster General, and Augustus H. Garland, senator from Arkansas, to be Attorney General. Cleveland thus fulfilled the party requirements as he understood them, but he also hoped that the pains he had taken to investigate had yielded him a hard-working group. He was de-

Daniel Manning (*Courtesy of the Buffalo and Erie County Historical Society*)

termined above all that a new respect for executive competence should be created.

The selections were well received by the mugwumps. Those who had feared a Cabinet of Democratic politicians were agreeably surprised. Most of the appointees were reform Democrats. Only Bayard and Manning were political professionals, and Bayard was thought of as too aristocratic to be approachable for favors. The politicians were not happy; but at this stage there was little they could do. When Cleveland was in the White House their political strength could be used to get their own way.

One other matter Cleveland studied seriously before his inauguration: the matter of "cheap" vs. "sound" money. It was a national question, probably *the* national question, then and for years to come; but characteristically he reached his decision rapidly once he thought he understood the facts. He found later that it was more complex than he had thought, having roots many years in the past.

There were a million square miles beyond the Mississippi where the federal government had everything to do—from keeping the peace to arranging for the use of land. There was a law that supposedly governed the occupation and use of these six hundred million acres. It had been passed in 1862—a part of Lincoln's program in the campaign of 1860—and was called the Morrill Act. But the idea of those days had been the straightforward one of opening land to settlers. The vast tidal movement westward that characterized the decades of the sixties and seventies was continuing into the eighties. Free land was by now becoming scarce, and competition for it was fierce. Other land could be bought—and people were paying more for it than they could afford.

There were several reasons for this Westward migration; a vast empty land seemed to offer new opportunities to the younger sons of Eastern farmers who could not be accommodated on the home place. The cheapness of the enterprise was an attraction too—many, perhaps most, of the first settlers went West without any capital at all, staked a claim, built a sod house and borrowed support money while they plowed the prairie and planted a crop. They paid little or nothing for the land in the first years—the government gave it to them; but later migrants were forced to borrow to buy their land, and then went further into debt for stock and machinery.

Farmers were not the only migrants; there were moneylenders too, and merchants who sold goods on credit. Settlements grew up and farmers were soon deep in debt to the townspeople. And as competition with the vast acreages of Canada began to be felt, and as droughts came, they were hard put to pay what they owed.

What the Easterners who came West were slow to realize was that the great plains were not the same sort of country they were used to. When the Missouri and the Mississippi were passed the prairies stretched treeless to the Rockies and beyond, a rolling upland region of grass that grew shorter and shorter as the wagons rolled Westward.

The grass grew shorter because there was less rain; and the strains of grass were special ones that had adapted themselves to long periods of drought. The plains uniformly turned yellow in early summer when the matted grass lost its spring green; and the dry winds blew across the empty miles all summer and into fall. There were years, and cycles of years, when there was so little rain that spring brought no green at all. Only the hardy grasses survived, having kept the soil covered as they dried and kept their seed viable until the rains came again. Inexperienced in these conditions, the pioneers plowed and planted as they had in the East; and in many years waited in vain for the rains to awaken their seeds. With crop failures following close upon each other they were unable, of course, to pay the debts they had contracted. Instead, they contracted more.

After years of this, what the farmers needed most was cash, cash to pay back their debts, cash to buy food and new equipment, cash to live on. They demanded that the government issue "greenbacks" (money not backed by metal reserves) and silver dollars (instead of the more valuable gold), and then to make this money available to them to pay back their debts. It was argued that if these devices were not resorted to, the dollar (backed by gold) would go up in value, be harder to acquire and thus make debts harder to pay. Too, additional borrowing would be impossible; enterprise would be stopped; development of the land would become impossible.

Those who had loaned them money, on the other hand, contended that greenbacks and silver dollars were simply not worth as much as sound gold dollars, and if a farmer paid back one hundred greenbacks for a loan of one hundred dollars in gold, he was not really paying back the full sum he had borrowed. They demanded that debts be paid back in gold or at least that if they were paid back in some other currency, it must be enough to equal the value of the gold they had loaned.

Conflict flared between the creditors and the farmers. The migrants were resentful anyway because their hopes had proved so empty, the promise of the land so unfulfilled. And it was not only the people of the plains who developed vengeful feelings directed at creditors and townspeople. Their relatives in the East often had to scrape up enough money to bring members of their families back home and heard the tales of hardship and felt the anger of those who had failed. They shared the resentment.

The controversy, of course, had deep repercussions in Washington. The "cheap money" forces were presented in Congress by vociferous advocates who on every occasion enlarged on the wickedness of the Money Barons, the creditors. They demanded that more dollars be printed so that debts would be easier to pay.

A focal point of this intractable issue just before Cleveland's inauguration was the Bland-Allison Act, passed in 1878. This had provided for the coinage of several million dollars of silver a month as a substitute for scarce gold. By now nearly two hundred million of the silver dollars were in circulation. During the depression of 1883, these coins began to return to the Treasury, and gold went out in exchange. Whenever anyone paid a debt to the government, it was in silver or greenbacks; but when the government paid its debts, gold was demanded. The cheap-money policy began to embarrass not only private creditors, but the government itself.

Since gold was an international standard, and since at least a hundred million dollars in gold was regarded as necessary to guarantee the government's continued ability to support the nation's currency, the constant drain of gold from the Treasury and the influx of silver and greenbacks had created a critical situation. The sound-money advocates, wishing to maintain the government's position (and, often, their own as well) advocated the repeal of the

Bland-Allison Act; this would check the decline in federal gold reserves. Unfortunately, however, it would also make it more difficult for the farmers to pay back their debts or borrow more money for the essentials they so desperately needed.

This was the dilemma Cleveland had to face at once. He had heard of the farmer's plight from the days when he lived in Holland Patent and saw many of the pioneers come back East, bankrupt and disconsolate. Nonetheless he decided that he must stand for sound money. His natural disposition as a conservative and his experience as corporation lawyer inclined him to this decision. He reasoned simply that debts ought to be paid in dollars of value equal to those that had been borrowed. True, this was the creditors' version of the issue; but it seemed to him only honest. If he sympathized with the debtors who now wanted an easier way to meet their obligations, he firmly believed it would be a fatal public policy. As usual with him, once he made up his mind he would not be moved from the position he thought correct.

So, even before his inauguration, he took action. He wrote to several congressmen, asking them to vote for the repeal of the Bland-Allison Act providing for silver coinage.

Politically it was a mistake. Two days later the House defeated an amendment for suspending coinage. This rebuff would probably have been expected by a politician more accustomed to the behavior of Congress and more sensitive to national opinion. But he had concluded that honesty was involved in the issue, and his mind was quite clear about it. As yet, of course, he was not President, and there was nothing he could do but suffer the rebuff in silence. But the matter would, he was sure, come up again when he was actually in the White House and in a stronger position to do something about it. Then he would see what could be done to make the dollar sound.

14

IN accord with custom, Cleveland took the oath of office prescribed in the Constitution standing bareheaded on a platform erected to the east of the Capitol. He repeated the solemn words after Chief Justice Waite in a resonant voice, and then made his inaugural address. To everyone's astonishment, he spoke without a manuscript or even notes. He had been thorough in his lawyer-like way, and he knew by heart what he meant to say.

His address was not long, but as with everything he composed, it managed to be dense and dull. He knew so little about the problems he was about to meet that he could not say much more than that he intended to give the country "a business administration." This had become a favorite phrase. He meant it to include a good deal, however, and this seems to have been understood. It was particularly an era when business was admired and its methods thought to be efficient and praiseworthy. As Cleveland put it:

The people demand reform in the administration of the government, and the application of business principles to public affairs.

For a presidential candidate, he had not been highly visible during the campaign of 1884, but now, in March of 1885, he became the central figure of the republic, elected to be the nation's chief of state for four years to come. He was impressive, no doubt about that; he weighed some three hundred pounds, and in the frock coat of ceremony he was monolithic. Under the heavy jowls there was a formidable jaw. It could be imagined that nothing would move him unless he had decided that it ought to. He would quite obviously be a good protector. But there were many in his audience who were apprehensive about that. They wished he had a more accommodating look.

The politicians, particularly, were afraid he meant what he said about withholding jobs from deserving Democrats. The farmers and their leaders were afraid he meant to fend off their attacks on gold. The industrialists and their friends in the Congress were afraid he would take the tariff plank in the platform too literally. The workingmen, just entering on a half century of battling for decent wages and working conditions, were afraid he would be unmoved by their miseries. Even Senator Robert M. La Follette was concerned. As he wrote of the inauguration in his *Autobiography:*

The contrast with Arthur [the retiring President], who was a fine, handsome figure, was very striking. Cleveland's coarse face, his heavy inert body, his great shapeless hands, confirmed in my mind the attacks made upon him during the campaign. . . .

All of them were right to be worried. Cleveland expected to reform nothing but government. He had no notion of expanding its operations; he intended rather to see that what the executive did was done well. This, he thought, was his first job. He went at it immediately.

It was reassuring to conservatives that he appeared to take the view that the President had very limited duties. This had been a matter of continued controversy since Washington's administration. Nearly every President at one time or another had quarreled with the Congress about spheres of power. And this difference had risen to a climax after the Civil War when the radical Reconstructionists had tried to restrict President Andrew Johnson and, when he resisted, to oust him by impeachment. They had failed by only one vote, and there was still on the books (somewhat amended) the Tenure of Office Act resulting from that attempted disciplinary action. It provided that the Senate would have to be consulted in dismissals as well as appointments by the President.

Presidents with little experience almost always began by thinking they could get along with the legislators better than their predecessors had managed to do. They were soon disillusioned—

Chief Justice Waite administering the Oath of Office to President Cleveland (*Courtesy of Historical Pictures Service, Chicago*)

the Congress always pressed for advantages and had to be met with counterattack.

What all Presidents came to realize was that the Constitution had made legislative opposition inevitable. Senators and representatives were elected by states or districts, the President by the whole country. Legislators were bound to take what Washington, in disillusionment, had called "local views"; and the President was bound to consider first the needs of the nation as a whole. Also, he was committed to the policies of his party, and congressmen felt free to disregard these if they happened not to suit their constituents.

In order to bring his program into law the President had to bargain. Usually he had to yield some favor, some appointment or even some undesirable amendment in order to achieve anything. Hence the continued controversy.

The President's difficulty was that his performance would be judged largely by legislative accomplishment while that of the legislators would be judged mostly by what they managed to wangle for their states or districts. They had invented numerous ways of not being counted, or of being counted only when it happened to be advantageous to them, on any large national issue. In this way they could escape responsibility; the President never could. It would not take long for Cleveland to discover this as other Presidents had; but it was obvious from his inaugural that his lesson was yet to be learned.

There were other lessons yet ahead. His address dwelt on the evils of strife and spoke of conciliation as though he hoped partisanship would be tempered by concern for the general good. In the same manner he hoped, he said, for an end to sectional rancor, a reference to the still lingering bitterness about the Civil War. But although his inaugural hopes were naive, it was generally guessed that he would turn out to be a "strong" President in contrast with all his predecessors since Lincoln.

One thing could have been predicted: there would be a conscientious and hard-working President. He himself felt that he not only had a good set of Cabinet secretaries but equally good assistant secretaries. He could begin with some optimism.

The White House itself was in better condition than it had

been for a long time. That beautiful structure, since its rebuilding after the British had burned it during the War of 1812, had had hard use. It was both home and headquarters for the Presidents; and it was open to visitors a large part of the time. But it had recently been repaired and refurbished. To Cleveland it seemed luxurious after life in the Albany mansion.

Considering the duties of the President, his working establishment was incredibly restricted and his time scandalously wasted by visitors with no real business that he needed to deal with. He cut these down somewhat by making a rule that congressmen and others demanding jobs for their constituents must go to the department secretaries. But the rule was often violated, and he continued to complain bitterly that they prevented his giving attention to more important matters.

He held two Cabinet meetings a week—on Tuesdays and Thursdays; and these were used mostly to direct the work of executive reorganization. Throughout the departments there were what the press had been calling "pockets of corruption"; and these he meant to clean out entirely. Beyond that he intended to set up the machinery for the "businesslike" administration he had promised. The worst of the festering situations were in the Navy and Interior departments. Both had long histories of waste, so long that waste had come to be accepted as inevitable. But Cleveland had dealt with similar situations in Albany and he knew what to do.

His familiar secretary, Daniel Lamont, came with him from Albany and they continued working and practically living together. They began with breakfast before eight in the morning, and the lights in the Oval Room where they worked were often still on after midnight. Presently Lamont, at Cleveland's invitation, brought his family to live in the White House too. This made something of a family life for the bachelor President—more than was supplied by his rather formidable sister Rose.

But he did have some social life. Two Buffalo friends came to visit during that first spring. One was John G. Milburn, prominent lawyer and supporter of Cleveland; the other was Shan Bissell, the friend and partner who had done so much to assist and protect him during his rise. It was to him that he wrote complaining of his harassments when they were more

Frances Folsom Cleveland (*Courtesy of The New-York Historical Society, New York City*)

than he could bear. It seemed, now, that Bissell was hurt because he had not been given a Cabinet post and because none of his recommendations had been approved. There was talk about this in Buffalo. It was said that the new President meant to punish all Buffalonians for what he considered to have been outrageous treatment in his home city. His friends, of course, had done all it was possible to do in his defense; nevertheless, it was a fact that no Buffalo man was taken into the administration. Even the Republican postmaster there, a federal appointee, was continued in his job. Cleveland was aware of the dissatisfaction, but, as he wrote to Bissell in June:

. . . if, in carrying my present burden, I must feel that my friends are calling me selfish and criticizing the fact that . . . I am not aiding them, I shall certainly be very unhappy, but shall nevertheless struggle on . . .

And, a month later, he wrote to Charles Goodyear of Buffalo:

I have been here five months now, and have met many people who had no friendship for me, and were intent on grabbing all they could get . . . but I have managed to get along with them as well as with my Buffalo friends . . . I am not going to say that I can get along without Buffalo or Buffalo friends. I care much—very much—for the latter. But by God! I have something here that cannot be interfered with; and if my Buffalo friends . . . cannot appreciate that, I can't help it. . . .

He ought to have tried harder to forget his personal annoyance. There were able men among his old acquaintances. Either he wanted to deny the soil out of which he had grown—the second ward and his German neighbors, Billy Drainger's and the Dutchman's saloons, the faithful companionship of Tim Mahoney and the rest—or some residue of guilt for what after all was his own dereliction, made him blame Buffalo and all Buffalonians for its revelation. At any rate, he cut himself off from twenty-five years of his life as a young and rising man.

But the separation was not complete, for in April there were other visitors who might in a sense be considered Buffalo friends. Oscar Folsom's widow and her daughter Frances came to the White House. The young lady, now grown to be a lovely young woman, was about to graduate from Wells College. The Folsoms stayed for some time and Washingtonians wondered whether

Oscar's widow might be about to end the President's bachelorhood.

The White House social regime was as simple as Cleveland could make it. He endured the functions he had to preside over; he ate the meals prepared by the French chef he had inherited from Arthur—and disliked every one of them so much that he wrote to his successor at Albany, Governor Hill, asking if he could not have the woman cook who had done for him at the Executive Mansion.

His only recreation, after he had made the sort of gesture new Presidents often made by decommissioning the small Navy craft held for presidential use on the Potomac, was to be driven about the country roads around Washington. He ordered his coach for late afternoon; and, as often as he could, took the air for an hour or two. His coachman reported that his habit was to get out and walk alongside for some distance, sweating and puffing. His three hundred pounds, getting to be more every day, were a heavy load to carry. Sometimes he had a companion—often it with Charles S. Fairchild, Manning's assistant in the Treasury, to whom he had taken a liking—but many rides were solitary ones. It was about the only time he had for meditation.

Buffalo is something of a resort city in summer. The Lake Erie breezes are cool and refreshing; Albany is not so agreeable, but still not torrid. Cleveland had never before experienced anything like the close and humid climate of summertime Washington. For days, even weeks, a blanket of heat covers the Potomac lowlands. Cleveland felt that he could not leave. His corpulency made him groan and complain, but he made no concessions. He kept his schedule and held everyone else to theirs.

In August, however, he reached the end of his endurance. But he went off to the Adirondacks, not to his old haunts near Buffalo. There he lived for a while the rough life he loved—he fished, mostly, or tramped through the forests until he tired, then sat on a convenient log and looked and listened just as he had so many years before along Limestone Creek or down around Lewiston where the Niagara pours into Lake Ontario after its tumultuous trip over the falls and through the rapids.

He felt fairly satisfied with his first months of responsibility.

He could see that he would have to compromise, possibly more than his conscience would approve, with the politicians. They were still pressing him. Even Manning, with concern for the party, was reminding him that unless his was going to be a one-term administration, he would have to keep the political leaders in his debt.

He had long thoughts to think, also, about some matters he had no experience with—relations with other nations, the irrepressible tariff issue; all that sort of thing. On only one issue was he sure he was right and determined not to compromise. His defense of the dollar had hardened into the conviction that it was a kind of cause to be defended as a matter of conscience.

He came back to Washington hardly rested. He was no longer suited for roughing it, and in September the heat was worse than ever. But Presidents for nearly a century had stood it somehow—although most of them had taken longer vacations than he had done—and so would he. It was not in the Cleveland character to be defeated by any physical hardship.

15

WE have already seen how Cleveland refused to bend to the ever-increasing demands for the cheapening of the dollar. But the plains settlers had other grievances, and he listened to these with more sympathy. Something could be done about them and he meant to do it.

The settlers were not only imposed on because of their debts, they were cheated in other ways. They often found their homesteads preempted by corporations with so much influence that they were dispossessed. Perhaps their claims had been staked on land that some tremendous transaction in Washington had already allocated to a railroad, a land company, a mining syndicate or some such corporate body. There was no way for the settler to be certain of his rights.

The reason for this was that in earlier decades national policy—the opening of the West—had called for transcontinental railways. But the railway men would not extend their lines into sparsely inhabited areas without subsidies. The government thus had to cede belts of land along the rights of way, sometimes many miles in width. This the railway could sell to recoup the cost of construction. As the population grew, the value of this land increased enormously and the speculators who had bought it found themselves growing richer and richer. Fortunes were made by such men as Jay Gould, Collis Huntington and many others whose names have a unique place in our history. If any homesteader had staked his claim to a part of that land, he was dispossessed without recourse.

Such opportunities for easy profit led to much of the corruption of government Cleveland found when he moved to Washington. It existed in many of the departments with favors to dispense, particularly in the Land Office of the Interior Department where settlement rights were issued. Permits bought from officials for a small price could be pyramided into fortunes. Sometimes the payment was made in political support rather than in outright bribes, but it had the same effect. Ever since the war there had been an era of easy compliance. No one seemed to care when land or mineral and water rights were given away or when they were traded among speculators. It was only now that the wrath of those who were excluded from the Western wealth, who found it preempted or who were dispossessed in favor of some nameless entity back East, was reaching the heat that demanded action.

The same Cleveland who would not concede cheap money to pay debts was moved to honest indignation by what he discovered in the departments he was responsible for. He instantly determined to stop the easy prostitution of government for private benefit. This was reasoning as simple as that concerning the sound dollar. The exploiters met their match in him, just as the alderman in Buffalo had; and without intending to, he became the worthy predecessor of more imaginative conservationists in a later generation.

The remedy for such a situation was simple: find out what the crooks were really up to and stop them. Another kind of politician would have made a crusade of it, with loud denunciations and much claiming of virtue. That would be Theodore Roosevelt's way. But Cleveland did not think a thing was done when he made a speech about it; it was done when the cure had been applied. There were no poses struck, but what was going on was halted.

In this case, Cleveland directed the Land Commissioner to stop all land entries (with a few exceptions) until an investigation could be made. There were howls from big ranchers, timber companies and the corporations who had carried out fraudulent surveys. The practice had been for cowboys and lumberjacks in the pay of these interests to make homestead entries and then to hand them over to those they worked for. In this way empires had been put together. Now this kind of practice was stopped. William A. G. Sparks, the new Land Commissioner, also reorganized the surveying system so that land markers could be depended on. The investigation showed such enormous frauds, and Cleveland was so detailed in his statement of the situation, that there was not much defense.

There was not much defense but there was violent reaction. When he compelled the cattlemen who had been fencing in the public domain to take down their fences and get out, there were political repercussions throughout the West. It had been customary to make deals with Indian tribes, too, and cattlemen were using the reservations as private property. This was done by bribing a few of the chiefs, sometimes ones who had little claim to represent their people. This was stopped too—and the howls of rage grew louder.

What Cleveland and his Interior people did was to save the public domain from public exploitation. They did not extend it; they did not develop it; the concept of great forests and parks was still in the future. But the destruction was ended.

It was not necessarily a reform that would last, for continued vigilance depended on honest management, and there was no guarantee of that for the future when other administrations succeeded Cleveland's.

Some guarantee might have been possible had more been done to develop the Civil Service. True, there was a Civil Service Commission, set up under the Pendleton Act, which was technically in charge of overseeing correct management of the service. But there had never been effective commissioners, and Cleveland's were somewhat worse than preceding ones.

He made some effort at improvement. He even offered a membership to Bissell, who would not take it. But since no one of stature wanted to serve he finally appointed an ex-congressman who did nothing at all to purify or extend the Civil Service.

Actually, despite all his good intentions, Cleveland reduced the number of political appointees very little. He worked hard to make them behave while he was the executive; he punished those who spent most of their time in political work rather than what they were supposed to do; but this was far from enough to guarantee that government work would be done by those who were qualified.

Cleveland and the Civil Service. Cartoon by Thomas Nast, *Harper's Weekly*, January 30, 1886 (*Courtesy of The New-York Historical Society, New York City*)

This failure must be put down to the growing irritation of party politicians who saw their machines being weakened because they could not dispense the patronage they were used to controlling, and who forced Cleveland away from reforms. Customs officials illustrated this. In Republican administrations the collectorship of the Port of New York had been the paramount political position in the country outside the post office. President Hayes had moved to clean up this pocket and had been able to dismiss Chester A. Arthur, who managed the Conkling machine from the collectorship. But Arthur was later made Vice-President, and then succeeded President Garfield when he was assassinated. The most important exponent of patronage had in this way come into control of the whole executive establishment; and it was his nation-wide machine that Cleveland had defeated—aided, of course, by the quarrel between the Republican factions of Blaine and Conkling.

But any President must think of reelection; he must also think of keeping his party in power; and after his initial cleanup of the worst situations Cleveland was compelled to pay some attention to the laments of his party associates. He did hear much on the other side from the reforming mugwumps who praised his early actions; but his colleagues warned him that the congressional elections of 1886 might be lost if he persisted in his drive for reform. He was reminded that his own election had been a close one; he was also reminded that mid-term elections for congressmen (who had to run every two years) were often disastrous; without a leader for the ticket, and with representatives running on their own, the party in power usually lost a considerable number of its members.

Cleveland was therefore much less strict about appointments after his first year. He turned over to assistants the job of making recommendations in the post office, the customs service and elsewhere. When his term was over, it could be seen that very nearly as large a percentage of former Republicans had been replaced by Democrats as would have been replaced by any partisan President. Cleveland's concessions to the politicians proved not to be the winning strategy that the politicians had said it would be; but that was primarily, they said, because of his mistakes in larger strategy. And perhaps they were right.

Part of the "larger strategy" centered in the labor movement. The hard times that had hit the Western farmers hit the industrial workers, too, and the stubbornness of employers in refusing to meet their demands led to periodic outbreaks of violence. Workers whose situations were desperate listened, as the farmers did, to agitators who preached the wildest doctrines—so wild that they approached anarchism.

Cleveland was at a loss to know what to do about the labor problem. Since his instincts were so conservative, and his associates drawn from among those who were employers—or from their corps of lawyers—he had no close touch with the real situation in industry. The factories of those days were frightful places to work in. It was before the time of electric power, before the time, also, of the efficiency movement. And collective bargaining was in its most primitive stage. The twelve-hour day was usual even in the hardest jobs. Factories and railroads had no concern for safety. There were many accidents; and injuries to employees were frequent. When a man lost an arm or leg, when he was made sick by dust or fumes or when he was worn out by hard labor, it was at his own risk. There was no assistance either for the family that became destitute when the laborer fell sick, was injured or grew old. Looking back from a time when shorter hours, cleaner and safer factories and collective bargaining have been made compulsory, it is hard to realize what had to be contended with so short a time ago in a nation already the richest in the world and rapidly becoming more so.

Why more was not done by so generous and genuinely sympathetic a man as Cleveland is hard to explain. Part of the reason, however, lay in his conception of the presidency; and to this we must turn for such explanation as there can be.

16

WHEN Cleveland said in his first inaugural that he meant to be a President who kept to his own duties he implied a policy so abysmally mistaken that it hampered his whole subsequent administration. For no President's duties are *only* executive: to execute the laws but not to help make them; to leave alone not only the Congress, but the states and their citizens; to act as a servant but not as a leader. He may have based his beliefs on a deep conviction that the three-branch government established by the Constitution imposed such drastic restraints on the executive; but whatever the source of his feeling, it denied him a position the country desperately needed when he took office, a leadership that could only come from the President himself.

It gradually developed, in his first two years, that he not only believed the President should not encroach on the Congress, but that the federal government itself ought to be severely restrictive in exercising regulatory and directive powers. And it was likewise not the duty of the federal government to care for its citizens in any respect whatever except to keep order when state and local powers had failed.

This resolution to keep the federal government within bounds lasted longer than his abstention from presidential leadership. For he quickly found that he must make known his views on several large questions. He found, moreover, that he must work and scheme to get his proposals accepted.

Of these views, the ones about sound money and low tariffs were the most important. So far did he go in these instances that he could be quite justly criticized as holding to his strict interpretation of presidential duty only when he felt that the issue was not vital. And this was a distinction that was always breaking down.

At any rate, his relaxation of principle after the lessons of his first two years did not extend to the duties of government. In 1887 he took occasion to express these views. It was characteristic that he did it in a veto message. There had been a disastrous drought in the Southwest and the Congress had passed a bill to furnish seeds for destitute farmers (the so-called Texas Seed Bill). He vetoed it, saying sharply that such subsidies were inadmissible and that he would not approve this or any similar measure. As he put it:

A prevalent tendency to disregard the limited mission of this [federal] power and duty should, I think, be steadfastly resisted, to the end that the lesson should constantly be enforced that though the people support the Government, the Government should not support the people.

This significant determination was natural to the sort of mind and temperament Cleveland brought to his position. But, it must be said, it was the same sort of view that was held by all the conservatives of his time—and, for that matter, later, because such a view would characterize for instance, Hoover in the thirties and Eisenhower in the fifties. These later conservatives were recognizably Cleveland's sort, but somewhat more moderate; they had learned that in a close-coupled industrial society there are many services no single individual can perform for himself or for his family, many risks he cannot meet, many rights he cannot protect, many opportunities he must have help in developing.

Cleveland would later be called a Bourbon Democrat, meaning that he seemed never to learn anything and never to forget anything—just as was said of the Bourbon aristocrats of Europe who were submerged in the tides of early nineteenth-century revolution. The term was not quite fair. If he never consented to the uses of government that later Presidents found necessary for the service of citizens, he at least did modify his view of his own duties as President.

No doubt he should have known to begin with that there was a built-in antagonism between the executive and legislative branches. Both in Buffalo and Albany he had had trouble with lawmakers. Perhaps the experience had been too short; perhaps he considered the federal government to be on an altogether higher level so that its legislators must be concerned with the public interest. This may have resulted from his lack of learning, his ignorance of history—even that of his own country. He was not a reader. He knew little of literature beyond that of the law; he seldom read for pleasure or for general instruction; and his knowledge of public affairs, even in his own lifetime, was incredibly limited. He was, indeed, it must be reiterated, the most unprepared President who ever succeeded to the office—the most unprepared, that is, in everything but his commitment to duty.

As his limitations gradually became apparent to him, he did attempt to educate himself by the familiar lawyer's methods, but even then only about issues he had to confront. He felt, after hard digging, that he understood money matters; and he made long and searching inquiries into the tariff problem; but it was still apparent to more sophisticated students of these matters that he had no genuine grasp of them. Study did not affect the conviction he arrived at in either instance, for he remained unshakable. If his conclusion was oversimple, that was characteristic of many of the crucial decisions he made.

About the labor problem, for example, and about foreign relations, he developed the same sort of opinions. About the one, he saw no reason for government to do more than restrain violence—or, at the extreme, to offer assistance in bargaining. About the other, he was a belligerent isolationist. What went on beyond the borders of the United States was hardly worth attention; when it was, the primary concern consisted of making sure the United States was left alone.

These sentiments or policies characterized the whole of his first two years; and if they were later modified, the modifications were not substantial—except in the case of his own prerogatives as President. In that matter he was forced to find new ground and to defend it. He discovered that the Congress he had to deal with was largely devoted to interests other than those of the public; and when these impinged on his prerogatives or obviously controverted the principles he believed in, he not only protested but in the end gave battle.

Senators at that time were still elected by state legislatures, bodies easily influenced, as Cleveland knew from New York, by those who had favors to gain and were willing to pay for them. There had developed among many senators an incredible tolerance about "working both sides of the street"—that is, taking pay from, or owning stock in, companies that needed or wanted legislative favors. Many senators were quite generally identified with railroads, steel companies, cattlemen, timber companies, financial concerns or various industrial combinations. The Senate was known as a "rich man's club," and obviously many of its seats had been bought rather than earned.

What could be expected of such a body when matters of public interest collided with the desires of businessmen? The businessmen prevailed!

For a different reason, the House was as venal. The shortness of terms made it necessary for members to carry on a continual campaign; and this made it necessary, in turn, for them to maintain organizations back home that would assure reelection. This was costly; and businessmen or others, such as veterans, who wanted legislative favors, were quite willing to provide the funds. So the lower House, too, often opposed the President, who was elected by a nation-wide constituency and who had to think of the whole people, not of a few.

Besides this, the House was so organized that members could oppose measures of general interest with complete success and without penalty. A small group from "safe" constituencies held committee chairmanships by seniority and blocked measures they found some objection to. Any sort of bill could be stopped unless it interested so many voters that there was strong public demand for its passage.

Very little of public advantage would come from such a legislative body acting without leadership. If the President did not take the lead, it simply would not be taken by anyone. Cleveland, as we have seen, was reluctant to lead, and compromised his principles only painfully; but he did eventually compromise and take the initiative in matters he felt to be of great importance.

He was much more effective when he was preventing "steals" such as he felt were represented by the numerous pension bills that came to him than he was in persuading the Congress to act on measures of public interest.

Congresses that would do nothing else were in the habit of setting aside two nights a week to consider private pension measures. These were cases that had been considered and rejected by the Pension Bureau; and as was well known, the bureau was lenient enough. The requests usually had little or no relation to actual service and were mere grants to constituents that congressmen traded among themselves. The volume of these was immense. They came to Cleveland for his signature, not in dozens, but in hundreds. He wrote painstaking vetoes. It was this that kept him—and Lamont—up until two or three in the morning. And he became known as a vetoing President as he had been a vetoing mayor and a vetoing governor.

This was not leadership. It was a presidential duty, but not a major one. And the country needed more. Cleveland found this out in one rancorous struggle with the Senate that taught him some lessons he needed to know. It concerned the Tenure of Office Act. This had been on the books since it had been passed to control President Johnson's Reconstruction policies. It had been somewhat modified when Grant had protested; but it was still a threat to presidential operations; and the Senate—where the Republicans still had a majority—tried to use it to show Cleveland that it was his master as it had been the master of his immediate predecessors.

In order to understand this very important incident in the long tug-of-war between the legislative and executive branches, the origin of the act in 1864-65 has to be recalled, together with the Senate's renewed attempt to make use of it twenty years later in Cleveland's administration.

It began, really, when Lincoln attempted to reduce the rancors left over from the Civil War. He meant to be conciliatory. He wanted the rebellious states readmitted to the Union on easy terms as soon as loyal governments could be set up. But the radicals in the Congress, supported by soldiers who would not forgive and forget and by Northern business interests that expected to exploit the prostrate South, wanted a vengeful peace.

It was their intention to punish the rebels, to set up military governments and prolong the military occupation indefinitely, making the terms of readmission strict and humiliating.

Lincoln was assassinated, just as the policy of conciliation was getting started, and when Johnson succeeded to the presidency he followed Lincoln's lead. But Secretary of War Stanton, who was allied with the radical group in the Congress, set out to oppose and obstruct him; and when Johnson dismissed him from office for contumacy, the congressional radicals were furious. It was then that they passed the Tenure of Office Act. In it they used one of the Constitution's silences as their excuse: In Article II it is said that the President may appoint officials of the government, but nothing is said about the procedure to be used in dismissing those he has appointed. The wording on the subject is this:

[The President] shall nominate and by and with the advice and consent of the Senate shall appoint ambassadors, other public ministers and consuls, judges of the Supreme Court, and all other officers of the United States . . .

The issue had arisen in Washington's first administration; and, after some deliberation, he had determined that the power to appoint must imply the power to dismiss. Since Washington had helped to write the Constitution, and since he had such overwhelming prestige, the Congress did not challenge him on the issue; and it had ever since been assumed that this settled the matter.

It was true, however, that the constitutional position on dismissal had never been made certain. If the Senate now asserted that the power to appoint did not imply the power to dismiss, no one could say that this was contrary to the Constitution. How such an interpretation affected presidential powers was not much considered except by assertive members of the legislative branch. When President Johnson refused to accept the act and dismissed Secretary Stanton anyway, he was impeached and brought to trial. The trial was an exhibition of malice and prejudice but it nearly succeeded. Only the refusal of one senator—Ross—to be intimidated defeated the radicals.

The trial was in 1868, and there was a new election that year. The Republicans nominated Grant, and he won as a war hero. Since Grant was their man, the radicals were less inclined to insist on their control of dismissals during his time. When Grant did protest on one occasion with some show of vigor, the act was amended in certain particulars; the amendments provided that the President might *suspend* an official at his discretion; it released him also from the duty to send the Senate evidence of misconduct to justify the action and, finally, it dropped the provision that the suspended official might return to his position if the Senate failed to concur in the President's action.

This was a good deal short of outright repeal. It still assumed a senatorial power that Presidents could not accept. Following Grant, there were three Presidents who were irked by the situation, but all were Republicans and the Senate majority made no real trouble for them. Now, however, it was different. A Democrat had finally become President; and since there was still a Republican majority in the Senate desiring to make as much trouble for Cleveland as possible, the remaining clauses of the Tenure of Office Act were convenient for that purpose. Moreover there remained in the Senate two of the original framers of the act who had been influential in its passage—Senators Edmunds and Sherman.

When Cleveland had been in office only a short time he discovered that a postal official in Rome, New York, had failed to make required reports and had mishandled receipts. In March of 1885 he presented a new appointment and asked the Senate for confirmation. That body adjourned without acting. Cleveland dismissed the offending postmaster, asserting a power denied in the original Tenure of Office Act. Thus began a struggle that went on for more than a year. But plainly the President had the public on his side, and in the end he won. His victory was so complete that within a year the act was repealed.

Meanwhile there had been attempts on the part of Edmunds and Sherman to force Cleveland's compliance by refusing confirmation of all appointments. They demanded that he not only show why his appointments should be approved, but that he should show why former officials were being dismissed. He would comply with the first demand, he said in a message, because it was clearly constitutional; but as to the other, he would not show evidence of any sort. It was his prerogative to dismiss for any reason that seemed to him sufficient—even if it was only because of incompatibility. He instructed his department heads not to comply with Senate requests for evidence.

There the matter stood. The senators at first thought their position tactically impregnable. Cleveland could hardly carry on his work if confirmations were refused to all his appointees. They forgot another clause of the Constitution. It read as follows: "The President shall have power to fill up all vacancies that may happen during the recess of the Senate by granting commissions which shall expire at the end of their next session." Several Presidents in similar situations had used this power; and it was clear that if he wished, Cleveland could appoint and reappoint until the end of his administration, thus keeping his own chosen subordinates in office.

It was partly this and partly the support Cleveland began to get from the public that ended the engagement in his favor. Again and again it had been shown in such disagreements that Presidents could prevail if they appealed to their nation-wide constituency on the ground that their powers were being impaired. The Senate was regarded with suspicion anyway; and Cleveland, if not overly popular with the people, was respected for his undoubted integrity. If he said that he was attempting to serve the public interest but was being hampered by the Senate, the conclusion was automatic that he was being opposed for no good purpose.

In a first two years that were generally empty of accomplishment, repeal of the Tenure of Office Act was a notable exception. Every President from then on would have cause to be thankful for Cleveland's stubborn defense of his power. President Jackson in a famous pronouncement almost fifty years earlier had put the position clearly. In a message to the Senate protesting a resolution of censure passed by that body, he had said sharply that the President was the "direct representative of the people," and that senators were not; they were elected by legislatures; and anyway, they represented states, not the whole nation.

The public had believed him, and they believed Cleveland. He had a chastened Senate to deal with in his subsequent years, and it made him somewhat bolder.

He even became something of a leader in a very modified and conservative way.

17

WHEN a President takes the inaugural oath he swears that he will "preserve, protect and defend" the Constitution of the United States; but also he has to say that he will "faithfully execute the office of President . . ." These are two quite different commitments. The one means that he will maintain the integrity of the governmental system represented by the document; the other means that he will accept the multiple duties imposed on him as chief of state, leader and mentor of its people, guardian of its safety, custodian of its honor and exemplar of conduct for true citizens—all this by implication besides the duties mentioned in the Constitution itself: to be commander in chief, to participate with the Congress in legislation, to "see that the laws are faithfully executed."

Some of the responsibilities not spoken of were understood by the framers, but others only emerged when the government began to operate. For instance, Washington had to set a style in being a leader and mentor. He had to be national guide as well as the people's conscience. Then there was the dignity of the office so important to the country's prestige in the world—the respect due from others. This last, Washington felt, made it necessary to set up an elaborate establishment where he and his wife could entertain in the most formal manner. He held levees (or receptions) at least once a week when his house overflowed with officials and prominent citizens. It was very tiring but it was thought essential to his position.

The precedent he established was almost kingly, so much so that some dogmatic democrats were viperish about his royal manners. But Washington was sure he was right; the new republic must fix its status among the powers. It was young and weak. France, Britain and Spain on its three borders showed daily how little respect they had for the upstart nation that had come into being by revolution. It was part of his foreign policy to show that colonial days were past and that an American President was the equal of Kings and Emperors.

He knew, too, if such others as Senator William Maclay of Pennsylvania, his most bitter critic, did not, that the people themselves should hold the man chosen to be their chief executive in the fullest respect. They must become aware that he was much more than the executive of their government. He must represent them at their best; he was set apart, dedicated to public duties, unassailable in integrity, worthy of trust in any crisis.

Presidents following Washington had reason to thank him for this example. Some—like Jefferson—had been scornful at first of his "airs." The ceremony and show, they said, were undemocratic; but Jefferson himself, and after him his followers, Madison and Monroe, learned in time how important the unmentioned elements of the presidency were. Thus fixed, the tradition had come down through the line of succession. It had been assailed by the frontiersmen who had come to the Capitol with Jackson; but it had been revived at once, almost, because Jackson himself was a man who understood leadership and the power of example. It had survived every attack and still in 1885 was much what it had been in Washington's view.

It was in these unmentioned requirements of the presidency that Cleveland was most deficient. His lack of formal education, his dislike for literature, his ignorance of history, his early associates and even his experiences in Albany had mostly been wrong for the preparation he should have had for his great office. He may have had some sense of insufficiency, but being very much alone and having no other resources than work, he did very little to make himself more capable of really filling the position he had attained.

There was in this some of the same narrowness that led him to misinterpret his other duties. There had been other Presidents —and there would be more—who had begun by saying that they would keep to the *execution* of the laws and allow the Congress to *make* them. These periods of indoctrination and testing are regarded by students of politics as danger periods for the republic: the months or, in extreme cases, the years when new Presidents are learning what is required of them—and, especially, that the Congress and the people expect to be led and even to be told what they must do to fulfill their duties as representatives and citizens.

This is so demanding a requirement, and so essential, that until it is understood, Presidents are bound to be in the deepest sense incompetent. And Cleveland was profoundly incompetent. It took him longer to learn what a President must be than it had most of his predecessors; and his gifts were not well suited to some of the most serious of his duties. He was conscientious; he was capable of hard labor; with these virtues, he set an example of devotion to his position. It was quite clear that with him public office was really a public trust. This was important after the slack years of the seventies, but it was not everything. The White House lost the glamour it ought to have as the social and moral center of the nation; the Congress did nothing because it had none of the leadership it needed; the Democratic party fell to pieces because it had no national head; there was no vision of the future and so no planning for it. The economy proceeded to expand because its businessmen made money out of expansion; but the industrialists had no direction, not even any indication of their responsibilities to the nation.

Gradually, however, Cleveland's illusions about the legislative branch were dispelled. His quarrels with senators and his discovery that the House was organized to oppose everything but to initiate nothing were appalling revelations to one with his simple and direct reactions. That the august federal legislators were much like the aldermen in Buffalo, and quite as devoted to local interests—and those not of their constituents generally, but of the individuals or businesses with whom they had the closest relations —was something he ought to have known early and would have known if he had ever taken any interest in matters beyond his immediate duties. But it shocked him to find it out.

1 3 7

What Cleveland eventually became was important and was good in the nation's history; but what he did not become was tragic. For this was a time when the predatory interests then taking control of the economy, and indeed of all American life, might have been brought under control and given a discipline that would have avoided much terrible dissension and many later tragedies.

True leadership would remain for later Presidents when industrialists and financiers had become so powerful that they could challenge the federal power and often defeat it. The "malefactors of great wealth" that Theodore Roosevelt would try unsuccessfully to bring into some sort of control were highly visible in the early eighties. But such men and their lawyers were Cleveland's most trusted friends and he saw no danger in their accumulations of wealth and power.

He thought he was doing his whole duty when he sat up most of the night and vetoed ridiculous private pension bills, for the vetoes prevented stealing from the government. The immensely greater stealing from the people that went on in other places he paid no attention to. It did not cross his desk to be acted on. If someone had said to him that something ought to be done about the practices of Standard Oil, the steel companies or the railroad companies as they formed and reformed their financial structures and made millions because they could then make their rates and charges almost arbitrarily, he would have been left cold. But nobody did say these things, and he found out about them only indirectly—when he saw how the industrial powers were brought to bear on the tariffs he sought to reform. The schedules would be written with complete indifference to the public interest. His attempted intervention was blandly ignored. He found out then some things he should always have known. He would prevent timber companies from cutting down publicly owned forests, and drive trespassers off the public domain, and from the Indians' lands. But about the important encroachments on the rights of labor and the needs of consumers he could not see that he had any duty.

Eventually he learned about his relations with the Congress and about the need for national leadership, but he only learned when it was too late to be effective. He completely wasted the period of the "honeymoon." (This is a time when Presidents are new and Congresses are still not settled into opposition, when determined leaders can get much done that they can never get done again.)

It is necessary to say even more about Cleveland's deficiencies. As a lawyer he should have known how delicately balanced are the powers outlined in the Constitution. Each branch is independent; but each branch, also, to operate effectively, must understand that it is expected, not only to cooperate with the other branches, but to require them to cooperate with it. There are unwritten principles of restraint and compulsion inherent in the structure. The President, for instance, must insist on his prerogatives and must resist all attempted aggressions. Aggressions will come; they are a certainty; and he must be ready, not taken by surprise. But too often Cleveland was not ready and he was taken by surprise. His practice as a lawyer had not required him to know the Constitution as a governing charter for the republic; and he had never studied under teachers who might have instructed him.

His quarrel with the senators over the Tenure of Office Act taught him part of the lesson he had to learn. When it was over he was a different President. He would never be other than a narrow conservative, taking his views from the traditions of his associates in the business and legal fields; and nothing could cause him to lift his eyes to a larger future for the nation and use the government to make that promise a reality; nothing could make him a charming and persuasive party leader who formulated programs and plans and persuaded his party to adopt them willingly.

Nevertheless he did change. He learned about the presidency as a bulwark of the people—at least in certain respects. And he learned something about leadership, even if he never attained proficiency at it. But he never really learned how to use his powers of office and those he possessed as party chief, and it is one of the tragedies of our nation's history that he did not do so.

His early failures were reflected almost at once in the congressional elections of 1886. There were severe Democratic losses of seats in the House; and the Senate, already Republican, remained that way. His performance as President was not approved.

After that it was not at all clear that there was a second term in prospect for him. He had achieved very little in his first two years. Could he do so much better that he would have a chance for reelection in 1888?

18

THERE was a notable change in Cleveland's way of living in his second year in the White House, as well as in his use of the presidential power. He was finally married to the young lady he had hoped so long to have for his wife. Frances Folsom had evidently been proposed to during her April visit in 1885. Her spring vacation from Wells College had lasted only ten days, but Cleveland had made the most of it. After she had graduated that year and had taken a trip abroad with her mother, she came back in the spring of 1886 to become the first lady to be married in the White House.

Washington gossips had expected her mother to be the one; and for once, they were really surprised. No wonder! Frances was twenty-two, and Cleveland was forty-nine. She was a very beautiful woman now, tall, graceful, self-possessed, charming; and Cleveland was enormous and coarse-looking, a middle-aged man, humorless and immersed in his duties.

He had always been shy in his social contacts; even in Buffalo he had seldom visited in the houses of his lawyer and business friends. When he was governor he had kept much to himself, suffering the ceremonials of his office with resignation. To think of him engaging in any of the amusements natural to a young woman of twenty-two was ridiculous. Yet the young woman had made up her mind without hesitation.

When Frances and her mother came back from Europe late in May, Lamont went down the harbor in New York to meet them and escort them to their rooms in the Gilsey House. It happened that Cleveland was reviewing the Memorial Day parade in New York, and it was noticed that he visited the hotel. The inquiring

The Wedding, June 2, 1886. The White House (*Courtesy of The New-York Historical Society, New York City*)

newsmen soon discovered the reason, and speculation broke out. As soon as Cleveland returned to Washington, a formal announcement was made and speculation turned into a furor of excitement in the capital.

The marriage arrangements troubled him. He was not a member of any church, although he had kept up his Presbyterian preference and went often to services; and it seemed to him unsuitable to be married in a public place such as a hotel. Frances and her mother had intended the marriage to take place at her grandfather's home near Buffalo, but he had died a short time before. A White House ceremony seemed the best solution. William Cleveland came from his country parish to assist.

The mansion would not be the same again. Neither would Cleveland, for that matter. The reticent and stolid bachelor would be softened and humanized by his new wife. It was a change that meant something for the whole country, and for the party as well. For Cleveland, although his worthiness was recognized, had wholly lacked that priceless quality of glamour a President must have. He had not gained the affections of his people—only their respect. And he had been kept from showing his humanity by the stern discipline he enforced on himself and those around him.

The marriage revealed a new man. The mean innuendoes about youth and age, beauty and the beast were quickly dispelled by Frances herself, who was so obviously happy in her marriage that hearts were soon won as well as heads. She was capable, too. She reestablished the social life appropriate to the presidency; she was a thoughtful hostess; she had taste and sureness of touch. It was soon being said that she was the most helpful presidential lady since Dolley Madison, and quite clearly she was. She introduced Cleveland to culture, to refinement and to social grace, introductions long overdue!

It was a time of peculiar worry for Cleveland—many problems needed his attention, and he felt he could spare only a few days for a honeymoon. It would have been thought that even a President, with all his cares, might have taken a longer break for so important a reason, but there was that conscience! Besides, in Frances he had a bride who had followed events closely and understood the circumstances. Now, and always, she was the President's companion.

There was, however, another reason. The curiosity of the public had its reflection in the behavior of the press. Reporters followed the newly married couple everywhere they went, peeking and prying, looking for the least item of interest to be exploited for their readers. The press was not in an admirable phase just then. It was the time when it began to be called "yellow." The competition between the Hearst and the Pulitzer papers resulted in appeals to the lowest instincts and the greediest appetites. The same newspapers that tormented the bridal couple—who had retreated to a small cottage in Deer Park, Maryland—would harass Cleveland's successor, McKinley, in another way. The egomaniacal publishers would practically drive him into the Spanish War in 1898. Now their reporters allowed Cleveland no seclusion even for a honeymoon.

Cleveland was furious about this. There was, however, little that he could do. It was before the time when Presidents were guarded as they would be later. He had very little privacy, something that has to be understood as one of the peculiarities of the slowly maturing democracy. He was jealously watched by hostile eyes as well as friendly ones.

Congressmen allowed him as few perquisites as possible. The White House itself periodically fell into disrepair under heavy use —it was open every day to hundreds of visitors who were quite apt to invade its living quarters as well as its public rooms; and every proposal for rehabilitation was sure to call out demagogic speeches from bucolic congressmen on the theme of extravagance. Callers could quite easily walk into the President's office. His salary was insufficient to support the establishment as it was expected to be kept; he was to have no pension when he was through.

Worse, he had no protection. His appearances in public were an invitation to the unbalanced partisans who always exist. Garfield, only a few years before (in 1881), had been approached without interference by a disappointed office seeker and fatally shot. Lincoln had been an easy target for his assassin in 1865. It was a situation, for the chief of state of a great nation, that would seem incredible to later generations. It could only be explained as

Mrs. Cleveland in her White House sitting room (*Courtesy of The New-York Historical Society, New York City*)

the high cost of a fetish for commonness that required a show of equality regardless of consequences.

The fashion for presidential "democracy" was fastened on the presidency by Jefferson under the influence of the French revolutionists, and confirmed by Jackson, who had ridiculed the aristocratic manners of the man he displaced—John Quincy Adams. Since Jackson, Presidents had felt compelled to make a show of economy and even meanness, although Arthur, Cleveland's immediate predecessor, had done something to modify the image. He had refurnished the disgracefully shabby White House and had lived in state more appropriate to the office than Grant, Hayes or Garfield had dared attempt. It is to be noted, however, that he was not reelected—not even renominated.

Cleveland was careless of his image. By preference he had lived by himself before his marriage. He would hardly have entertained at all, except for a few associates, if it had not been required of him. And, indeed, he had not until his new wife established a quite different regime. When Cleveland became President he made little effort to acknowledge the presence as neighbors in Washington of some distinguished Americans. There was, for instance, John Hay, who had been Lincoln's private secretary as a young man and, as an older one, would be Theodore Roosevelt's Secretary of State; there was also the well-known historian, George Bancroft. Just across Lafayette Square from the White House, Henry Adams, grandson of one President and great-grandson of another, had built his home. Hay was just finishing his biography of Lincoln, and Adams had retired from his Harvard professorship and was the center of an intellectual circle that Cleveland might have taken advantage of. He made no such attempt. He would have said he had no time, but the work of investigating fraudulent pension claims might have been delegated; he might have given the country a vision of its possibilities in the new age of productivity that was obviously beginning; more conversation with the company available to him would have made him a better President.

Frances could not really change her husband in these respects. She did bring him contact with people and ideas he had never considered before, and she eased his lonely concentration on the minutiae of his work; but she could not make a visionary out of the lawyer and she could not give him an education he had never had. Perhaps he would have been lost in conversation with Henry Adams; and after the conversation was over, he might have felt that Adams had seen all too clearly his deficiencies.

If his marriage was a gain for the President as well as the man, one other event was a serious loss. In March of 1886, Manning was forced to give up his work in the Treasury. He was a man whose corpulence and capacity for work matched those of Cleveland; and he held the same opinions about questions concerning finance and the tariff. He was in every way a dependable helper. Moreover he was a party man. As the head of his own considerable New York organization, and as continuing custodian of the Tilden tradition in the party, he brought Cleveland a support he badly needed.

Manning had always warned Cleveland that he must pay attention to his party duties. Political leadership was an integral element of the presidency as it had developed in the American tradition. And although Cleveland knew all about local organization, he was inclined to suspect that the corruption he had uncovered in Buffalo and in Albany was a characteristic not only of Tammany but of all other local organizations. He felt forced to regard the bosses as his enemies rather than his allies. That this was no way to ensure the party's continued success and his own continuation in office Manning kept reminding him.

He had Charles Fairchild to take up the duties in the Treasury but he had no one to succeed Manning as the kind of political adviser he badly needed. The mistakes he made in 1886 and 1887 might well have been avoided if Manning had been with him still. For mistakes were made. He did perceive that he must make concessions to the politicians and he was still somewhat equivocal on tariff reductions as a concession to the Northern Democrats who were protectionists; but he was rigid about the protection of the dollar. And it was this last that was disrupting the party.

Frances could not help with the economic problems; but she could and did make his relations easier with the congressmen who had been offended when, as they felt, he was unreasonable about political concessions. Dinners, receptions and entertainments at the White House under her management were events approved by everyone except a few carpers. It is true that the newspapers were still mostly hostile. But this was more because they were looking for something to play up as sensational than because they had anything against Cleveland. And even the papers were won over by the First Lady's charm, grudgingly at first, but with more enthusiasm as time passed.

As other Presidents had, Cleveland, after his marriage, longed for a more homelike living place than the White House. No other chief of state in the world was so constantly exposed, and as government activities multiplied, so did the exposure. When the country had been younger and Washington less a capital and more a country town, this had not been such a problem; by now it had become a constant irritation. It was another of the congressional neglects that left the President without such a country retreat as other heads of government possessed. In desperation Cleveland finally purchased a small house in what was then farming country two miles north of Georgetown. He decided to spend part of his own small fortune to buy the place and thus escape from any critical comments there might be if he used public property.

The house was on high ground on the Tennalytown Road (now Wisconsin Avenue) overlooking the city. It was a small stone structure that had to be considerably enlarged; but the grounds were large enough to furnish the seclusion he longed for. Frances was delighted with the opportunity to alter and furnish the place and manage a home of her own. She called it Oak View. Before they heard of this, reporters began to called it Red Top—from the color of the roof—and that it remained, at least to the public.

From its porch the Clevelands could see in the distance the austere shaft of Washington's monument and the Capitol dome; not far away were some famous old houses: Woodley, the stately home of the Key family, and Grasslands, the estate of Secretary of the Navy Whitney, as well as others. It had a lovely prospect of forest and hills and, below, the Potomac basin where the White House stood. It was a real home, the first Cleveland had ever had. Washington was now a city of some hundred and fifty thousand people, but Frances was able to make something of a farm of her twenty-seven acres. There were cows in a pasture and flower and vegetable gardens around the house. Cleveland enjoyed his morning and evening drives to and from town—it was about three miles to 1200 Pennsylvania Avenue—and even appeared now to enjoy the entertaining Frances arranged.

Still his worries multiplied; the cheap-money advocates became, if possible, more insistent; the tariff was a puzzle he seemed unable to make up his mind about; and as new tests of the administration approached and potential rivals appeared, his record came again under scrutiny. Especially the Grand Army of the Republic, infuriated by his repeated veto of pension proposals, brought up his failure to serve in the war. There were false stories about the sufferings of the substitute Cleveland had bought. Brinske (or Benninsky), it was said, had been wounded and had suffered neglect, and there were several ingenious variations on this theme. Actually the man, who had been a casual laborer in Great Lakes ports, had been injured, but in an accident, not in battle, and had ended his service quietly as a hospital orderly. But the facts did not interest the detractors.

The jibes over his lack of military service kept recurring, and sometimes they were embarrassing. There were such serious threats of insulting demonstrations that he did not attend the annual encampment of the G.A.R. This, however, he turned against the threateners by saying that whatever was thought of him personally, it was intolerable that the President of the United States should be treated with disrespect. Yet the publicity attendant on this and other such expressions of disfavor were sinister forecasts of what might come in the campaign of 1888.

When he had written his first inaugural, he had made a commitment no politician of experience ought ever to make. He had said that he favored limiting the presidency to one term. This had been a fashion in earlier days when equalitarianism had demanded the sharing of government jobs among as many partisans as possible, and when it was fashionable also to believe—or at least to say—that any man was equal to any task. Cleveland's statement would now have to be dealt with or be deliberately ignored.

There are many reasons why such a suggestion is unwise for any President, but one reason was apparent to anyone: he was the only available Democrat. If he did not run, the Republicans would come in again and the familiar control of government by speculators and exploiters would be resumed. Both for the party's sake and for the country's, he could not go through with his expressed intention.

This may not have been a serious concern; he had not really made a firm commitment to one term, only expressed an opinion; and it was obvious that the nomination would be pressed on him. But what worried him more, as he entered on the final phase of his first term, after the disappointments of the congressional elections in 1886, was what he would be elected *for*. He could claim to have cleaned out the "pockets of corruption"; the departments were now in good order; the Navy was on the way to rehabilitation; the stealing of public land and its misuse by cattlemen and timber companies had at least been brought under control. But he could not honestly say that either on the money question or on the tariff issue he was much farther ahead than he had been in the beginning. And these now seemed to him much the most important issues of the day.

Generally speaking, everyone knew he was for sound money; and they knew also that he believed in lowered tariffs—just why, we shall discuss in the next chapter. But he had not carried the party or the country with him. Nor was he really prepared to expound and defend his attitudes.

There was, for instance, the momentous puzzle of adjustment to a Treasury surplus, something very few nations at very few times had ever had to deal with. And there were other phases of the two issues that he still needed to analyze if his own mind was to be entirely clear.

19

WE must imagine that during these early years in the presidency Cleveland was trying earnestly to understand some large policies—ones as mayor and governor he had never needed to understand. They were, however, ones a President must deal with every day of his life; especially the money and tariff issues had been and would continue to be questions that determined prosperity or depression and, as well, conflict between one region and another and one class and another. Politicians would take sides about them and would find themselves committed, often, to more conflict than they had foreseen. Cleveland was no exception and, as we have seen, he realized it very quickly. What he did not realize was that solutions—both economic and political—were far more complicated than he had been led to think by those who at first advised him. He, too, was soon committed to more than he had anticipated.

As we have noted, from the first he was inclined to accept without too much question the morality of the gold standard. It did not occur to him that the soundness of the dollar might be achieved at the cost of unsoundness in the whole economy. It seemed to him, very simply, that the bankers were right who wanted their loans repaid in currency worth as much as when the loans were made. He did not see that a rigid gold standard might be increasing the value of dollars and so favoring creditors; nor did he see that it might be stifling activity and making life harder for farmers and workers. Because of this, he would never really find out why Populism—the radical farmers' movement—was sweeping so irresistibly through the farm states.

He would not show much interest either in the causes of labor unrest. These causes ran deeper than just the unreasonable demands of workers for more and more pay. They were related to the changes in industry, in shipping, in mining and in communications. The efficiency movement was just getting well started. Its effect was to reduce the cost of making things. But also it reduced the need for manpower, and workers resented being replaced by machines. They also felt that they should share in the profits from increased productivity. Employers granted these demands only grudgingly. Often they allowed disputes to become small civil wars with their workers locked out and their properties guarded by hired armies.

Unions were the workers' device for strengthening their bargaining power. This collective action was resisted too. The organizers were pictured as anti-American. When strikes happened, the government—local and federal—usually had to intervene to keep order. But keeping order meant that the strikers were suppressed. Property was protected, but workers' rights—if they had rights—were not.

And about this matter of rights, Cleveland, as a lawyer, shared the prevalent attitude. No such privilege as collective bargaining was recognized in the Constitution. It was something that had not yet been needed in the United States. So Cleveland, presiding over the expanding nation at the time of its most critical adaptation to the conditions of modern economic advance, lingered with others of his class and condition in a past that was simpler, and whose moralities and customs were derived from that time.

He was a fair man, and we must assume that there were reasons for his lack of understanding. We can guess at some of them. He was an Easterner, a lawyer for business interests and unfamiliar with conditions in the West. And there is a curious absence in all his career of evidence that he took an interest in agriculture or in the industries of the expanding economy.

Village boys were familiar with farms and farmers, seeing them every day as they did; yet there was always an antagonism between village and farm; and this was as true in New York as in the West where Populism had its home. Easterners, however, had better access to markets and had not acquired their farms so recently. Their debts were smaller, usually, and their resentment less bitter. But Eastern merchants sold goods to farmers and bought their produce. They sold for as high a price as they could get, and bought for as low a one as they could manage. They gave credit too; and in collecting their debts, the same sort of antagonism was set up as always exists between those who must pay and those who must be paid.

The times were speculative; everyone was betting on a more prosperous future. The West was being occupied and funds were being borrowed by the occupiers. When these debts came due, the usual conflict between debtor and creditor arose. When repayment was difficult for all the debtors, because their speculation had not paid off, they were apt to make common cause—to feel that their creditors were being hardhearted; they appealed for help wherever they thought they could find it. In a democracy that help could best come from the government, and congressmen from the farm states were pressed to find ways that would make debt payment easier. We have seen this pressure operating even before Cleveland took office. It became stronger as his term went on.

To grasp the basis of this issue, so bitterly disputed by 1886, it is necessary to understand the "quantity theory of money"; it can be explained in a series of theorems:

All dollars available are exchanged for all commodities available. (Commodities *include* services.)

If there are 1000 dollars and 1000 commodities, *and all are to be exchanged,* each dollar will buy one commodity.

If there are 500 dollars and 1000 commodities, each dollar will buy two commodities. The price for each commodity will be one half dollar.

If there are 1000 dollars and 500 commodities, each dollar will buy one half a commodity. The price of commodities will be doubled. Each will be worth two dollars.

Variation on either side of this equation raises or lowers the value of each dollar and, correspondingly, the value of each commodity. The fewer the number of dollars, the more commodities each will buy; the greater the number of dollars, the fewer commodities each will buy. Prices will go *down* if the number of dollars decreases. Prices will go up if the number of dollars increases.

Since the debtors were the producers of commodities and the

dispensers of services, they naturally wanted an increase in the number of available dollars since more available dollars meant that they could get higher prices for their bales of cotton or bushels of wheat. The creditors (the banking and business interests), on the other hand, resisted the infusion of more dollars because that made each individual dollar worth less, and when they collected their debts, each of the repaid dollars would buy fewer commodities. The debtors wanted a rising price level, creditors a falling one. The debtors wanted more dollars, the creditors fewer.

Events during Cleveland's years were affecting both sides of the equation. On the one side, the number of commodities was being increased by the expansion of production, an increase that was as true of farmers who were raising more cotton, corn and wheat each year as it was of the steel mills and factories whose products were multiplying. This increase tended to increase the number of commodities in relation to the number of dollars, and the price for a given commodity was consequently lower, since there were fewer available dollars to buy the increased number of goods.

On the other side—the money side—the dollars available as a medium of exchange had been increased in a number of ways. New deposits of gold had been discovered several decades before but production had now slackened; when the slackening became obvious, silver was added to the coinage. There was much more silver, and this could increase considerably the number of dollars. The debtors saw this, and several years before had succeeded in getting through congress the Bland-Allison Act mentioned earlier.

This, quite naturally, led to the conclusion that if silver with an intrinsic value far below that of gold could be used, why not something with even lower intrinsic value or, even, none at all? In the crisis of the Civil War, a good many paper dollars had been issued that represented no value at all except legal provision that they must be taken in payment for debts—and this meant payment for commodities as well. This resort had been resented by creditors, of course, and "greenbackism" had become almost a swear word in financial circles. There was still a quantity of old greenbacks in circulation; now the demand for more greenbacks became shrill.

Every day Cleveland was faced with some phase of this controversy, and the Congress seethed continually with demands on the one hand for still more dollars and, on the other, for fewer. There were slogans. "Soundness" was one, and a good one for creditors. But there were many picturesque epithets for the collectors: "Barons of Wall Street," for example, in reference to the men of the financial center in New York; or "gold bugs" in reference to bankers everywhere.

There was another complication. It had to do with quite another set of circumstances, but had a complicating effect on both the labor movement and the money question—this was the tariff. The issue here was one between manufacturers, who wanted "protection" from cheaper imports, and consumers, who wanted the lower prices that would result from foreign competition. The low-tariff advocates were many, and they included not only ultimate consumers but many manufacturers who used commodities such as steel, for instance, in making finished goods, and who, with low tariffs, could buy the raw product more cheaply from abroad. So there was a division of interests.

But this was complicated, too, by a theoretical controversy; "infant industries" were spoken of. It was argued that tariffs were necessary to encourage new economic ventures; and much the same argument was used about protecting American wage earners against competition from goods produced by workers abroad whose wages were much lower than their own. This was persuasive and the labor movement, on the whole, was protectionist. Economists had another view. The "infant industry" argument, they said, was being used to protect not new industries but old ones wanting excessive profits. And as for wages, American workers were so much more productive that their earnings would be higher than those of foreign workers if their employers paid them what their productivity warranted. The only result of protection, then, was that American consumers paid more than they ought to pay for their goods, with resulting profits to "big business" and no advantage to wage earners.

There existed a Free Trade League with the well-known economist, David A. Wells, as its president. Meetings, charged with emotion, were held periodically, and protectionists were excoriated as profiteers and exploiters of both workers and consumers.

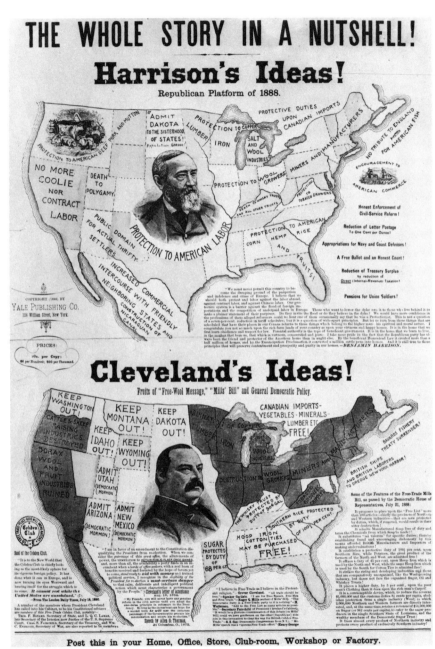

A Republican view of the issues (*Courtesy of The New-York Historical Society, New York City*)

The Congress was divided on this issue as it was on the issue of money, and there was the familiar tendency of senators, particularly, to represent the protectionist interests rather than the consumers. Higher and higher tariffs had been legislated all through the Republican years since the Civil War. The Democrats had always said they were for lower tariffs if not for absolute free trade. But a faction led by Senator Samuel J. Randall of Pennsylvania was as frankly protectionist as the Republicans—who were assumed to be the party of finance and big business, just as the Democrats were the party of farmers, small business and debtors. Many other Democrats were only theoretical free traders; they tended to be protectionist when the interests of manufacturers in their districts or states were in question.

The connection of this issue with the money question was that the high tariffs of recent years had brought in so much revenue, and the expenditures of government were at this time so moderate, that a "surplus" was accumulating in the Treasury. And, curiously, having too much revenue was proving to be a much more difficult problem than having too little of it had ever been. A government that had a surplus was either taking in more revenue than was needed or was spending less than its resources warranted. Which was true? Should revenues be reduced or should expenditures be increased?

As Cleveland studied this, he was forced to conclude that the surplus dollars could only have come from continual withdrawals of revenue dollars from circulation by the Treasury. Dollars taken out of circulation were reducing the total quantity and changing the equation between them and the goods and services they were used to buy. Prices were tending to fall, farmers were being squeezed by having to pay debts in dollars of increased value and unrest was rising in the West and South.

This might have been a situation normal to a Republican regime; but Cleveland was a Democratic President. On the money issue, he had been at odds all along with the majority of his fellow Democrats especially those in the West and South, as well as with the tradition of the party. On the tariff issue, should he take an antiparty position as well? Should he favor protection? Or should he favor lower tariffs?

As a sound-money man, he should also have been for sound tariffs—that is, ones favored by industries and bankers. But as a Democrat, and as an honest man, he came to quite another decision. It seemed to him that, on the evidence, the low-tariff advocates were right in saying that protectionism was not necessary to support American industry and maintain high wages. Also he felt that it was resulting in exorbitant profits for the interests sheltered behind the high duties.

This conclusion accounts in large part for what happened in the campaign of 1888—this and the dissensions in the party resulting from it.

There was furious controversy about both issues, and even the facts became confused. That more money was being taken in by the Treasury than was going out did not mean that the government debt left over from the Civil War had been paid off: there were still bonds outstanding. There also were millions of greenback dollars in circulation. The surplus revenue could be used to pay off the bonds and retire the intrinsically worthless greenbacks. This would be the "sound" course. But this would reduce the number of dollars and would tend to depress the prices of commodities— such as cotton, wheat and corn—and would make dollars scarcer when debts had to be paid. Rising regional and class conflicts were involved in these issues, and the country, as well as the Democratic party itself, was torn with the dissension.

During 1887, Cleveland kept getting warnings from the politicians that both the tariff and the money issues were dangerous and that he had better find some middle course that would give as little offense as possible to either side. But this was not in character for him. Once his mind had been made up he was forthright about both issues. He stayed sound on money, but on the tariff he came down—and came down hard—on the side of reduction.

The situation was this: governmental revenue in 1886–87 was about 371 millions, and this was 103 millions more than was expended. Revenues, mostly from whiskey and tobacco taxes, furnished 118 million of the total; and customs duties furnished 217 million. There was the possibility here of reducing the surplus by lowering the taxes. Also, if customs duties should be reduced, the reductions could be made mostly on luxuries: sugar, silk and wine, for instance, and this would still leave protection for manufacturers.

Cleveland rejected the opportunity. In a closely reasoned State of the Union message to the Congress in December 1887, he set the pattern for the campaign of the year to follow. The tariffs on *necessities* must be lowered. Consumers were being made to sustain exorbitant profits because of protectionism. It was intolerable. So he argued in his blunt and heavy style.

This was a considerable change from the soft attitude he had taken before. It clearly resulted from the study he had given the question and conclusions he had reached on his own. It caused a sensation—and a line-up of opposing forces. It now remained to be seen whether the voters would support him for reelection. The politicians were apprehensive. Cleveland himself seemed to think that at any rate he had done the right thing. If the voters did not agree, he could not help it.[1]

[1] It is suggested that illustrative material on these issues—tariffs, money and the labor movement may be found in contemporary newspapers and in economic histories of the United States.

20

I T was obvious that Cleveland had given up the idea of serving only one term. There was too much at stake. He should have seen this earlier; in fact, he should never have mentioned the matter. That he had might count against him in the coming trial of strength; whether it actually would remained to be seen.

He felt that he could rely on support from some sources that might well have been hostile. It was not in his nature to be really conciliatory, but he had made an effort. He had tried to win over the Southerners, for instance, by giving them numerous positions in the government. There were several in his Cabinet. As one Northern newspaper pointed out with some annoyance, there were three former Confederate colonels in Interior alone. He hoped, also, that although he had done nothing especially favorable for labor, he would have such support as the leaders were able to assemble in payment for his sympathy with their grievances.

In this last matter, the labor leaders had reason to feel that the Republican party, being traditionally allied with business interests, would never do anything to assist their cause. Cleveland had at least spoken for peaceable solutions to a number of problems, including the grievances of labor in its battles with Gould, Huntington and other railway owners. Samuel Gompers was appearing as the most responsible leader, and he had shown an awareness from the first that a favorable governmental attitude was necessary to union progress.

The depression of 1873, and the slow recovery from it, ought to have taught everyone that such economic ordeals were not inevitable, that they could be prevented or, if they happened, that recovery could be assisted by governmental measures. But these lessons were still ignored. Even the economists had no over-all ad-vice to offer. Still, Cleveland need not have taken the view that no matter what the consequences, unless some violence occurred there must be no government interference.

He was learning. His self-education about money and about the tariff, it is true, were forced by circumstances. He was being pulled both ways on both issues. The soft-money advocates, to-gether with the silverites, were eternally agitating. There were enough of them in the Congress to pass resolutions advocating one or another of the ways to increase the amount of money in circu-lation; and even Cleveland, with his prejudice for soundness, could see that the Treasury surplus was causing a restriction that was hard on the debtor class. This was a government policy that affected the economy. A hands-off policy was making the trouble. But, of course, it was not *really* a hands-off policy, or so Cleve-land felt. The trouble was being caused by another government policy—the protectionist tariffs that brought in so much unneeded revenue.

When he had to consider these problems with the seriousness they demanded, Cleveland finally figured out the course that might have been expected of him. Money should be left alone—that is, no measures to increase the number of dollars should be taken, but tariffs should be lowered. Lowering tariffs, in his view, was really the opposite of government interference; it was a reduction of inter-ference. This accorded with the conservative view that held so closely to *laissez faire*.

As the controversies became more acrimonious—and as the surplus continued to increase—this reasoning of Cleveland's gradu-ally became a conviction. During the summer of 1886, he began to have more prolonged and more earnest conversations with congressional leaders. He reminded them that the Democratic plat-form had declared for lower duties, and that the Democratic tradition was one of free—or, at least, freer—trade. It was time the obligation was met.

The Congress had recessed without taking any action. He thought of calling a special session and consulted Speaker John G. Carlisle about it, but Carlisle was opposed. The party, he said, was too divided, and if a decision was pressed upon it, there would be more division. Wait, he urged, until after the congressional elections and see whether there might not then be more support for reductions. But the elections went against the Democrats.

Matters stood this way when in the summer of 1887 Cleveland made his first presidential tour of the country. He did not visit all its regions, but he went into the Midwest and into the South, areas that were strange to him; and he learned some things that he should have learned before he became President at all.

Many American Presidents had made such journeys. Washington, the first of them, went by carriage on an arduous processional into Northern states he had not seen since the Revolutionary War, and continued on into New England, where he was almost a stranger. Other Presidents had understood that they must acquaint themselves with regions they had only heard of, meet the people, try to comprehend their problems, learn more about their needs. In 1887, it was still not an easy undertaking. There were railways now; and a President could travel in a private car with family and associates. But the ceremonial was just as exhausting and there was just as much difficulty in seeing beyond the crowding politicians to the people themselves.

Cleveland went as far north as St. Paul, as far west as Omaha, as far south as Montgomery (the first capital of the Confederacy), on to Atlanta and north through the Carolinas.

Whatever he might have preferred to do, he had mostly to shake thousands of hands as reception lines filed past, make speeches to crowds gathered to see and hear the President who had until now seemed so remote and visit sights selected by prideful local dignitaries. This was the custom, and he followed it faithfully. At Chicago there was a procession stretching for miles, and there were huge crowds as a result of a holiday throughout the region, declared for the occasion. That night Cleveland was said to have shaken six thousand hands, an incredible feat even for a man with his stamina. At Madison, Wisconsin, he managed to do a little fishing, but this was almost the only such interlude on the whole trip.

The demand for speeches was met by a series of them that turned out to be wholly unsuited to his audience. Instead of being folksy or inspiring, Cleveland had evidently used reference books

Benjamin Harrison (*Courtesy of The New-York Historical Society, New York City*)

to compose reviews of local history—something everyone in the audience knew better than he. True, this did at least keep him from offending the politicians or getting into controversies that might be embarrassing. But he also succeeded in boring his hearers mercilessly, and this would do him no good in the next election. He came back to Washington exhausted. He felt that he had done a duty, at least, and certainly he had shown himself in country quite strange to him. He had learned a little, perhaps, but mostly he had simply performed a necessary but unpleasant chore.

Before undertaking his official trip, he had had a pleasanter experience. He had gone back to visit, as President and with a new wife, the country he had known as a boy and later as a frequent visitor from Buffalo. He spent some days in Clinton, in Fayetteville, in Holland Patent and in Forestport, where William was pastor. In these villages he was able to do what he had not done for years: sit on front porches, stroll down shaded streets, stop in stores for talks, go for rides with the doctor as he made his country rounds. The grocery at Fayetteville was decorated in his honor, and he made an informal speech, mostly of reminiscences.

These experiences, one pleasant, one a tiring duty, carried him through the hot summer. It was the end of October 1887 when he began again to work on his State of the Union message to the Congress. This address in December would fix the issues for the campaign of 1888. It proved to be his most important state paper, and also the most disastrous. It would disrupt the congressional session, split the party and give the Republicans the chance they had not thought they would have—and it would not result in lowered tariffs. That was the issue he had been studying so earnestly, calling the party to its duty and insisting that the issue be settled by a national referendum. All his earnest thoughts went into his message.

He was defeated in the election of 1888. It was close; he had actually a popular majority; but not a majority of the Electoral College. He was beaten by Benjamin Harrison, grandson of President William Henry Harrison and son of a second Harrison who had been a member of the Congress. It was a mistake all around for the American people.

The campaign itself was not a notably exciting one, although toward the end, Republican funds made it appear so by organizing parades and meetings, by setting many speakers to work and by circulating millions of pieces of pamphlet material.

What was more important was that the Republicans worked hard and the Democrats did not. Perhaps, also, the country responded to the protectionist arguments so positively put and now so familiar. Perhaps they meant to reject Cleveland's demand for revision. More likely, lowered tariffs were not convincingly argued for. The Republicans had some success in making out that Cleveland was an outright free trader when in fact he was moderate in his views. He meant to depend as much on the argument that the high tariffs constituted unnecessary taxation to be borne by consumers as on the argument that industries did not actually need protection. But that was not the impression that prevailed among the voters.

The Republicans spent vast amounts of money to convince workers they would lose their jobs if tariffs were reduced, and actually the most radical of the labor leaders, Terence V. Powderly of the Knights of Labor, campaigned for Harrison.

Small businessmen were told that hard times would surely follow Cleveland's election, and most of them believed it.

The farmers were inclined, as usual, to vote against their own interests. Lower tariffs would have permitted an increase in imports of manufactured goods, and these would have paid for more exports of farm products. But they did not see it this way. This was becoming a persistent phenomenon of American politics. It was doubtless mixed in farmers' minds with the desire to be conservative—and the Republicans were that. At any rate they repudiated the Democrats.

Cleveland himself did not actively campaign. He had taken positions that were not popular. He had opposed easy money; he had been unsympathetic to veterans' demands; he had been unfriendly to local politicians who wanted to be on the public payroll; and he had been only nominally interested in labor. But he stubbornly considered that his high office precluded active pleading for support. On the whole, the Democrats were on the defensive throughout. They had to defend a record consisting mostly of a return to integrity in government, together with principles that the President had argued for but had not been able to put into practice. He might be respected, but he was not accepted as a leader.

Besides, the campaign was badly managed. In 1884 there had been much better organization than there was in 1888. Then, A. P. Gorman of Maryland, as chairman of the Democratic Executive Committee, had himself been an enthusiastic believer in Cleveland's worth and the issues he had defined. In 1888 the campaign was managed by Calvin S. Brice of Ohio, who did not much believe in lowered tariffs. He and William H. Barnum of Connecticut, who was a member of the Iron and Steel Association, were mostly in charge. One was a corporation lawyer and railroad financier who had grown wealthy in the manipulation of securities, and the other was an extensive owner of iron ore fields. Both would be injured by lowered tariffs and neither cared to center the campaign on this issue.

The Republicans, however, believed hotly in their cause. Their chairman was the notorious Matt Quay of Pennsylvania. Quay had absolutely no scruples, and he was a newly elected United States senator, whose backers were manufacturers and ironmasters. He was assisted by John Wanamaker, the merchant, one of a group of Philadelphia conservatives who dominated the party in that state. These were not only hard protectionists, but shrewd and effective managers. They raised the largest sums ever yet used in a campaign, and filled the mails with propaganda. They did more: they bought votes, and bought them where they would count most.

This last was still an unfortunate feature of elections in those years. There were fixed rates; there were customary procedures for registering hired voters in doubtful precincts; and there was an organization for getting them to the polls. Both parties had local machines skilled in these practices. Tammany was experienced in such work, but in the 1888 election there were complications and all of them seemed to favor the Republicans.

One of these had to do with the familiar antagonisms of the foreign born. These were as important in this campaign as they had been in the previous one—except that this time they favored the Republicans. The Republican effort to picture Cleveland as a British stooge (lower tariffs, it was said, would benefit England) was made credible by a curious incident having to do originally with a dispute over Canadian fisheries. This led the British minister, Lionel Sackville-West, to make a diplomatic blunder. Cleveland had won the applause of New Englanders as well as the Irish by demanding a retaliatory law against the Canadians who were restricting American fishermen in their waters. But when Sackville-West was asked by an inquirer to say whether the incident showed prejudice against the United Kingdom, he failed to see the trap. He told his questioner, in effect, that Cleveland was not hostile to British interests and that is would be all right to vote for him. Such interference, as it was called, in a domestic matter by a foreign representative was inadmissible; and it was used with enormous effect to convince the Irish that Cleveland was actually a British sympathizer. Cleveland demanded the minister's recall at once, but the harm was done.

Harrison himself made speeches and preached protectionist doctrine; also, in the middle of the campaign, Blaine returned from Europe and began to tour the more doubtful states on Harrison's behalf. There were no Democrats who could compete successfully with these two for attention, and it was apparent to the Democrats in the closing days of the canvass that the election was likely to be lost.

Cleveland actually had upward of a hundred thousand votes more than Harrison; but they were distributed in such a way that the electoral vote went against him 233 to 168. Cleveland had been a good President, by his own estimate, and did not deserve to lose, especially to a Republican who promised nothing but a return to the deplorable conditions of the postwar era. But his mistakes were obvious; he had not accepted his duty to be a party leader and he had not tried earnestly enough to carry the country with him on matters he believed to be important. He had failed in these obligations because his view of the presidency had been too restrictive and he had not used the government to redress the intolerable injustices of farmers and workers. He had not proved that he was the President needed by the country in his time—for a former one, yes, when simple honesty in office was enough—but not for the disturbed years of the eighties.

2 1

I T has to be said that Cleveland was not much inclined to blame himself for the Democratic defeat. He felt that the stand he had taken had been right and that he had done all that he could have done without sacrificing principle. Over and over he was assured by his close associates and by the mugwumps that protective tariffs did involve the government in the support of monopoly, the exploitation of consumers and restriction of free enterprise; also that the reform he had stood for had not really been defeated in the election; in the end, he was told, they would surely prevail. He preferred, naturally, to believe these reassurances. He even believed, after thinking it over, that his tariff argument had influenced the Republicans and that Harrison would prove to be a moderate.

About this last he was wrong. The most extreme tariff bill ever written would be passed during the succeeding administration. This was the McKinley Tariff Act, named after a congressman from Ohio who would himself someday be President. Reform would have to wait. But his friends were right in another—a long-run—sense; a discussion had been begun that would eventually have some of the results Cleveland hoped for. This is often the way in American politics.

About other matters, as he was preparing to leave office Cleveland expressed some convictions no one guessed he had been developing. He was beginning to understand that more was going on in the country than he had allowed himself to consider as presidential responsibility. In his last message to the Congress in December, he identified certain issues that before then he had ignored. There was trouble coming, he said, because the rich were getting richer and the poor poorer. There was outrageous evidence of this in the cities where palatial homes of the wealthy stood just next to the wretched houses and filthy tenements of the poor. Employers were virtual dictators, and workers were condemned to "unremunerative toil." He used language he had seldom used before; it seemed almost to echo that of the more radical labor leaders. How could the speculators and financiers brag about their achievements he asked, when "citizens" were struggling far in the rear and were being "trampled to death beneath an iron heel"?

The leaders of American industry, he said, must be blamed; corporations should be the servants of the public; in reality, they were fast becoming the people's masters.

Could the man who expressed himself so strongly now about the injustices of industrial society be the conservative defender of sound money, the same President who, when he had entered on his office, had restricted himself to purely administrative duties and felt that government itself ought not to interfere in such matters?

Experience, it seemed, had broadened his views, aroused his sense of justice and redefined for him the part Presidents and the government itself must play in the country's affairs. The December message, so forthright as to constitute an indictment, was an exercise of leadership he had before professed to avoid. His struggles with the monopolists over the tariff had apparently embittered him; but his defeat had not reduced him to submission. Defeat had never done that to Cleveland. He was a tough fighter who had learned that a President's fighting cannot only be defensive but must often be aggressive.

Harrison would be a cold and ineffective President. He would consent not only to the McKinley tariff, but to the savage suppression of labor organizations. And, being a veteran himself, he would give in to the demands of the Grand Army for dependents' pensions that Cleveland had ridiculed and had consistently vetoed. He would also yield to the silver producers' demands and approve an act providing for further purchases and coinage of that metal. This last was not consistent with Republican tradition, but Harrison was from Indiana and he was a politician too. He had heard the farmers' protests, and even though the moneyed men disapproved, he risked splitting the party to keep rural support.

Cleveland, looking on, sympathized with Harrison. He had found out now something of how strong a man it took to be a defender of the public interest and how wise a one to make decisions. He knew how many temptations there were to surrender when favors were requested and when friends and supporters could be favored by sacrificing principle. He knew that presidential independence and responsibility were often denounced by those who should have understood their necessity, and that weakness was praised by those who should have reproached Presidents for showing it.

The man in the White House had to be his own conscience. More than that, he had an obligation to carry the country with him, to be an educator, calling the democracy to its duties and insisting that the right and not the wrong should be supported. This could not be done as Cleveland had tried to do it, by working through the night to guard the Treasury and frustrate those who meant to exploit their fellow citizens. He must go out to lead and carry his people with him. It had taken a long time and the reality of defeat to teach him these things, and of course he had not fully realized them yet. His final message had shown, however, a new conception of presidential duties. He could do no more now than warn of troubles to come, but this he did in the same uncompromising way that he did everything he felt to be right.

Apart from the defeat of the causes he had been learning to defend, he had reason to feel that his first intentions as he had entered on office had been fulfilled. The administrative reforms he had set out to make had been completed. A new Navy was in the making; the despoilers of the public domain had been frustrated and many of them punished; the post office and the customs service were more efficient than they had been in a generation; abuses of the pension system had been checked; and above all, the presidency had become an example of industrious and devoted service, untouched by any suspicion of use for private ends.

It had not been enough—he knew that now; but what had been accomplished was important, and it gave him satisfaction.

Otherwise, and in a personal sense, he could lay aside his worries with relief. His working habits as a public servant had never allowed him any real rest; his conscience had kept him at tension that never relaxed. At the end of his term he was as near absolute fatigue as a man could be and still keep going.

During the last two years the pressures brought to bear on him, not only during the campaign, but in the effort to influence his executive actions, were of a sort calculated to infuriate him. Then, too, his marriage and the obvious loyalty and helpfulness of his young wife had been challenges to his detractors. They must destroy the image that threatened to spread of a devoted husband whose wife had found in him the embodiment of her womanly ideals.

His enemies had organized a campaign of vilification. It cannot be denied that the political arts have often included the use of such devices. They had been used on many Presidents, sometimes with devastating effect. Never had they been more unscrupulously pressed than in the campaign just past. Tough as he was, he felt at the end a weariness with prolonged effort that amounted to disgust.

The deepest annoyance caused by this sort of attack is that nothing direct can be done about it; no answer can be made. The whispering goes on under the cloak of confidence. The gossip can be utterly malicious, the lies outrageous and the attributions irresponsible. Such innuendoes came close to destroying the image the Clevelands were entitled to—of domestic virtue and married happiness. Cleveland was pictured as gross, dissipated and unfaithful. He was said to treat his wife with inhuman cruelty, even beating her and locking her up. These outrageous stories worked on Cleveland's always short temper with more effect because, although it did not show outwardly, he was so grateful to his wife for a happiness he had thought he would never have.

To be subject continually, over a considerable period, to such determined detraction was the best reason Cleveland knew for willingness to give up his office. The persistent circulation of these stories and the hints and innuendoes of an unscrupulous press could be guessed to have had a considerable part in his defeat. Worst of all, he was a man who, although he had few illusions about the depths politicians will descend to, still hated to admit that the democracy he served could be so subverted by unscrupulous professionals. And when he had to admit it to himself, he could show no outer awareness of its existence. He could not combat calumnies; he could not even see any way to make the purveyors of filth and scandal ashamed. If scandalmongering succeeded, it was justified in the professional politicians' view. This was the test.

Everything considered, the prospect of release was one the tired man could look forward to with some eagerness. He could now find a place to live with his wife and the enlarged family they hoped for, in the decent peace and retirement enjoyed by ordinary people. But where? He thought of several possibilities, and many suggestions were made of employment and association. One of these he ruled out. He would never again live in Buffalo, where the Reverend George H. Ball had made a sensation of his weakness, where the press had succumbed to the attractions of sensation and where his friends had been slow to defend him. He still counted some Buffalonians as confidants—Bissell and others of the legal fraternity—but they were not enough. Then too, Buffalonians had been among the worst of the office grabbers; and when he had resisted, he had been talked of among the Buffalo politicians as ungrateful. He had not been willing to promote and favor his old associates—and nothing worse can be said of a professional politician.

This feeling about him in Buffalo was strong and he knew it. It had come to be, as he said in a letter to a friend, "the place I hate, above all others." The city that had for so long been his home was thus closed to him for future working and living. If what he wanted was anonymity and the sort of employment he was best fitted for, his friends in New York told him the biggest city was the best place to find them. He finally agreed. He was offered, and accepted, an association with the well-known firm of Bangs, Stetson, Tracy and MacVeagh. He did not become a full partner, but he shared their offices and used their facilities. His life changed. He became what he had never been able to become before, a man with plenty of work to do but not too much, with a home and friends and a wife who kept him entertained with lively interests of a broader sort than he had ever known before. He was a distinguished citizen at the age of fifty-two.

It is probable that the New York City interlude, lasting four

The Republican Club in 1887 (*Courtesy of The New-York Historical Society, New York City*)

The Favorite Sport (*Courtesy of The Firestone Library, Princeton University, Princeton, New Jersey*)

years, was the happiest period of his mature life. He came downtown to his office in the morning on the Sixth Avenue elevated, stayed in his office until lunch time, then went with friends to the Downtown Association. Toward evening he walked part way uptown to his home on Madison Avenue near Sixty-eighth Street. He and Frances entertained only a few friends and enjoyed New York's attractions in a restrained way. He went out sometimes for dinner or an evening to the Century Association. This was a staid and exclusive club where he felt sometimes that his qualifications were inferior to those of the intellectuals around him, but it was the sort of company he enjoyed.

His two closest friends were Francis Lynde Stetson, the senior member of the firm where he had his office, and Richard Watson Gilder, the editor and literary arbiter, with whom he had become acquainted at a White House social occasion and who had introduced him at the Century Association. His common interests with Stetson were the basis for a solid friendship. Stetson was counselor for many large corporations, those formed by the House of Morgan, for instance, and he and Cleveland saw things in much the same way.

It was Gilder who induced the Clevelands to consider Buzzards Bay instead of the Adirondacks as a summer retreat. They took first a small, and then a larger, house there; and it became for them a second home. Gray Gables, it was called, in accord with its weathered appearance. Possibly it ranked above Oak View in Washington in the Clevelands' affections. There were, for neighbors, the Gilders, the Joseph Jeffersons (he was the well-known actor), W. W. Appleton (the publisher) and Richard Olney (who was to become Secretary of State in Cleveland's next administration).

Cleveland's favored occupation was still fishing. It is quite accurate to say *occupation* rather than *recreation,* according to those who fished with him. He was a really serious angler. We know, of course, that this was nothing new. From Green Lake to the Niagara River, and later the Potomac and the Adirondack waters, he had perfected his technique and allowed the art to take hold of his affections as no other diversion had ever done. Buzzards Bay offered plenty of opportunity and he made the most of it, going out early and staying until an hour when his companions had long since been ready to quit. There was an irresistible attraction about the solitude, the quiet, persistent taking of every advantage and the satisfaction of the catch. In earlier years he had liked to hunt, and he still went after birds in season; but now he had grown older and less agile in the woods and marshes. Fishing just suited his capabilities as it had always suited his temperament; hunting was for unusual excursions with friends who had elaborate equipment and private preserves.

It was during these years that the children began to appear. The first was a daughter, Ruth. The event caused in the new father an upsurge of an almost uncontrollable emotion. It gave him a new prospect in the world to think of his own children as being part of its future. It tended to lift him out of the has-been category and to revive his ambitions. As he wrote to Bissell, who was also expecting his first child:

I feel an impulse to write you. And I feel, too, that unless I make an effort, I shall write in a strange fashion to you. I, who have just entered the real world, and see in a small child more of value than I have ever called my own before; who puts aside, as hardly worth a thought, all that has gone before—fame, honor, place, everything—reach out my hand to you and fervently express the wish—the best my great friendship for you yields—that in safety and joy you may soon reach my estate.

This famous man, ex-President and still the most prestigious figure in his party, might have occupied himself, during these years in extending his influence, in keeping up contacts—in behaving generally in the ways an elder statesman and party head would be expected to behave. He might have traveled widely—abroad and at home, for instance; but he had no such desire. He preferred the quiet of a few places, a close circle of friends—and his family. What he stood for, he felt, was known to everyone. There was no need to insist on attention and no need to go on repeating what he had already said, bluntly and candidly and with no possibility of misunderstanding.

To this there is, however, a note to be added. In 1891, during the summer, he did make a visit to Buffalo. His friends there,

Mrs. Cleveland with Ruth (*Courtesy of The Firestone Library, Princeton University, Princeton, New Jersey*)

realizing how he felt toward the city generally if not toward them as individuals, tried their best to convince him that everything was changed by now. He was met at the station by Bissell, Tim Mahoney and a few other old friends who took him to a new hotel— the Iroquois. He wandered out to some of his former haunts and drove out to call, at last, on the Allen family in the familiar house in Black Rock. He made two speeches; and especially when he spoke before a German society, the papers said, he was listened to with "breathless attention." There was a crowded reception too. On the whole it was a success, and he was touched by all the efforts at reconciliation.

Would this city he had once loved so well and served so faithfully ever seem like home again? Regretfully he acknowledged that the wounds had actually not healed. He could not bear to consider living among the old associations. And, actually, he would never try. Buffalo would go on claiming him as the city's most honored son. But he would never again acknowledge the relation.

22

IN spite of the retiring life he lived, Cleveland gradually became the center of Democratic hopes for regaining control of the federal government in 1892. He did nothing very active to bring about his own nomination except to make a few speeches—in nearby cities—defending the familiar principles of good government, sound money and lowered tariffs. His detachment was weakened, however, by a series of events, considered by himself and his friends to be sinister. They began in 1891.

The events had to do with the control of the party. They had as their background the familiar controversy between debtors and creditors, now taking on definitely regional character and becoming more and more angry. It looked as though the agrarians actually thought they might capture the party, using as their front, David B. Hill, who had succeeded Cleveland as governor of New York. Hill had now been elected to the United States Senate through the efforts of the machine Democrats in the legislature. In the coalition behind Hill, Tammany was prominent, and the chieftains hated Cleveland as much as ever. They had no real concern for the Populists in the farm states; but they would always back a man, no matter who he stood for, if they thought he could do them some good.

Ever since Hill had supported Cleveland in order to become his lieutenant governor, and then supported him for President so that he could succeed as governor, he had had in mind the possibility of succeeding him also as the Democratic candidate for the presidency. This was the time. If his supporters could capture the delegates from New York State and make a deal with the aggrieved radicals in the West and South, they might control the Democratic national convention. Tammany would have New York and all the federal jobs. The Populists could have all the rest.

This possibility was as plain to the conservatives who had been Cleveland men as it was to Tammany, and it grew more so as the strength of the radicals increased. The conservatives began to coalesce and organize as early as 1890. The names most prominent among them were familiar ones. There were, for instance, William C. Whitney and Charles S. Fairchild, who had been in Cleveland's administration and who were close to the bankers and promoters on Wall Street. Backing them as well were the Straus mercantile family, Henry Villard, the railway financier and, less important but of later interest, James Roosevelt, who would be the father of a Democratic President.

A meeting of the conservatives was held early in 1892, at a time when agitation in the trans-Allegheny country had become really frightening. Present along with the Easterners were Congressmen John G. Carlisle and William L. Wilson, both prominent in party affairs. They all agreed that Cleveland was the safest possible candidate and probably the strongest. They were certain, also, that they could again enlist the mugwumps who had been so helpful before. In advance of this meeting, Villard had gone to see Cleveland and was able to say at the meeting that the former President would accept the nomination if it should be offered.

Of course they all knew that he would not only consent, but would gradually be aroused, as he always was, to make a fight. It would be his own kind of fight. He would not make frantic public appeals, would not make political bargains and would never compromise to get an advantage. He would, however, state, in his blunt way, the policies he stood for, and he would defend them as moral necessities. It was true that during his New York retirement he had grown even more fixed in his opinions, more belligerent about the money issue and less disposed to grant his opponents any sort of virtue. His association with the Wall Street crowd had been intimate and was well known. But it was also known that his integrity was unimpaired.

His candidacy would polarize the issues as no other candidacy could, and it would certainly cause the party to lose many adherents. The split might even give rise to a third party, since the radicals could hardly become Republicans, who were even more conservative than the Cleveland Democrats. If they got no encouragement from either party, they might form one of their own. But the Easterners believed they were stronger than the Western faction and that the others would have to come to a compromise with them.

Hill was the worst threat. He was dangerous because he was known to be unscrupulous, and this made him unpredictable. There had been passages in his career that were reminiscent of those in the careers of the discredited Republicans—Blaine, for instance; and these might be a handicap in a campaign. But his defects would almost certainly be overlooked by the radicals if he accepted their terms on the money question. The Clevelandites were sure he would, and they were more afraid of his candidacy than any other.

But Hill and his supporters outsmarted themselves. Their plan was first to capture the New York delegation, then to make their deal with the politicians in the South and West. If they came to the national convention with all the New York delegates pledged to them under the unit rule, they could offer an initial strength and could then persuade others by offers of support for easy money and the promise of jobs. To do this they had the state committee, headed by Edward Murphy, call a convention for February 22. This was some two months earlier than was customary for the state convention. The delegates, for this reason, would be chosen in local caucuses when snow still prevented free travel. Little groups of local politicians, most of them machine Democrats, could choose Hill supporters without much opposition. But the maneuver was too blatant. A wave of indignation followed that surprised the Hill forces.

Democrats outside New York also reacted violently to this sharp practice. It resulted in a review of Hill's career much more searching than his supporters had expected. Nevertheless, the convention was held, the unit rule was imposed and the New York delegation was instructed. The proper description for the meeting was supplied by the press: it was called a "snap convention," and those who attended were called "snappers." This catchy term played a considerable part in discrediting the whole Hill movement, but actually it began almost at once to disappear. The efforts of Whitney and Fairchild in other states, as delegates began to be chosen, soon told. In Rhode Island, the first state after New York to have a convention, the delegates selected were all for Cleveland —in spite of the best efforts of Hill's followers. This was at the beginning of May, and Massachusetts followed soon, with the same solid support for Cleveland. There was a final struggle, of more importance, in Georgia, where the silverites and others were thought to be strong. But Cleveland's stand for lowered tariffs had traditional appeal for Southerners, and it resulted in a delegation that was overwhelmingly favorable to him.

When the Democratic convention met in Chicago, the Republicans had already nominated Harrison for a second term, although they knew his candidacy would be weak, and the prospect was that Cleveland could defeat him—as, in the popular vote, he had done in 1888. Tammany was sullen. The attempt to displace Cleveland had failed miserably, a result contributed to by a large unofficial delegation that came from New York to Chicago under the direction of Whitney, thus assuring everyone that Tammany was wrong in claiming that Cleveland could not even carry his own state.

Cleveland headquarters in the Palmer House were from the first lively with the prospect of victory. The votes for favorite sons, and those supported by the silverites, were overwhelmed by the obvious tide rolling up for Cleveland. Before the first vote was completed, it was all over. The result was: Cleveland, 617, Hill, 114 and Boise (the Farmers' Alliance candidate), 103.

The campaign that followed was a quiet one. Neither Harrison nor Cleveland was a charismatic leader, given to exhortations. Each had a record to stand on. Each respected the presidential position that one had held and one was still holding. The torchlight parades of other years, the attempts to impugn either candidate's morals, the impassioned speeches—all these were kept down.

There was one novelty. This was the Populist ticket headed by James B. Weaver. The agrarians had finally despaired of capturing either of the major parties and had launched one of their own. Weaver, together with his colleague, Mary Elizabeth Lease, the woman agitator who counseled farmers to "raise less corn and more hell," did best in the South and West. They had real hope of carrying Georgia and some other states—Wisconsin and Kansas, for instance, and, although the hope was not realized, they did attract more than a million votes. More of these were lost to Harrison than to Cleveland, however, because their main strength was in the Midwest, where there were more Republicans than Democrats.

The real reason for the lack of excitement in the campaign was that there was after all so little difference between the parties and even, as the electorate saw it, between the candidates. Both Republicans and Democrats of the Cleveland sort had their base and found their support in the wealthy and conservative people who were tightening their control on the economy and on its politics. The Republicans were on the defensive because of having passed the McKinley tariff during their four last years. Its protectionism was outrageous, and everyone knew that its various schedules had been dictated by the interests most affected. Andrew Carnegie had been consulted, for example, on the steel and iron duties, and they were fixed to suit him. As a result, he had grown so rich and powerful that he could live in almost royal state. He dictated policies to his subordinates from the castle he maintained in Scotland, and Republican politicians made pilgrimages to this seat of power.

Cleveland had no such direct affiliations. He insisted that he must be independent and he was. He was a forthright enemy of protectionism. His message to the Congress in 1887 had shown that, and he still stood on its declarations. But he was no free trader. He stood for moderation in this as in most other matters. His affiliates in the business world were not so numerous as those of the Republicans and they tended to be of a somewhat different sort. The mugwump group were either wealthy, lawyers for the wealthy, or respectably allied with the wealthy as university people or members of the clergy. But they were reformers of a sort. They believed in honest government.

Whitney was most like the Republicans, and his energy in Cleveland's behalf seems to have been largely personal rather than ideological. He was remarkably efficient in political organization as well as in business, however, and Cleveland was glad to utilize his talents. The campaign of 1888 had suffered from inefficiency and lack of energy. Whitney managed the one in 1892 and made a very different job of it. He got every vote that was available, and there were enough to make a victory.

It was quite a remarkable victory when all the returns were in—much more impressive than anyone had anticipated. Cleveland even carried Wisconsin, Illinois and California; and Ohio was lost by a very narrow margin. Altogether, Cleveland had 277 electoral votes to Harrison's 145.

The chief reason for Cleveland's victory seems to have been an undercurrent, hardly noticed on the surface, running against Harrison, the more conservative of the two conservative choices. Many voters who shared Populist sympathies did not vote for the Populist candidate (the Populists were, after all, a regional party, without substantial support in New York, New Jersey and New England) but rather threw their support to Cleveland as a protest against Republican subservience to an arrogant elite of the wealthy.

This arrogance had been clearly demonstrated during the campaign months and may well have had more to do with the result than any of the politicians' efforts. Aside from the farmers' revolt in the West, there was an even more violent revolt in many industrial centers. This was the summer of the Homestead strike at the Carnegie steel plant outside Pittsburgh. There Carnegie's manager, H. C. Frick, deliberately provoked a confrontation that ended in a conflict of arms between the unionists of the Amalgamated Association of Iron and Steel Workers and a private army of Pinkerton operatives hired to attack them. These mercenaries were fully armed and instructed to kill.

The issue was the recognition of the union and its right to bargain collectively. The steel men were determined to stop once and for all the spread of unionism. They meant to establish the open shop, to hire and fire as they pleased, to pay the wages they preferred and to maintain the conditions that seemed to them reasonable.

But the wages and conditions were far from reasonable, as could be seen by anyone who visited the works and the homes the workers lived in. The twelve-hour day with a swing shift of twenty-four hours once a week at the hardest labor; wages that would maintain a family only at the barest level of subsistence; and surroundings that were the familiar filthy slums of the mine and factory towns—these were the intolerable conditions that caused rebellion.

At the same time, the industrialists were able to dictate to legislatures and executives, making whatever legislation was passed convenient to themselves, and were amassing fortunes so huge that their size could not even be estimated. There were no income taxes, and the government was not yet supposed to go in for welfare measures. Workers injured or grown old were simply discarded and their families allowed to fall into the most desperate circumstances. The employers were the dictators of the Republican party and had been since the Civil War, when the foundations of their power had been laid in profits from war contracts.

Cleveland's one strong statement of the campaign was a rebuke to this group. In his speech accepting the nomination, worked over carefully and spoken in the heavy sentences he characteristically used, he referred directly to the condition of the workers. They were, he said, suffering hardships owed to "the exactions wrung from them to build up and increase the fortunes of those for whose benefit subsidies were furnished by law."

Apart from the Homestead strike there were similar violent labor battles in the mines of the Tennessee Coal and Iron Company and in the Coeur d'Alene region of Idaho. President Harrison was appealed to when struggles between workers and strikebreakers threatened to destroy property. Troops were sent and the strikers were defeated. And there was trouble in the railway yards of Buffalo that had to be suppressed by the state militia. Everywhere government, moving to keep order, managed to intervene on the side of employers. The unions were helpless, their one weapon, the strike, being nullified by government interferences.

These were the events that may well have elected Cleveland in spite of his well-known conservatism. When the campaign was over, he was sobered by the prospect. He really had no answers in his mind for the problems he would not be able to evade. His principle of a noninterfering government was, he saw, likely to be tried to the limit. What he would do when he, instead of Harrison, was asked to intervene in the violent differences dividing Americans, he did not know. It was therefore in a sober and restrained way that he celebrated the Democratic victory with his more jubilant friends:

While we find in our triumph a result of popular intelligence which we have aroused, and a consequence of popular vigilance which we have stimulated, let us not for a moment forget that our accession to power will find neither this intelligence nor this vigilance dead or slumbering. We are thus brought face to face with the reflection that if we are not to be tormented by the spirits which we ourselves have called up, we must hear, above victorious shouts, the call of our countrymen to public duty, and must put on a garb befitting public servants.

23

CLEVELAND'S somber expectation that there might be serious troubles during his second administration proved to be justified. The depression of 1893—one of the worst in the nation's history—was well begun even before his inauguration. Banks, as well as other businesses, were failing in large numbers, the blight of unemployment spreading, prices falling, farmers not only unable to sell their crops at more than cost, but losing their farms because they could not pay their debts. The whole country was sliding into one of those periodic sinking spells that had so often tormented the free-enterprise economy.

There were demands that something remedial be done. The seething unrest was even worse than any disturbances in the similar but milder depression of the seventies—worse, because population had increased and cities had grown, industries had expanded and farming had extended farther across the Western plains. There were pools of miserable people in the city slums and in the company towns around the mines and ironworks; the farmers and workers were in a mood to hold the big industrialists and Wall Street accountable for all their troubles; and Cleveland was associated in their minds with employers and bankers. It seemed a miracle that so conservative a man had been elected—until Cleveland was compared with Harrison.

Opinion was polarized by the money issue. This question had been argued so long, and so many politicians—and others—had taken positions about it, that there was general agreement about one thing. The way to recovery was to be found in action one way or the other on this question. That too much or too little money was a sufficient explanation of the industrial paralysis hardly anyone questioned. It was accepted that action about it would lead to immediate improvement.

No one really seems to have done much analyzing. Actually, a whole generation would pass before more realistic descriptions of business cycles would be made and really remediable ways of preventing recessions, or of recovering from them when they had happened, would be worked out.

Looking back from a later generation, the discussions during hard times, the charges and recriminations, the imputations of blame, the impassioned demands for action seem curiously childish. It simply has to be accepted that the nation had grown faster than its understanding of itself. Like children, men looked at their deplorable condition and found themselves willing to grasp at any sort of plausible explanation. Politicians made the most of the panaceas offered for betterment. They encouraged people to believe they had cures for their ills.

The adherents of the cheap-money cure were the most frenzied. At least half the Democratic members of the Congress were convinced that this was the answer; and as the troubles worsened, their demands for action grew more insistent. On the other side, the sound-money people contended that the government purchases and coining of silver (authorized by the Sherman Silver Purchase Act of 1890) had underminded the gold standard, had reduced the prestige of the United States, had led to a serious drain on gold reserves (as it had), and that what had to be done was to repudiate the silverites, reverse the silver coinage legislation, stop the outflow of gold and reestablish a sound, gold-based currency.

Cleveland, being a sound-money man, felt it necessary to repeal the Sherman Silver Purchase Act and, as the troubles of winter became worse in spring, was convinced that somehow he must prevail on the Congress to accept his conclusion. He resolved on a special session, seeing that a crisis concerning the Treasury's gold reserve could not be held off until the Congress met for its regular session in December. He was urged to call the session at once after March 4; but he had to make sure of his ability to get the repeal passed; and for this he had to wait. Nervously and impatiently, he held off. The special session was not convened until August.

Meanwhile the agitated debate went on. The old Populist orators went on even more excited rampages than during the presidential campaign, and they were joined by new—or newly prominent—demagogues. Among these were some of enduring prominence, such as William J. Bryan, who would capture the next Democratic nomination (in 1896) and would be a formidable figure for a whole generation. This was indeed the beginning of a decade when divisiveness and sectional hatred would disrupt old political affiliations.

When the 1900s came, the business cycle would not yet be understood; indeed by then there would be a kind of resignation. It would be concluded very generally that these recurrent sinking spells were in the nature of things, that they must simply be endured and suffered through. That recovery would come in its own time seemed as certain as that another recession would presently recur. It was like the seasons following one another. But people in 1893 were not yet ready for this fatalism. They still saw both preventive and cure in money.

The conviction on both sides was like the unshakable belief of a chronic invalid in some nostrum. Cleveland knew a majority of his party did not agree with him that the gold standard must be protected at any cost. He was sure they were wrong, but he could not be certain that he could get even a compromise from them.

On this one subject Cleveland was convinced beyond argument, and he put it high among his categories of importance. But he was well enough aware that many other issues he had never settled for himself were waiting to entrap him in their complexities. He could only justify his second presidency by considering who might become President if he did not. He would at least be more dedicated than any of the Republicans would have been. He would not give away the President's power, much less sell it. He would use it for the country's good, not his own or that of his friends.

He took the oath of office on a day of snow and wind and was driven without any sort of elation to the White House afterward. What he had to do first was the sort of thing he had avoided whenever he could. He had to exert leadership, and he was still reluctant to persuade congressmen to vote as he felt they should. Using the power of his office to bring the reluctant members around to his support was distasteful, but there was no way out of it.

He was not able to form the Cabinet he wanted, and his depression was evident in this January 1893 letter to a friend:

I am dreadfully perplexed and bothered. I cannot get the men I want to help me, but strange to say, my greatest trials come through those professing to be near and attached friends, who expect things. I hope the skies will lighten up by and by, but I have never seen a day since I consented to drift with events that I have not cursed myself for yielding; and in these particular days I think I curse a little more heartily than ever.

The Secretaries of State and Treasury and the Attorney General, upon whom any President must especially depend, were second choices. Bayard, who in his last administration had been Secretary of State, now wanted the ambassadorship to Britain; Fairchild would not take back the Treasury post; and George Gray refused the Attorney Generalship. In their places, Cleveland finally chose Walter Q. Gresham, John G. Carlisle and Richard Olney. Gresham was a Republican, and his appointment was meant to please the mugwumps and to induce nonpartisan support for foreign policy; Carlisle was a long-time Democrat with extended congressional experience and was, besides, a man of undoubted brilliance, but he had had no experience in administration; and Olney was a Massachusetts lawyer with a formidable reputation among the corporate interests he mostly served, but was hardly known among the political fraternity.

These most important posts proved to be not too happily filled. Gresham proved to be a weak Secretary of State although he seemed always to mean well. He had poor health, and was extraordinarily tactless in dealing with the Congress when, as a Republican, he might have been expected to be most soothing; and the more partisan Democrats were offended by the appointment.

They did approve the choice of Carlisle for the Treasury, but they knew him to have a weakness. He rather frequently went on sprees of drunkenness and disappeared for days or weeks at a time. As Cleveland had hoped, this weakness was curbed when he became Secretary. But there was another difficulty: he had once been "wrong" on the money question, tending to side with the silverites. True, if he had now changed his mind, it was not because he was influenced by the financiers, but because he had really become converted.

It was Olney who was the most remarkable of the appointees and destined to be the one who would influence Cleveland in making the worst mistakes of all his public life. (One involved the Pullman strikers in Chicago and the other a foreign relations confrontation that might have resulted in war. We shall discuss them later.) He was a Yankee of the same general origin as Cleveland. He might have been an Adams. Like them, he was irascible and opinionated, but also extremely able and aggressive. He reinforced Cleveland's most reactionary impulses and persuaded him to accept ones that were even more reactionary.

The lesser departmental posts were filled with some difficulty too. Bissell was finally induced to take the Postmaster Generalship where he could be of assistance in the rush for appointments that must somehow be handled. Lamont, the faithful private secretary of other years, was now a wealthy man, having speculated to good effect under the guidance of Whitney; and since nothing less than a Cabinet post would attract him, Cleveland out of affection appointed him to the War Department.

A Confederate veteran, Hilary A. Herbert of Alabama, was made Secretary of the Navy. Agriculture went to a man from Nebraska, J. Sterling Morton, who, in spite of his origin, was a sound-money man. Finally, Hoke Smith of Georgia, a lawyer and the proprietor of the influential Atlanta *Journal,* was appointed to Interior. He was well known in his region but had hardly been heard of elsewhere. Cleveland satisfied himself that Smith would stand fast against land grabbers and exploiters of the public domain. Besides, he had helped keep Georgia Democratic when it looked as though Weaver and his Populists might carry it. Smith wanted the secretaryship badly and used every avenue of influence to get it. Cleveland had some doubts, but gave in when he failed to find a better candidate.

They all went to work with vigor, following their chief executive's example. Cleveland had to select a new private secretary, and he finally chose Henry T. Thurber at the recommendation of a friend. It was a mistake. Thurber was neither as industrious nor as knowledgeable as Lamont had been. The President had to depend

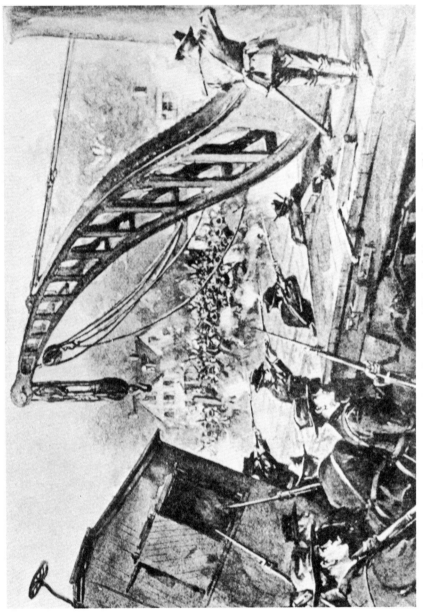

Pullman strike, 1894 (*Courtesy of Historical Pictures Service, Chicago*)

on others outside his White House family for many of the services Lamont had performed so well. He did, however, have a young confidential secretary who was growing into usefulness. He was Robert Lincoln O'Brien, whose talents would increase and whose attractive personality would charm a wide circle of friends throughout a long life.

Thus equipped, not so well, certainly, as he could have wished but, he hoped, well enough, Cleveland braced himself to meet the trouble that burst upon him at once. On March 5, 1893, there was a panic in the financial centers. Stock prices plunged, banks failed and there was chaos throughout the business community. Then there rushed upon him frantic appeals to do something. He knew well enough that there was unemployment and misery as well as fear among industrialists. Should he merely wait out the crisis as chief executives had done in the past, or should he attempt to influence matters in such ways as might be useful? And if he decided something must be done, what could it be? He got no help from anyone about this.

His need for finding his way in the storm was infinitely complicated by the time-consuming selection of his associates, preceded, as always, by the most careful investigation. But even worse was the harassment by the office seekers, already at its height when he moved into the White House again. It had been building up ever since election. His predecessor, Harrison, ostensibly a cold and reserved President, who sought to give the impression of being above the battles of Washington, in reality had abased himself before the Republican bosses. He had allowed them the purge they demanded at the beginning, and it had continued throughout his term. Naturally the Democrats wanted now to clean out the Republicans and give the jobs to Democrats. It could not be argued that they would be replacing more efficient civil servants. The Harrison appointees had been chosen wholesale and with pratically no regard to ability. The politicians asked, with some asperity, whether Democrats could not perform as well, especially if some effort should be made to establish a standard of competence. And there was really no good rebuttal.

Cleveland occasionally still used his old chilling answer when some outrageous request was made: "I was not aware, sir, that the post was vacant." But actually he felt that the waste of time, when matters of importance had to be studied and decided, was more than he could condone. He resorted to a rule that job seekers were not to be brought to his office by congressmen. He also announced that he would appoint no one who had had a job in his previous administration. But this was not enough, and finally he had to say firmly that Bissell and others had the whole responsibility for appointments and that he would positively not deal with them further.

For this he had the excuse, in his own mind, that he would not be eligible to run again and had no need of a personal political organization. There was no prohibition against third terms; but the custom, fixed by Washington, was regarded as inviolable. Even if he had no third campaign to think of he would need party support if he was to prevail on the issues then coming to a decision; and his determination to escape from political involvement was modified by the permission he gave his subordinates to dismiss Republicans and appoint Democrats almost at will. For this he was bitterly criticized by the good-government people, but they really had a weak case. What was needed was a deeper reform—a reworking of the entire civil service structure so that incompetents would be excluded permanently. Before he was through, Cleveland made a certain contribution to this reform, but just now his other troubles were uppermost in his mind.

He was going through an ordeal that was worse for him than it would have been for a less conscientious man. He had determined in his first presidency what the scope of his duty was and what was the reach of the federal government itself. This had simplified many problems. In principle, he was required to leave legislation to the Congress, and the federal government was properly confined to actions clearly national in character. He had found, however, that neither of these rules could be followed consistently. He had been forced to compromise. If policies adopted by the party and approved by election were to be made into law, the President was involved in their implementation as much as any representative or any senator. Was he not more involved? As President Jackson had so firmly insisted, the President was the one official who was elected by *all* the people. He therefore bore a special responsibility for their interests. He could never be merely permissive. He must lead.

If what was needed in this national crisis was action on the money question, the Congress would have to reverse its former legislation. Ought he now to keep clear or ought he to join the battle? It was a much easier decision than it would have been in 1885. Without knowing what would actually make the situation better, the people who had elected him and, indeed, *the whole people,* looked to him for the protection of their interests. If he thought the Sherman Silver Purchase Act ought to be repealed, he clearly must use all his influence to see that the repeal went through.

For so solid and determined a man, and one so devoted to principle as he understood it, this process of persuading, of bargaining, of using patronage and favors, of threatening reprisals, if need be, was distasteful in the extreme. He kept as aloof as he could. But actually he engineered the attack himself with close attention, and he used every means he could devise to influence the voting.

The repeal passed the House before August was over and, after long and tedious debate, also passed the Senate at the end of October. Would it have the effect predicted for it by Cleveland's sound-money friends? That remained to be seen. Certainly by now the country had reached the very nadir of exhaustion and despair. Never had the economy been so prostrate. Perhaps there was no way to go but up, and perhaps the recuperative force of energies suppressed for so long a time would gradually have an effect. This had happened before.

Cleveland seemed strangely little elated by the legislative victory. Quite possibly he had lost confidence in the single change he had so ably advocated. He was a puzzled and unhappy President as fall came on. He was also a sick one, as we shall see. His powerful and enduring constitution was undergoing its first real trial.

24

AS Cleveland had reluctantly to recall, the Constitution written by the framers in 1787 had provided for a President elected by the whole nation. He thus owed his authority to the same source as the Congress. He was in no sense subordinate. Yet his salary, his aides and his home had been left to be provided by the legislative branch. The Congress was jealous of his power, and Presidents had therefore always been handicapped by having a personal establishment too small for the work it had to do. The President even had embarrassingly insufficient funds to maintain his official home, continually invaded by the public, in the style expected of him. By Cleveland's time, the situation was becoming worse than embarrassing—it was impossible.

Mrs. Harrison had insisted on, and the Republican Congress had consented to, a certain amount of White House refurnishing. But basically the structure was in bad shape. The old rafters were sagging, the pipes and wires were so interlaced and complicated that the risk of fire or collapse was serious and offices had encroached on the living quarters until there were hardly rooms enough for the family, to say nothing of any distinguished visitors who were expected to be entertained. There was now electric lighting instead of gas, thanks to Mrs. Harrison, and there was now—and it seemed an enormous change to Cleveland—a telephone switchboard and several phones in different parts of the house. In his former incumbency there had been one phone attached to the wall, and he had had to go to it whenever he had need of calling someone or whenever someone had called him.

There were seven servants, including a coachman and a nurse, about one third the number necessary for decent maintenance and, for business purposes, Cleveland still wrote most of his correspondence, and all his public papers, in longhand.

In spite of the difficulties, however, Frances Cleveland came back quite happily to the White House. When she had left to make way for the Harrisons, she had told the head usher that he must take care of everything so that when they (the Clevelands) came back, everything would be the way she had liked it. She found it somewhat changed, but not in ways she could not correct to suit herself. The important consideration was that now little Ruth and her nurse had to be accommodated. And, it was apparent, there would soon be another baby to find room for.

As before, Cleveland was so annoyed by the intrusions on family privacy that he looked again for a place he could call his own. Oak View had been sold and could not be retrieved. He tried to get the Admiral Porter house on H Street, but failed. He finally leased Woodley, the lovely estate that had belonged to the Key family. And this, during the four years of the second term, was the real Cleveland home—paid for by himself and a constant reproach to a penurious Congress who chose this singular way to express its jealousy of a competing branch.

Frances Cleveland was not a complainer; she accepted the situation as she found it and tried her best to meet the social obligations of the presidential family. These included a set series of formal dinners and receptions, averaging several a week—for the Supreme Court, for senators and representatives divided into manageable groups, for the Cabinet and other members of the administration, for ministers and consuls representing the nation abroad, for the diplomatic corps and for such distinguished visitors as might come to Washington. For these last, if they were chiefs of state, special honors were obligatory—such, for instance, as were arranged for the Infanta Eulalia (of Spain's royal family) in June of 1893, lasting several days and involving fetes appropriate to the occasion.

The spring social season that year was a lively one. It did not matter that the country was in trouble and that the trouble was deepening, or that the President was worried as he had never been before concerning his responsibilities. The dinners must be given, the receptions arranged and protocol carefully observed. These were the duties of the President's wife with her small staff of servants and with little of the assistance from experienced officials that would become available in later years. Other Presidents' wives had broken down under the strain and several had become either imagined or real invalids, thus escaping the burden.

Not this President's wife! She carried herself gallantly, was always good-humored, even gay; she met the inevitable small crises without becoming flustered and won the affection of everyone around her. Even Cleveland's enemies growled that he was stubborn and wrongheaded, but that his wife almost made up for his boorish crudeness.

When summer came and the Potomac bottom lands steamed in the humid heat, the Clevelands again retreated to Gray Gables on Buzzards Bay—or Frances and the baby did. Cleveland had to deal with a Congress fuming under the assaults of a public that demanded some relief from its fears—redress without infringement of any of its privileges—and being called into special session for the purpose. Shortly after it met, all the Clevelands returned to the White House, and a week later another baby daughter arrived. This was the first President's child to be born in the mansion, and the excitement over the event was considerable. There was some tendency expressed in the press to reproach Frances for not having borne a son, but the parents themselves were well enough pleased.

It was while worry about the depression and the forthcoming special session was at its deepest, and while he was concerned about his second child, that one of the President's worst ordeals was forced upon him—the sudden finding of a growth in his mouth that his doctor feared might be cancerous. It was imperative that it be removed without delay.

The discovery was so untimely as to be very nearly disastrous. The dependence of the American people on their President is something they do not fully realize, ever, until something happens to weaken his authority. This may be the discovery that he is incompetent for his duties; but people are slow to accept this, since they are inclined to make him a hero and since they realize how far his detractors will go to discredit him. It may be something that happens to undermine their confidence in his ability to act as their representative, their strong defender. He is better than they, he possesses more wisdom, he is their mentor and guide. It is a relationship peculiar to our system. And, because it is so much the vital element in the system, any weakening of the presidential strength is a tragedy of enormous consequence.

People do not usually recognize that they are so dependent on the President. They may speak of him familiarly, sometimes seeming not to hold him in appropriate respect. They will criticize his actions and advance opinions contrary to his. But let anything happen to threaten his authority or weaken his strength, and the reaction will be almost universal. The fundamental concern will at once become apparent. The man in the White House must be present and in charge.

Obviously one of the worst hazards in this dependence on the vital center is a breakdown in health. A President who is not inhumanly strong and powerful cannot be the President provided for in the Constitution. From the first it was impossible for the conditions to be completely met, even when the government was simple because the nation was small; and it had become much less possible with growth, expansion, and the assumption of place among the great powers of the world.

The truth was that about half of the Presidents in the line leading up to Cleveland had been less capable than was required to meet even the minimum of competence. Some had been fading into age, as Taylor and Harrison had been; some had never been fitted for the position—as Buchanan conspicuously had not; some had been incapacitated—as Garfield had been after his wounding by an assassin.

The nation had had the luck to have vigorous Presidents in some of its crises—as when Jackson stopped dead a movement in the South toward secession, or when Polk made certain that the country's territories should stretch to its natural border on the Pacific. But this had not always happened. A succession of weak Presidents had allowed the situation to develop that finally ended in the terrible War between the States.

Cleveland, himself, had followed several Presidents—Grant, Hayes, Garfield and Arthur—who had fallen short of the constitutional requirements of the office. It was these deficiencies, emphasized by their inability even to stop the corruption of the executive establishment under their control, that had given Cleveland his chance for a career in high office.

Under the feeble direction of these Presidents, the industrial system had grown to be stronger than government itself, so that the men of vast wealth dictated policy; it was their conception that government existed to further their interests, and they had no scruples about buying elections, keeping officials in their debt and generally seeing to it that they were not interfered with even when they exploited their workers with inhuman cruelty, manipulated markets so that they could accumulate speculative fortunes and treated consumers as mere conveniences to their businesses.

Cleveland was in no one's debt; he felt most strongly his responsibility to the people, and he meant to do his duty as he saw it. He had not seen it as a reformer of institutions, only as a reformer of government, one who meant to impose honesty and efficiency in public service.

This was a limitation; and he was President at a time when decisions were pending about the subservience of government to big business, about people's expectation that their political leaders would stop the drift toward complete control by private interests. He was little inclined to see the situation as the radicals of his time saw it; but he was coming to see that monopolies were dangerous and must be curbed, that workers were ill treated and must have a better life, and even that farmers were in difficulties that they themselves could not resolve.

That the silverites should prevail because it would enable debtors to pay off their creditors in devalued dollars still seemed to Cleveland dishonest; and he considered it his first duty to work for repeal of the legislation, passed some years earlier, that was steadily depreciating the currency. Even his scruples about his own powers as President—his reluctance to interfere with legislative prerogatives—weakened as the crisis became worse. If a sound currency would save the country from disaster—and he had concluded that it would—he would do his best to establish it.

This was why he called a special session for the purpose of repealing the law for the continued coinage of silver.

And now he was sick, perhaps seriously so. A sick President was a tragedy for the American people in any circumstances. When they were beset by depression that amounted to disaster, and when something needed to be done that might set the conditions for recovery, it would be almost the final calamity if the President should be lost to his duties. It would be bad enough even if the people merely suspected that he might be absent—that he was not there in the White House carrying on sturdily day after day in their interest, using such wisdom as he had and exerting his will to coerce reluctant cooperators. To have it known that he was incapacitated was unthinkable.

It must be prevented.

25

TO understand the President's agonizing experience in the summer of 1893, it has first to be realized that the country was demoralized in a way that had seldom happened before. The depression of 1893 had no clear resolution. It was the first of the general sinking spells since big business had begun to take over the economy and to dictate its policies. That of '73 had been serious, but it was a postwar phenomenon. This of '93 came upon a country at peace and in the midst of expansion.

The worst controversy was the continuing one between those who wanted an increase in the supply of money and those who felt that the nation's future depended on its "soundness"—meaning the maintenance of the gold standard. Advocates of neither policy had any completely convincing arguments. As the heat of argument increased, the demagogues became more shrill and the conservatives more sullen and stubborn; but neither could claim a consensus. Taking the country as a whole, it was a nearly even division.

Throughout the West the picturesque Populist figures who were bidding for leadership became more and more shrill and incoherent. They finally fell to preaching hatred, almost undiluted; reasoning, they found, did not stir the crowds. The gatherings at country picnic grounds, on village commons and in the halls of small cities were more like revival meetings than forums for the settlement of public issues. There was shouting and waving of arms. But there was reason too. The Populists had a point. As later generations learned, the supply of money *was* too restricted. Briefly, these were the farmers' complaints:

Expansion 1880–1900 (50%)
300,000,000 cultivated acres

Mortgage Burden

Number: 2,300,000
Amount: $2,200,000
Interest Rates: 8 to 15%
Annual Charges: $200,000,000

Prices

Steady fall; but with farm prices falling fastest.
1893: Wheat, 50¢ a bushel in Chicago
                  30¢ at the local elevator
          Corn, 20–30¢
          Cotton, 7¢ a pound
            50% decline in three years

Average Value per Acre of Ten Crops

1866–70	$14.70
1871–75	14.05
1876–80	11.89
1881–85	11.33
1886–90	9.97
1891–96	9.71

Taxes

All federal revenue derived from indirect taxes on consumers' goods
(⅔ by tariffs). No income tax on large fortunes or profits.

Railway Rates

Shipping grain Midwest to Atlantic ports average rate 10–12¢ per
bushel (after 1900 average would be 5¢)

Money Supply

Production of gold steadily diminished. Continuous reduction of currency supply.

There was no agreed settlement in Cleveland's time or in that
of his immediate successors. There could be none short of actions

no one had yet conceived, and ones hardly anyone would have approved even if Cleveland or his advisers had conceived them.

Depressions were inherent in the uncontrolled and undirected system of free enterprise, as much part of it as their opposite, the booms. That brakes should be applied to the booms and stimulants to the sinkings was as yet only a fugitive idea in a few minds. And the more drastic idea that both could be prevented by stabilizing measures and by the manipulation of the money supply was still a long way in the future. The freedom to venture, to buy and sell, develop, exploit and abandon anything and everything an individual could get hold of was an unquestioned privilege. Privacy of property was regarded as a literal, an *absolute* right; and these were beliefs held by both sides of the argument.

At this very time, Europeans—Germans in particular—were devising systems of social insurance. They were influenced by the desire to have strong and united nations. They were beginning to realize, too, that such measures would help to stabilize the economy and give people a sense of permanence—and gratefulness to a beneficent government; but such conceptions were foreign to the pioneering spirit that still dominated America, especially throughout the West. Even the worst ranters of the plains drew their arguments from a different philosophy. They wanted more freedom, not less. They wanted the creditors punished. They wanted an unlimited coinage, not a managed one. They wanted to grow all the crops they could coax from the soil and they wanted a good price for all they produced regardless of demand. They did not see that free enterprise had betrayed them. They wanted more of it, not less.

Farthest from the thought of Wall Street, likewise, was any notion of stability. Financiers wanted to gather and use venture capital, loaning it to the actual venturers—including farmers— at a high interest rate and getting it back in dollars worth as much as (or more than) those they had loaned. Their idea of a sound economy was one that was safe from the schemes of inflationists, one they could build speculative empires in to rule as they liked. This was their conception of free enterprise. If some impecunious small people were hurt by it, that was their lookout.

Repeal of the silver-coinage act would seem to a later generation a small and almost irrelevant event in the progress of the economy. The continued infusion of silver into the currency tended to cause domestic inflation and the loss of gold to other nations, and inflation was what the agrarian radicals wanted. Actually, speculators had no reason to fear it either. It was as stimulating to growing industry as to an expanding agriculture. The real trouble was that it did not work evenly. Some prices rose while others fell. Those producers whose prices were falling had low incomes and could not buy from those whose prices were rising. When buying slowed, there was unemployment. When men in factories and mines did not work and get wages, they could not buy farmers' products. When farmers could not sell at profitable prices, they could not pay their debts. If their creditors then took their properties, the farmers became indigent. All this made everyone angry. Recrimination and incitements to violence resulted.

Nothing anyone wanted to do at the time promised, really, to have any permanent stabilizing effect. Only such tremendous undertakings as the curbing of monopoly power, the control of speculation, minimum levels of wages, guaranteed prices for farmers and a system of social insurance could remedy the situation. But no one had this sort of vision—at least no one in the political forum, or, if he did, dared to suggest such a radical cure. After some years of agitation and argument, and now in the midst of deepening depression, it still seemed to Cleveland and his adherents—the conservative wing of the Democratic party— that a beginning of recovery could only be expected when silver coinage was stopped and the drain of gold to other countries was checked. The special session he called on June 30 to meet on August 7 was intended to bring this issue to a conclusion.

It was doubtful if he could win. His own party continued to be equally divided. Republican votes would be needed to provide a majority. Meanwhile the country was in the throes of something approaching civil war. At least this was true in the farm states; and it was not much better in the East, where strikes were continually breaking out and being fought with clubs and guns.

The depression seemed to have started in agriculture, but now its effects were being felt in industry. There was rebellion. Men were being wounded and killed at the gates of factories. Carnegie in

The President at his desk (*Courtesy of The Firestone Library, Princeton University, Princeton, New Jersey*)

his remote Scottish castle was telling his manager, Frick, in Pittsburgh, not to compromise, but to hire even more mercenaries and suppress the rebellious workers—with such force as was necessary.

When the nation is in trouble, the President is always involved, even though the trouble seems to be outside his responsibilities. He must keep his head, act with restraint and judgment and try to find ways of calming the agitated belligerents. That is what is expected of him. Even those who disagree with his policies and would not support him at the polls expect it. Since Cleveland had been President for a previous four years and had had four years in retirement to watch Harrison as he went about his duties, he knew well enough what was required of him. He knew that he ought not to have become President if he was not willing to accept the primary responsibility. He knew that the nation looked to him and that in its time of trial he must not fail. In his heavy, conscientious way, he accepted his duty without reservation.

It was in these circumstances that one day he felt in the roof of his mouth a sore spot that during succeeding weeks did not heal but seemed to become worse. When he asked first Dr. Robert M. O'Reilly, the White House physician, and then Dr. Joseph D. Bryant, who had become the family's doctor, to examine it, he was told that it must be removed at once.

He was just making up his mind that a special session of the Congress would have to be called and that only his presidential influence, exercised with all the force at his command, could cause his proposal to be accepted. The operation would be a serious one. It might have what Dr. Bryant called "an unfavorable result." But it had to be done, and it could not wait until the impending struggle was over.

The call for the session went out on June 30. On that same evening Cleveland was boarding the *Oneida,* the yacht belonging to Commodore E. C. Benedict (one of his New York friends and a stout supporter) with the prospect of an operation aboard her. The *Oneida* was familiar to him. He had spent many days and weekends on her before.

There were no more than ten or twelve people who knew what was happening. Those who did know were a dentist, five doctors, Lamont and his wife, Benedict, Grover's own wife, Frances, (although she was not with the party), and an unknown number of the yacht's crew. Why the secrecy? Because, as every one of those with knowledge of the event seems to have realized, the American people would be deeply disturbed to learn that their President was not the strong, capable guardian they depended on. It is one of the remarkable facts of the nation's history that what happened was for nearly a quarter of a century not known for certain except by the few people who were involved. Dr. W. W. Keen told about it himself twenty-five years later. Dr. Bryant and the others never said anything, and Cleveland never made any reference to it.

The party went aboard the *Oneida* as she lay off Pier A in the East River. The operation was to be next morning. Cleveland sat on deck and smoked several cigars, chatting with the doctors and the Lamonts. Then he went to bed in the owner's stateroom and slept without a sedative, something that would seem incredible in the circumstances if Dr. Keen had not testified to it himself. The President even spoke of his troubles with the Congress and with office seekers. But if he said anything about the weight of his responsibility or cautioned those around him about the need for secrecy, there is no record of it.

That Dr. Bryant, who managed the whole affair, was well aware of these considerations is quite apparent from surviving letters he wrote to Lamont and to his assistants about the arrangements. Neither he nor any of the others knew what they might find behind the "sore spot"; but cancer was a frightening word, and it was likely that it was a malignancy that had to be dealt with.

For Dr. Bryant, and the surgeon, Dr. Keen, who bore the responsibility, the risk must have been felt as much as by the President himself. If there should be that "unfavorable result," what would be said of them for having consented, not only to the concealing of a presidential illness, but to so risky a procedure as performing a major operation on a private yacht instead of in a proper hospital? Both were deeply involved in something that, if it did not turn out well, might cause the gravest charges.

In the morning the main cabin of the yacht was stripped, the President was seated in a chair against the mainmast and the procedure was begun. The beginning in itself was something to be worried about. The patient was a corpulent man of fifty-six; in appearance he was a likely candidate for apoplexy, but the surgery was to be so extensive that a general anesthetic was imperative; the risk had to be taken. As Dr. Keen told it afterward, he himself began with nitrous oxide and, when the President did not lose consciousness easily, went to ether. This took some time; but there seemed to be no weakening of the pulse, so the operation proceeded.

First the dentist removed the upper bicuspid teeth on the left side. Then the incisions in the roof of the mouth were made and the growth exposed. It was more extensive than had been anticipated. It filled the whole of the antrum and there had to be the utmost care to see that all of it was removed. It was not, however, necessary to make any incision from the outside, and the growth seemed not to have extended to the other areas of the sinus. But the whole of the left side of the jaw was removed.

The physicians realized that this in itself was a serious matter. Cleveland had questioned them closely about his ability to speak in a more or less normal manner after the operation. They knew well enough why he was anxious; it was because of his concern that no one should know of the President's cancerous growth, always likely to recur. The operation left an enormous gaping wound, but all of it was inside, betrayed only by swelling; and this it was hoped would be reduced quite soon. Would the wound heal, and could an artificial jaw be fitted? No one knew, as yet; that could only be told when some time had passed. Meanwhile the mouth had to be filled with packs. He would be able to speak only in mumbles.

All that was generally known of the President's trip on the *Oneida* was what was told inquisitive reporters: that he had boarded her in New York and, after a few days of cruising, would be landed at Buzzards Bay, where he would vacation at Gray Gables. Dr. Bryant's presence was not remarkable, because he was often seen with the Clevelands. But there were rumors; and one Philadelphia reporter found a source of information.

A quite circumstantial account of what must have happened appeared in the Philadelphia *Press*; but this was not until the end of August, and, by then, Cleveland had appeared a number of times in public and could be seen to be at least alive. That he was not well was quite evident. The members of his Cabinet who began to visit him after a month could see that something serious had happened. His weight had gone down and left him looking haggard; he was pale and listless; and he continued to have difficulty in speaking, partly because his mouth was still stuffed with packs, but partly because there was a subsequent minor operation for the removal of still more tissue that it was feared might be affected. It was not until the end of August that he was ready to be seen again by others than those of his official family. By that time he had been fitted with an artificial gutta-percha jaw by Dr. Kasson C. Gibson of New York and was enduring the pain of learning to wear it without outward indication.

The story insisted on by Lamont and others was that Cleveland had had some teeth removed and that there was nothing more to the story than was published. Cleveland's stoicism in wearing the painful appliance seemed to support this version; and everyone involved lied manfully—except, as some of the others believed, the dentist, who may have given the story to the *Press* reporter.

For the two months from the end of June to the beginning of September, Cleveland remained more or less secluded at Gray Gables. On August 7, the Congress had met and had heard the message asking for repeal of the silver-buying legislation. This action, the message said, would erase all doubt that the government intended to pay its obligations in the currency recognized by all civilized countries. Since the act had been passed, it was noted, the government had bought more than 147 million dollars' worth of silver and paid for it in gold. If this went on the whole stock of gold would be displaced by silver. The country would then be on a silver standard; and how this would affect its standing in the world it was easy to see.

Considering the passionate talk that was prevalent concerning this issue, the message was extremely moderate. No names were called, and no blame was attributed to anyone. When it is recalled that the message was prepared while Cleveland was suffering agonies from his healing wound and worrying about the spread of the cancer (for the growth had been identified as a carcinoma), it seems a remarkable production. It carried an immense weight of prestige, and it was evident that the best efforts of the silver orators would be needed to offset its influence.

The distress of depression deepened that summer until something like despair settled over the whole country. Circumstances calling for a strong presidential leader and for following his lead were never more apparent. If he demanded a measure, there was a strong disposition to support his demand.

The silver people did not give up easily. The West was far from Washington, and the agitation for cheap money was still rising. An individual known as "Coin" Harvey began the publication in Ohio of a propaganda paper that was widely circulated. In Chicago, just before the special session began, there was a meeting of the American Bimetallic League; it was attended by a formidable number of influential Westerners. It resolved that since the depression was as acute in the gold-standard countries of the world as in the United States, the silver circulating under the Sherman Act could not be blamed. It also called attention to the clauses in the platforms of both political parties at their last national conventions, favoring silver coinage.

The atmosphere was electric when the congressional session met. Eloquent speeches were made by the silverites, the most remarkable being made by young William Jennings Bryan of Nebraska. He spoke without notes in a singularly powerful and moving voice —one that was to be heard in the future by millions of Americans —for three hours. In it he displayed an amazing facility for marshaling his sentences into finished paragraphs. He appeared to have at his command an unlimited amount of factual material, and he could present it as though it was a fascinating description of events. His speech was supplemented by those of the old silver advocate Richard P. Bland, and several others. Altogether, the silverites had the best of the oratorical contest.

On August 28, however, when the voting came, the administration's lobbying and the weight of Cleveland's influence—although after his message he had not participated in the debate—sufficed to win. The Repeal Act passed by 239 to 108. It was a remarkable victory, and Cleveland was relieved. Then, when the Senate worked over the measure, debated it at length and finally on October 30 voted 48 to 37 for passage, it seemed a really notable victory.

The trouble with it was, of course, that if it had been left to the Democrats alone to decide, the administration would have lost. The party was deeply and dangerously split. Also, it did not cure the depression.

26

S O M E of the dullest reading in American history has been produced by economists expounding their views on the tariff question. And the politicians, if not quite so dull, command as little interest. Their resort to complicated calculations and to prolix speeches based on fictional figures, is easily recognized for what it is—arguments for positions favorable to the special interests they desire to serve.

There were undoubtedly those who proceeded from principle. The lowering of tariffs seemed to Cleveland, for example, a way to stop the mulcting of consumers by monopolies and a way to allow the free enterprise he believed in to become really free. There were also those who, as a matter of principle, believed in protection, one argument being that it prevented foreign producers from selling goods in our markets produced in foreign factories where labor was exploited, and another that it sheltered infant industries while they established themselves. A more general claim was that it brought the various parts of the economy into relation with each other instead of with foreign regions. Nationalists argued vigorously that protection helped to make the nation one. Cleveland rejected all these claims.

But the truth is that these theoretical considerations were not very important in battles about the tariff in the years 1893–94. There were speeches that presented, with considerable eloquence, the alternate theories; but everyone knew from the first, what became more and more nakedly exposed as the acrimony deepened, that the struggle was for advantages—crude, hard considerations of profitability. What it came down to was the interest of this or that business and how strong that interest was when it came to controlling votes in the House or in the Senate.

It has to be said that the subservience of senators to the industrialists was much more naked than that of most representatives. The representatives more often owed allegiance to *general* interests —cotton, wheat or pork, the coal or iron industry, the city consumer or the workingman. In the Senate, there was much more actual representation, hardly concealed, of such *special* interests as the sugar trust, the ironmasters, the coal operators, the textile manufacturers or the lesser but still powerful businesses actually allied with some senator. It was still a time when there was amazingly little criticism of actual financial involvement by legislators in businesses affected by the acts they voted on.

Senators made money by speculating in the securities of concerns they were about to give some advantage; or they represented clients who had something to gain or lose from measures they might or might not support. Most often of all, they relied on the interests they favored to keep them in office by supplying campaign funds, keeping the state legislatures (by whom senators were elected) in line and maintaining their home organizations.

These weaknesses in the democratic system were well enough known, and they were beginning to be examined critically. The democracy was not so complacent about its political institutions as it had been a short time before. Cleveland himself was witness to that, since his election had been a sort of protest against this sort of subversion. After the tariff battles of 1893-94, the criticism would rise to a roar of protest. It was an early manifestation of the disgust that would result, after some years, in a constitutional amendment (the seventeenth, ratified in 1913) providing for the direct election of senators. Just now, however, those who had helped legislators, and especially senators, in their campaigns were demanding, without the least sense of shame, a return of votes for the heavy investment they had made in the elections.

This nauseated Cleveland, who long ago had set himself against such dishonesty. There were, however, several difficulties in his situation. One was that he still had a lingering reluctance to invade the province of the legislative branch. Another was that members of his own party were deeply involved along with Republicans. Still another was that his victory over the silverites had alienated some of those who might now have been willing to assist in lowering the tariffs.

It was with many misgivings that he returned to the tariff struggle he had begun in 1885. He was driven by conscience and by his pledges, but he had no illusions about winning. He had lost his second presidential campaign on this very issue; still he felt himself compelled to go on.

The prospect in the House of Representatives was better than that in the Senate. Partly this was because of the respect commanded by Congressman W. L. Wilson of West Virginia, who would have charge of the bill. Wilson was chairman of the Committee on Ways and Means, but beyond that he was known to be a dedicated public servant at a time when there were altogether too few who were not suspiciously linked with the lobbyists. These had descended on Washington in regimental numbers, an invasion regularly expected when controversial legislation was being considered. When even the smallest item, the slightest change, could make a difference of vital importance to a business, as in this bill, no effort or expenditure would be spared. When scruple was no consideration, it was cheaper to buy or to "influence" a vote, or several votes, than to suffer the loss that might result from adverse action.

Scruple, also, as a matter of hard fact, was always easy to define almost out of existence. If a congressman fought to keep duties on coal or sugar or iron ore (three that Cleveland thought should be on the free list) he could say to himself, if he came from a district in Pennsylvania, Louisiana or Michigan, that he was acting in his constituents' interests. And if, in return, he received a promise of support for reelection or was made an attorney for one of the concerns affected, it was a reward he could tell himself was deserved. He would have resented its being called a "payment." In his mind he was not being unscrupulous at all.

There were fewer direct bribes in the Congress than were being disclosed repeatedly in the state legislatures and the city governments of that time; but delicate feelings about such matters were all too rare even in Washington. William L. Wilson was different from many of his colleagues. His was a conscience so discriminating that no suggestion of any taint was ever attached to his reputation. He lived within his salary austerely and simply; he was industrious and well informed. It was because of these characteristics that he commanded such respect. In his academic way (he was a former professor) he had constructed the schedules of a new tariff bill with the greatest care. It was now one that he could conscientiously defend. It was calculated to forward the public interest and that alone.

Wilson by now was frail, ascetic and growing elderly. His advocacy would not be aggressive, but Cleveland knew that it would be effective. Any representative who opposed his proposals would find himself on the defensive merely because he had challenged the bill's author. Only a few of those most committed to the monopolists would care to risk such open opposition.

Wilson, besides his purity of motive, had other advantages in getting approval of the bill. One was that it was moderate. It was much more modest in its reductions of the present duties than outright free traders could approve; still it was so reasonable that it would be hard for any but extreme protectionists to argue against it. Proof of this was that Carnegie himself, at one stage, wrote a letter to the New York *Tribune,* expressing approval. He had some reservations, but he did say that business would do well to accept reductions in exchange for the stability of conditions that ought to follow the bill's passage.

Another advantage was that, under pressure of representatives from the Western states, an income tax provision was written into the bill as an amendment. This placated some of those who were most resentful about their defeat on the silver issue. Among these was Bryan, who was an ardent advocate of getting revenue in this way.

This amendment was important. Almost two thirds of the government's income came from duties on imports (the rest came from direct taxes on consumers' goods). If tariffs were reduced, the loss would have to be made up. That taxes on income were fairer than any other way of raising revenue was admitted, although the present proposal did not have the "progressive" feature of later ones. (The *percentages* to be levied were the same on all incomes that were taxed.)

Wilson's advantages, however, had certain offsets. The worst obstacle was the state of the country—in deep depression and falling deeper into it with every month that passed. It could be argued that it was a time to try desperately for recovery, not for reform. Changes in the tariff could hardly affect economic activity immediately or dramatically. Indeed, their effect was disputable.

CLEVELAND'S DEPRESSION

1893

Bankruptcy of railroads and businesses
Collapse of the stock market
Wave of bank failures
Closing factories created unemployment

1894

600 more banks failed, mostly in the West and South
Bankruptcies three times those the former panic year of 1873
Deficit in government revenue, forcing the issuance of bonds
Another stock market decline
Unemployment still more serious
Virtual paralysis of production

1895

Prices continued to fall, reaching the lowest point since the Civil War
Much of the railroad mileage in receivership
Commercial bankruptcies equaled those of 1893
Demand for relief of the unemployed by public works ignored
Sources of charity exhausted

1896

Continuation of the depression
Unemployment at the highest level ever known
Strikes frequent
Suffering in city and country the worst of any year

Nevertheless, after only a few weeks Wilson's bill passed the House by the remarkable vote of 204 to 140. There were ten

Populists voting for it along with the Democrats; but to Cleveland's consternation, there were eighteen Democrats who refused to go along. This was a split in the party that would certainly show itself more seriously in the Senate.

Wilson's closing speech was one of the memorable ones in legislative history, sincere, eloquent and convincing. It ended:

. . . This is a roll of freedom, and in the name of honor and freedom, I summon every Democratic member of this House to inscribe his name upon it.

When he finished speaking, he was carried into the corridors on the shoulders of his colleagues, among them Bryan and John Sharp Williams. It was the supreme moment of a noble Democratic statesman.

The Senate, as is the Senate's habit and as Cleveland feared, was not impressed by the action of the House. In this instance, deafness to House enthusiasm was something more than indifference. There was, by now, a prevalent and positive dislike for Cleveland. There is nothing unusual about a coolness between the President and the Senate; but the violent and open opposition now evident was more than the usual stiff hostility. It was so strong that trouble was predictable over any request Cleveland might make. Besides, the party balance was nearly even. There were forty-four Democrats, thirty-eight Republicans and three Populists (three seats were vacant). And of the Democrats, several could not be counted on. Presidential power, even if strongly exerted, would not influence such a body.

The first outright defiance of Cleveland was shown on a different issue: refusal to confirm a nomination for the Supreme Court. Rejection of a second choice followed. The nominees were both well qualified, and there was no real reason advanced for failure to confirm. This was notice to Cleveland that the tariff bill would be rewritten to suit the special interests. He was discouraged. An early aggressiveness about the appointment changed to conciliation; he gave in and nominated a senator, an appointment not likely to be rejected.

But the concession seemed so out of character that instead of helping, it made the Senate more confident. It was a measure of

Cleveland's concern about the tariff bill, but it did not keep it from failure—far from it.

The struggle, after the introduction of the bill and referral to the Finance Committee, went on for five wearing months. Finally, at the end of August, a measure so mutilated that Cleveland would not approve it was passed. It was a clear and humiliating defeat, and one he would not be able to reverse in any future engagement. If he tried, the humiliation would be repeated.

The first reverse in the battle had come in a caucus held by the Democrats. This had lasted for three days, and there had been so many implacable opponents of the bill that serious compromise was recognized by its supporters to be inevitable. Especially the Louisiana and Alabama senators refused to accept free imports of sugar, coal and iron ore. Cleveland's supporters arranged that Senators George Vest, J. K. Jones and Roger D. Mills should form a subcommittee to meet the objections if they could. They reported in March an amended bill with moderate duties on the three commodities. Immediately, however, it became clear that even moderation would not be acceptable. Not only coal, iron and sugar lobbyists, but all the others were demanding the same protection they had had in the past; and their senatorial friends were responding. The most extreme protectionists formed a coalition and agreed not to vote for any bill that did not satisfy their principles; with lobbyists looking over their shoulders, they felt the need of mutual bolstering.

This made any lowering of duties seem unlikely, but Senator Jones took it on himself to find out exactly what compromises would have to be made if any bill at all were to be passed. He felt by early May that he had reached a conclusion. He had a list of 403 amendments that seemed to satisfy enough senators to make a majority. A caucus was called again. Forty-three did accept the Jones version, and the bill was reported to the Senate. During the subsequent debate, the forty-three held together and a bill passed in early July. But then the sugar trust demanded and got an amendment that would cause their schedule to become effective much earlier than the others, and this opened the whole bill to debate again. Another flood of amendments resulted; and when final action came, there had been 634 changes from the Wilson bill.

Nearly all of these were indefensible favors to special interests. It had become more a Republican protectionist measure than the moderate one the Democrats had been pledged to pass.

Cleveland was outraged and said so; and the House leaders were furious because so little of their work had survived the Senate passage. They did think, however, that in the conference sessions with the Senate they might be able to get some important changes. In this they were disappointed. As far as the senators were concerned, they would have been as happy with no bill at all, so why should they compromise? Actually the House members forced adjournment with the resolve that no agreement could be reached.

Within a few days, however, certain members started a move to accept the Senate measure, and in spite of all that Wilson and a few others of the faithful could do, a motion to recede from disagreement with the Senate passed. Weaker party members felt that bad as the bill was, it could be presented as an advance over the existing Republican tariff.

During the period of disagreement in the conference, Cleveland had been persuaded to make public a letter he had written to Wilson denouncing the Senate measure, which read in part:

There is no excuse for mistaking or misapprehending the feeling and temper of the rank and file of the Democrats . . . Every true Democrat and every sincere Reformer knows that the bill in its present form and as it will be submitted to the conference falls far short of the consummation for which we have long labored . . . Our abandonment of the cause or the principle upon which it rests means party perfidy and party dishonor.

He could hardly pretend after that to be even moderately satisfied with what had been done. In a final gesture of disavowment he refused to sign, and the bill became law without his approval. He might have vetoed the bill, prolonging the fight, but evidently he had given up.

What had become of the fiercely determined advocate of reform?

True, he had spoken of "perfidy and dishonor," but to dissociate himself from the whole affair—even though Democrats in the House had decided to give in—was not the act of a leader.

In fact, this defeat marked the end of such leadership of the party as Cleveland had established. A majority of the members had refused to follow him, and more of them would now refuse. It was indisputable that they had repudiated the platform, but this they ignored. How could the party offer itself to the electorate as a coherent organization based on principle in any future election? Cleveland knew well enough what would happen in that year's congressional elections—what the Democrats deserved they would get. But how did he excuse his own weakness? He never explained.

27

T H E tariff defeat was not Cleveland's only distress in 1894. Far from it. Tremendous tidal forces building up reduced the tariff failure to a minor wave in a menacing flood. Cleveland believed that the protective duties represented a cynical use of government for private advantage, and that they were one source of the corruption he hated. But government was being used in so many ways by the piratical financiers and trust builders that the tariffs could not be considered even the most important.

As this conviction finally became firmer, his zeal for tariff reform slackened, and during the last stages of the Wilson bill's passage he avoided battle. What, after all, was the use of expending all his effort on one battle when a whole war was at issue? Something much more drastic than a single measure would be needed. What was necessary was to go to the deepest causes of the disease and see whether a cure could not be found.

He saw that when the industrialists talked of a freedom, what they meant was a freedom that allowed them to do as they liked with the power they accumulated from not allowing freedom to their smaller competitors. It is probable that he did not reach in his thinking to the heart of this paradox. But he was profoundly shocked by having to conclude that those who were the strongest advocates of laissez faire were the monopolists.

No one was in so good a position as he to see that the nation was becoming a headless colossus. It stretched now from coast to coast, a vast expanse of mountains, valleys, plains and shores. Its climate varied from the sub-tropics of the Southeast to the chill uplands of the Canadian border.

The wide Mississippi Valley was the richest agricultural area of the world, and it was pouring out its products in a deluge that overwhelmed the markets. Manufacturing towns steamed and roared with increasing activity—at least they did in good times. Cities were gathering millions. Railways were extending in thousand-mile leaps. Mines were spewing minerals. Forests were furnishing the lumber for vast building efforts. Nothing in all history had prepared men for what was happening in America.

The riches of the continent were being taken over by enterprisers who wanted no check on their activities, no examination of their impact on social life, no limit on their profits—above all, no definition of direction or purpose; any such definition, they feared, might in some way guide or channel their progress.

Suggestions for government interference were called "socialistic," and this was considered a sufficient rejection. The industrialists wanted to charge what they liked, produce what they pleased and hire and fire their workers without interference. This was their "free" enterprise. It had begun before the Civil War, had developed under forced draft to produce the materials of that war and then afterward had expanded explosively as population increased and spread across the empty areas of the country. Those who did well by aggression insisted that theirs was "the American Way."

The time was bound to come when the expanders and exploiters would begin to have collisions and conflicts even among themselves and would need some mutual agreement about rules. Besides, objection was building up to their fiercely individualist methods. By Cleveland's second administration these had grown loud. The catastrophe of panic and depression sent people scurrying for answers to questions they had not even asked before. And the answers were bound to be as hastily made up as the questions. Besides there was the suspicion that what had happened was caused by lack of rule and direction. "Freedom," "liberty"—these were not acceptable guides if they produced chaos.

Cleveland, feeling that simple honesty called for gold dollars and lowered tariffs, was not at first conscious that a larger issue comprehended the small causes he was backing. It was now being borne in on him that more, much more, was called for. He had brooded over this as he had waited, after election, for his inauguration. His forebodings were confirmed after his new term began by the cynicism of the Congress as the tariff bill was cut to pieces. Businessmen had been allowed to write that bill to suit themselves. But that was no more than a small evidence of their power. They were consolidating their hold on the industrial empires as they had on the railroads and the public resources—the land, the forests and the mines.

Gigantic trusts were shaped as the House of Morgan put together all or most of the enterprise in one or another industry, paid for them what was necessary, issued securities to cover the whole (plus generous pay for their own services) and sold to the public the securities they did not keep for themselves. They could then argue, and did, that they must be allowed to charge the prices or rates (if it was a public utility) calculated to produce a suitable profit. This was so usual that a name was invented for it. It was called "watering."

There was, of course, a good argument in favor of bigger business. It was this: the larger the scale, the lower the costs. Many facilities could serve several enterprises as well as one; this was especially true of management, of sales organizations, of financing. But also there were savings in the elimination of duplication; plants could be merged or devoted to specialization; because of their increased volume, more machinery could be introduced and processes could be "rationalized."

There was another important saving: a large organization could deal with its employees more impersonally, selecting only those whose efficiency was up to standard and rejecting the rest. It could also eliminate any troublemakers who were inclined to press for higher wages, better working conditions or, especially, who were inclined to join the union movement. Unions were dangerous because they increased workers' bargaining power. They provided a common front for employees against employers who preferred to deal with workers each by himself. These individuals might be weak because they had to think of their families' livings and feared to risk their jobs. But this was what employers counted on. This was the way to profit, power and expansion.

These problems would be tormenting the nation long after Cleveland's time. Many engagements would take place in the long struggle of consumers for fair prices and decent standards, of workers for the right to join together and bargain collectively, of conservationists for the controlled use of irreplaceable resources, of savers and investors for honest financing and, indeed, of society itself for the rule of law in the economic sphere.

There was no suggestion yet of government direction or planning, of making an effort to see what ought to be done and making rules to see that it was done. There was growing resentment among ordinary people at the miseries imposed on so many millions for the benefit, it was supposed, of a few wealthy and powerful monopolists. The tendency, it will be seen, was to blame someone, not some arrangement, not the system or the rules it ran by. During panics and the periods of paralysis following them, lasting for years sometimes, it was seen that things ought not to be the way they were. A nation so resourceful, so capable of immense feats of production, that showed itself so lively and aggressive should not suffer such sinking spells. Its workers and their dependents ought not to be left to starve and freeze through long winters in filthy slums; its farmers ought not to live in shacks on land they held only at the sufferance of their creditors. Workers ought to be able to sell their labor and farmers their crops at rates and prices that would support them.

Workers were now asserting that they would defend their elementary rights even if they had to fight. They might be shot or clubbed or starved (while their employers were sheltered behind the protection of the police) into submission once, and yet again, but they would not give up.

Farmers were saying that they must not be expected to carry the whole risk of planting and tending their crops and then finding them unwanted or wanted at a price below the costs of production. Thoughtful people, who were neither wage workers nor farmers, were beginning at least to think of these problems. The trouble, some could see, was not particular, it was general. It was not because anyone was bad; it was because the system of things was wrong.

If some order was to come out of the chaos, if there were to be rules and standards, some sense of direction, some guidance toward a future that made use of, and did not waste, the vast potentialities of the nation, government had to shape and regulate, give direction and guidance. But this was where most Americans balked. There was a general and firm belief in initiative, but not in direction. It was thought that individuals should be allowed to do as they pleased with their talents and their property. It was even thought—or always *had* been thought—that if freedom prevailed, all would be well. Trouble came from limiting freedom.

Americans lived under a constitution wholly shaped to protect individuals and their possessions *against* government. There was no mention of duties, only of immunities; no suggestion that people had responsibilities for each other's welfare, only prohibitions against interference with liberties. Unless a man disturbed another man seriously, unless he behaved outrageously, he was immune to check or discipline. He need not contribute in any way. He need only pursue his own interest and look after his own dependents. It was assumed that he ought to be able to do this with no more help than was needed to protect him as he went about his occupation.

The government was shaped to this theory. Members of the Congress were elected from particular districts or from their states, and they were in Washington to look after the wants of their localities and their constituencies. Such national or general needs as there might be were assumed to be sufficiently protected by the competition that arose among the representatives of localities. They had no expressed duty whatever to consider the interest of the whole. If they did, it was incidental to their main business of forwarding the prosperity of their friends and neighbors back home.

The President, with the Vice-President in reserve, was the single representative of the entire nation. He stood in relation to all the people as each legislator did to the few voters who had elected him. Upon him fell the responsibility for the Union, for its welfare, its security, its continuation.

This was an exposed position. It had from the first been subject to attack and attrition from the jealous legislative branch. Senators and congressmen bargained for local advantages against a President who must see that the entire nation survived and prospered. The position of the Congress had been reinforced by the desire of business, grown immense and powerful, to be let alone. Since businessmen wanted to go about their profit making without interference, they feared and distrusted the presidency. Whoever occupied that office was their natural enemy—their enemy and the enemy of the congressmen and senators. It was inevitable, under the Constitution, that legislators should become the allies of their supporters, the men with money.

So Cleveland saw the situation as the tariff bill made its slow way through the House and Senate.

Consider his position as it was borne in on him that, what it was his duty to do, it was impossible to do! Presidents were *not* elected because they would be strong leaders, capable of directing their party and seeing to it that party pledges were redeemed; capable, also, of responding to the people's needs and wishes. Their potential power had been sapped at the source by the growth and enforcement of the theory we have spoken of before—that policies should be made by the Congress, and that it was the President's business to execute them when they had been embodied in legislation: that and that only.

It has been noted that Cleveland was one of those who had agreed to this view, and now we see the result. He had intended to purge the executive of corruption and waste, but he had not intended to define and enforce national policies. If he now saw the error in this, it was far too late to change anything much. Even in the presence of country-wide economic paralysis, with all its consequent misery, there was little that he could do. His departure from the tradition of presidential abstention when he decided to fight for sound money and moderate tariffs had been only partially successful. Sound money had been defended for the moment, it was true, but with no certainty of long-run acceptance. Tariff legislation had been, on the other hand, a complete defeat. He had felt compelled to turn his back as he saw the final bill coming to him for approval or disapproval. He retreated to Gray Gables, stayed there oftener and longer than he ever had before, and spent his days on the bay fishing. He was disillusioned and humiliated. He returned to Washington only when duty demanded it.

He had, he felt, been betrayed by the business system he had served as a lawyer. He had seen that his theory of the presidency was one put forward by those who feared a powerful leader with the people's welfare at heart. They wanted a President who was no President. It was, for him, an impasse. He saw no way out.

To begin with, he was not a man of imagination. If something had gone terribly wrong, he still felt it was because the institutions he believed in had been subverted, not because those institutions were faulty. His rage was directed at the trust makers and the crooked financiers, and at the politicians who thought of jobs and reelection, not of the national good. The rearrangements and reinterpretations that were called for would, besides, have to be set against the dangers he saw in the proposals of the leaders produced by the Populist cause. They talked not only of cheap money; they went on to advocate public ownership of the railroads and the indiscriminate punishment of businessmen and financiers. There were even suggestions that public ownership should not stop with utilities but should reach to other productive facilities. Was a railroad so very different from a steel mill?

So he was at dead center. He was a President who could not *be* President because he could not accept the manifest destiny of Presidents. He sat and fished. He could think of nothing else to do.

There were times, however, during the rest of his presidency, when his principles of noninterference seemed so insufficient that he exploded out of their confines into protest or action. His frustration, as the depression went on and on with no evident betterment, approached the conviction of guilt.

There were three occasions during 1893-94 when he acted to protect the dollar. The first was the repeal of the silver-purchase bill, when he used all the influence he could gather.

Then, as silver continued to substitute itself for gold and the reserve dwindled, he sponsored a bond issue of fifty million dollars. Hard times had depleted the Treasury, and the government's obligations could not be met with ordinary revenues and so it must borrow. The gold reserve of a hundred million dollars, necessary to maintain the monetary standard, kept leaking away either to foreign speculators or to those who collected silver and greenbacks to trade at the Treasury for gold.

It was an unfortunate time for borrowing. The bankers who had to underwrite the bonds doubted the Treasury's authority to issue them; and when they did subscribe they paid in gold got from the Treasury in exchange for silver or notes. So the gold reserve was depleted in the act of enabling the Treasury to meet its obligations.

Then, too, the bond issue made the silverites furious. There were heated speeches in the Congress; and Senator William A. Peffer of Kansas, for instance, shouted that Cleveland and Carlisle had now allied themselves openly with the money barons. There was, he said, idleness, destitution, hunger and desperation in every state and in every city. And, with many millions in the Treasury, the administration sold the people's credit to appease the clamor of the misers in Wall Street. Senator William M. Stewart of Nevada spoke similarly of the iron hand of contraction and the dictation of British financiers. Others joined the chorus of denunciation.

Then a little later, in spring 1894, the House passed a bill sponsored by Congressman Richard P. Bland of Missouri for issuing coins to cover the seigniorage accumulated in the Treasury. (The Government purchased bullion for less than the value of the coins made from it. The difference between the value of the coins and the value of the bullion was called seigniorage.) Using the seigniorage in this way would give the government more silver dollars; but also, it would further threaten the gold reserve. The accumulation in 1894 could have been coined into fifty-five million dollars. Cleveland had to consider the fact that the bill had passed both Houses with majorities supplied by Democratic votes. In vetoing it, he was not only rebuking the silverites, but his own party. Its advocates had used every means they could devise to persuade him it ought to be approved; he had been adamant, but he knew the costs in loss of influence might be enormous.

He had violated the principle of allowing the Congress to make its decisions without presidential interference. In the matter of seigniorage he had felt so strongly that he had abandoned it completely. He feared that the two thirds necessary for passage over his veto might be found. He summoned Speaker Charles F. Crisp to the White House and practically ordered him to cut off debate so that the persuasive silver orators could not speak. Crisp demurred, saying that some of the most important party members would have to be suppressed, and that such an arbitrary action would jeopardize his own political standing; his state of Georgia favored silver and his reelection might well be made impossible. The President, aroused to anger and pounding his desk, demanded to know whether the Speaker of the House was really willing to sacrifice the country's welfare to protect his own political future, whereupon the shamed speaker gave in. Next day, certain that he would be punished for his arbitrary action, he nevertheless did cut off debate, and there were not enough votes to reject the veto. This could be put down as a victory, as could the passage of the Sherman Act repealer. But both were costly victories indeed. The spring of 1894 was one of deepening disaster. Unemployment increased, the farm situation grew worse. There began a series of strikes, affecting the largest industries, brought on by the desperate situation of the workers; and the disorder in the farm states became epidemic.

Both the workers and farmers felt that Cleveland had joined their enemies. He was rapidly becoming more and more unpopular. He had borne this sort of disapproval before; but always he had had the clear justification of righteousness to sustain him. This was different. His justification now had to rest on policies he had stuck to because he had once *thought* them right; he still *knew* them to be traditional; but he was no longer able to satisfy his conscience. One thing was certain; they had not worked. Matters were growing rapidly worse.

At a time in the history of the nation when imagination was as much needed as integrity and resolution, the President had none. He could stand firm against the erosion of the principles he believed in, but that standing firm was the very thing that prevented him from conceiving measures that would save the farmers and workers from the suffering that had grown intolerable. When he could not even stand firm any longer, he was a tragic figure.

28

CLEVELAND was still being excoriated about his veto of the seigniorage bill when a strike more serious and extensive than any that had yet happened began in the soft-coal fields. Many sections of the country were involved: Colorado, Pennsylvania, Alabama and many other states. It proved to be disastrous for the miners. They had no reserve funds, and their families were already destitute. After weeks of defiance they could hold out no longer, and they went back to work at the same pay they had been starving on before.

Later in that same April, an even more sinister strike broke out. This involved the railwaymen of the Great Northern, a transcontinental system, only recently opened after being promoted and built by James J. Hill. The strikers were led by Eugene V. Debs of the American Railway Union, and because, under his management, the strikers had real cohesion, most of their demands were granted in the settlement. This gave Debs a prestige that would be significant in future strikes—notably that at the Pullman works later in that same year.

Even earlier there were other troubles, each part of a pattern. A textile strike was accompanied by violence that showed all too plainly how far the disintegration of industrial society had progressed. Then there was the march of "Coxey's Army," an incident still recalled to illustrate the desperation of a people tried too far and reacting against the arrogance of employers with public authority behind them.

What "General" Jacob Coxey wanted in the beginning was the issuance of unlimited amounts of paper money; but it was obvious that those who joined him wanted the same redress of grievances that several other "armies" were demanding. Their focus on money was not a firm one. These were the unemployed, men without the means to sustain life, living from day to day as outcasts. They were hungry most of the time, and ragged; but, even worse, they were conscious of having failed in an obligation they had been taught to honor—the support of their families.

If Jacob Coxey believed that a descent on Washington could change Cleveland's mind, he was mistaken. On this subject, the President was adamant; and he had come to regard the easy-money advocates as at best mistaken and, at worst, demagogues who were encouraging debtors to evade their just obligations. The Coxey crowd, and others like them were flotsam, eddying in a flood of trouble. Some of his friends were frightened, but fright was not in Cleveland's nature. He judged his course to be right. He would not be moved.

Those who marched with Coxey knew little about economics, but, like others, they were attracted vaguely to the miracle of money got by fiat. Because the times were so disordered, a protest, if it was coherent and organized, seemed to them likely to result in some sort of relief. By the distressed millions, their adventure was at first looked on with hope; by the beleaguered elite, it was regarded as a portent of dreadful change. A "march" was equated with "revolution." For these reasons, it was taken far more seriously than was warranted by its strength. Hungry and under-clothed men are unlikely subjects for discipline; and although the gathering could be called an army when it started from Massillon, Ohio, only a remnant of some three hundred arrived in Washington.

By that time, the issue Coxey had been demonstrating about had been disposed of: the seigniorage bill had been vetoed. He was left without a cause. The towns along the way, alarmed and defensive, had been relieved to see the army pass; during the first days, newspaper reporters had gone along to report the incidents of the crusade. But it was soon apparent that most of the marchers were scarcely more than tramps, and their cause could hardly be taken as seriously meant. Soon they became more comic than dangerous, and most fell out when ridicule was added to hardship. When they reached Washington, it was in an atmosphere of anticlimax. Coxey, himself, was arrested for trampling on the grass of Capitol Hill.

But the strikes were another matter. There was nothing comic about the hatred and the will to violence they exposed. Of all of them, the worst, and the one recalled in later years with more shame and wonder than most of these needless small wars, was the strike that began at the Pullman works just outside Chicago in June. Like some of the others, before it was over it had broken through the orderly processes of social custom.

These processes seemed to the workers by now—as they seemed to the poorer farmers—weighted in favor of an elite in business and banking and against those who did the hard work of the nation. To the workers, the most important ethic of industrialism was that those who did its work ought to share in its product, ought, indeed, to be paid enough to support the children who would make up the nation of the future. Also, the conditions of their work ought not to violate their sense of independence. They were being reduced to a subservience, they felt, that recalled the serfdom of earlier centuries. They labored under the discipline of likely discharge for the least infraction of rules, or even for arguing about the rules themselves. They had no recourse. They might even be blacklisted and be unable to get a job with any other employer. Since there was no unemployment insurance and no refuge at all for their families, the distress of discharge, or even the threat of it, was cruel. It was not only cruel, it sapped the vitality of the nation.

The one defense workers possessed was that of organizing and bargaining collectively. This recourse was rejected by employers with a fierceness that seems savage in retrospect but that was defended by most respectable people during several generations. The denial of any such right was supported by press and pulpit.

Property, however, was to be protected at all costs, and property too often was defined as *operating* property—that is, there was a public duty to keep factories going, protect them from striking workers and even to guard the armies of strikebreakers so often recruited to break the will of the protesters.

In the long and tragic history of the battles workers had to undertake before unionism was made acceptable and collective bargaining was legalized in a series of laws in the 1930s, the Pullman strike was one of the most savagely repressed. Cleveland was appalled by its violence; but, like most of his friends, and certainly his lawyer friends, he judged that the violence originated in the strikers' refusal to work according to order. That there were orders they could not obey and still protect their most elementary rights, he, no more than others, admitted.

Ordinarily, however, such affairs were no business of the federal government or of its chief executive. Police powers belonged to the states and to the cities. The President might be concerned, but only in the extremity of actual insurrection could he act, and then only if asked by the legislature or the governor of the threatened state—and, moreover, with the sole object of restoring peace. Article IV, Section 4 of the Constitution states the principle this way:

The United States shall guarantee to every state in this Union a republican form of government, and shall protect each of them against invasion, and, on application of the legislature, or of the executive (when the legislature cannot be convened) against domestic violence.

Why Cleveland was moved to exceed the customary behavior of Presidents during the Pullman strike, and to exceed, perhaps, his constitutional power, we shall see.

He had just returned from a fishing expedition on the lower Potomac with two friends (one was Dr. Robert M. O'Reilly and the other, Captain Robley D. Evans, the "Fighting Bob" of the Spanish-American War). His wife and children were at Gray Gables. It was the twenty-eighth of June.

The grievances of the Pullman employees had been building up throughout the winter and spring. Many of the employees had been laid off and many others put on part time. Wages were cut by 25 per cent and members of a protesting committee were promptly fired. The workers were forced to live in a company town, paying high rents, being strictly disciplined and most probably losing their homes if discharged. When they had paid their rent, they had left out of their pay about 75 cents a day for all other expenses.

Yet in 1893 the company had distributed two and a half million dollars in dividends to its shareholders and held undivided surplus

Eugene Victor Debs (*Courtesy of The Tamiment Library, New York City*)

profits of about twenty-five million dollars. Pullman himself, of course, was one of the richest men in the country.

In the light of these facts, a national convention of the American Railway Union, with a membership of one hundred fifty thousand, led by Eugene V. Debs, asked for arbitration. It was refused. The workers then determined on a boycott against all Pullman cars (the cars were leased by the company to the railroads). In retaliation, the twenty-four railroads belonging to the General Management Association, determined to crush the strike. The G.M.A. hired strikebreakers, who were also made federal officials and who quickly moved in to take over the strikers' jobs.

A confrontation followed at once. In Chicago, twenty thousand railwaymen struck, and on the lines running west, forty thousand more left their jobs. Railway traffic in the areas virtually halted.

Cleveland learned of all this from the newspapers. The turmoil was pictured in the press as a consequence of orders given by Debs, and the strike was pictured as a battle between capital and labor unequaled in American history.

Chicago citizens, according to the *Tribune,* were terror-stricken. The hysteria that was to characterize reportings all through the strike had begun. There were prophecies of revolution and of descent into anarchy. Suppression was urgently demanded. Rioting, it was said, was completely out of control—but at the same time was being expertly commanded by Debs!

Cleveland had not heard much about the situation until then. He was soon briefed by Attorney General Olney, who seemed to share the general fright and who joined in the demand for suppression. Olney had very quickly seen the basis for federal action. The mails were carried by the railways, and any interference with them was a federal offense.

The fact was that, far from being a man of warlike inclinations, Eugene Debs was a pacifist. He had counseled his own followers to avoid overt acts that would precipitate physical conflict. The union boycott involved merely the refusal to move any Pullman car; the men merely had to walk off the job. But in such a situation, incidents quickly enlarge; and on June 29 a train was stopped at Hammond, Indiana, and strikers compelled the crew to leave its Pullman cars on a siding. By Olney's definition, this amounted to the use of force. Other such incidents followed. They were pictured as holdups and the union men as bandits.

On June 28, 29 and 30 the *Tribune*'s headlines seemed almost to scream with fanatic fear: DEBS IS DICTATOR, MOB IN CONTROL, MOBS BENT ON RUIN! The strike was no longer one against the Pullman Company or the railroads; it was against the public. Revolution had arrived. The other newspapers followed the *Tribune,* and the chorus spread across the country.

There were steadier counsels. Governor John P. Altgeld of Illinois advised Cleveland that the state was capable of handling the situation and that the reports of disorder were exaggerated. Such citizens as Clarence Darrow, the noted lawyer, were on the side of the strikers; Darrow, always moved by injustice, even resigned his position as a railroad lawyer to help the workers. But the voices of sympathizers and moderates were drowned in the swirl of unreasoning panic. There was a demand for savage reprisal that would support almost any disciplinary action the President might determine to take. In fact, the demand became hard to resist. It became harder as Olney, the Attorney General, insisted on repression.

In what happened afterward, it is important to recall that Olney had long been looking for a chance to discipline the unruly workers of the country. He had actually been attorney for several of the railroads most affected and still seemed to feel that he represented them. He was generally reactionary in such matters. He had, for instance, expressed outrage when disturbances earlier in spring had accompanied the movement of Coxey's Army, and when even more insubordinate bands of men from the West had seized trains and started them rolling toward the capital. He had then ordered federal marshals to prevent such seizures and, when they were unable to carry out his orders, had advised them to ask for help from his own Department of Justice in getting court orders; then he had ordered the Army to enforce decrees of the courts.

Olney was again made furious by the Pullman outbreak. He wanted Cleveland to send troops at once; but when the President was reluctant, he resorted to the strategy he had already used. He arranged for the attorney of one of the railroads to apply for an injunction; at the same time he instructed the district attorney in

Chicago to argue for it. The advice was passed on to the federal judges and they not only granted the restraining order but assisted in drafting the application they were about to grant.

The strikers were now outlawed; they were in conflict, not with their employers, but with the federal government itself. Their confrontation was actually with the Army. In all of this Cleveland was involved without having full information or any advice to counter that of Olney.

Later opinion about the small war that followed is that Cleveland was misled by Olney, that the violence was more in response to provocation than to the initiative of the strikers and their supporters and that the intervention was conceived and carried out as a lesson in discipline administered to an unruly element of the population. If Cleveland realized the distress of the workers or their hopeless conviction that their government had no interest in making things better for them, only in protecting property and suppressing their attempts to obtain justice, he showed no sign. He rested on his own conviction of a duty to restore order.

For a few days after the restraining order was issued there was comparative calm. Then, as soldiers began to appear, there were clashes between them and gatherings of strikers and their friends. These sometimes turned into battles. The strikers—and now their supporters—began to blockade railroad tracks, burn freight cars and stop passenger trains on a large scale. Several buildings at Chicago's Columbian Exposition were set afire, and it was assumed that the strikers were responsible. On July 7, seven strikers were killed and many wounded by gunfire from the troops.

Cleveland now was aroused and assumed the powers he possessed as commander in chief. The White House turned into a headquarters with Olney and Secretary of War Lamont in continuous attendance. Olney was communicating with the Department of Justice officials in Chicago, who by now had enlisted an army of deputies. These, it was afterward disclosed, were paid by the General Managers Association, but were certified as federal representatives. Actually they were strikebreakers. The whole of the Army at midwest posts was also thrown into the conflict.

Washington reporters afterward recalled that Olney had seemed well content with what was happening. The lesson was being taught. For Cleveland, once he had been convinced of his responsibility, suppression of the strikers was a duty he carried out with his customary bullheaded energy. Olney had interpreted the disorders as an attack on authority in general, planned by anarchistic leaders and carried out by their supporting mobs. Cleveland accepted this version of events and had no scruple thereafter about suppression by force. He had the right, he felt, if a legal basis must be found, of seeing to it that the mails of the United States were moved. He said in the midst of the rioting that if it took the whole Army and Navy to deliver a postcard in Chicago, the Army and Navy would be used. This was a declaration that stirred the nation. Many good citizens approved.

As Eastern newspapers joined those of Chicago in arousing fright about anarchism, there was a general alarm throughout the country much like the fear of the Chicagoans who felt themselves threatened. Cleveland had never been so popular as he was after that bloody week in July. He is not treated so kindly by historians who have examined the sequence of events. These include the fact that both Mayor John P. Hopkins of Chicago and Governor Altgeld opposed federal intervention. It was recalled, also, that some of the judges, as well as Olney, were former railroad lawyers, that there was certainly no anarchism involved and that Debs was anything but a man of violence.

Besides, it was abundantly shown in a later official investigation made by Carroll D. Wright, and fully documented, that the policies of the Pullman Company were calculated to bring on just such a revolt as had occurred. Actually, the report said in an admirable summary, the real blame rested "with the people themselves and with the government for not adequately controlling monopolies and corporations, and for failing to protect the rights of labor and redress its wrongs."

This was a rebuke to Cleveland as well as to Olney. He ought to have moved to control these monopolies and to have redressed those wrongs. History had caught up with him and he had not been ready. But at a moment when otherwise he was isolated and weary, it seemed he was suddenly approved in a wave of gratitude that gave him comfort in his loneliness. It did not last. Within a few months, he was again the most unpopular of Presidents.

29

LOOKING back, it does seem that the inadequacy of Cleveland, who had many virtues, was an inadequacy of the nation itself and of the best men it had bred. It had not come into maturity; neither had they. It was not prepared for its responsibilities and its men did not even see what the responsibilities were. Democracies must have leaders who are the people's prophets and who act as their mentors. A prophet must see ahead and turn people's minds to the future. A mentor Cleveland was—a stern and determined one. A prophet he was not.

The productive machine, pouring out goods both from farm and factory, the railway systems being extended everywhere, the growing cities and the increasing population—all made problems of new dimensions. They required that some control and direction should be given that no individual and no corporation could furnish. This was because in the philosophy of free enterprise, each was supposed to compete with others to make profits; and none had any responsibility for general order or service. Only a public agency could furnish the general framework and formulate the rules. And public agencies must be invented and managed. This new role of leadership was not accepted by Cleveland.

In these changing circumstances, there still prevailed the same beliefs and virtues that had guided the pioneering settlers and the first industrialists. Cleveland had these. In his first administration they had given a needed check to the exploitation of government by those who were subverting it. But there was a subtler subversion, and he was gradually coming to understand that monopolies must be regulated and that there must be some better ways of handling labor problems. He still did not understand fully what was happening all around him. The transformation of the economy had occurred in his lifetime. But he had not really followed it. He had worked for the corporations and had been friends with their officials. It was distressing to conclude that their disruptive management was causing the disorder now appearing everywhere.

Now, in his second term, when he had new issues to contend with, he had only industry and virtue to meet them with. If he had been a reader, even, if not a student in the academic sense, he might have read what William D. Howells was saying about the society they both lived in; he might have learned from Hamlin Garland that the farmers of the plains were not the sort he had known as a boy in central New York. He might have learned from any of a number of different writers that theirs was a changing world. But he did not read and he did not truly understand.

There were politicians who might have met the challenge of national change better than Cleveland. There was, for instance, Governor Altgeld, with whom Cleveland had an exchange of bitter recriminations. Altgeld contended that the state had been excluded from opportunity to control the Illinois troubles by the intrusion of federal power; and it can be seen now that Cleveland's reply—that since the mails were being tampered with, the federal government had every right to intervene—was something thought up after the fact. He had failed to understand that a profound issue desperately needed solution.

There was a Supreme Court decision in 1895 that upheld Cleveland's calling out of the troops to meet an emergency, a decision that still stands as one of the supports of presidential and federal powers. But that decision did not uphold Olney's resort to injunction and the use of private armies as federal enforcement officers; and it did not exonerate the President for having made a faulty judgment. He might have forced the railroad managements to accept some sort of conciliation and he might have used his prestige to convict them of the injustices they were committing. Instead he used the power of his office to uphold their right to exploit their workers as they judged to be most profitable.

If the point is easily sustained that Cleveland was badly prepared for his new economic responsibility, he was even worse prepared for his duty as the arbiter of foreign policy, both by temperament and by preparation. It will be recalled that he had never journeyed abroad, and this implies much—first of all, a lack of interest. He was indifferent to other cultures and past civilizations. And, as well, he lacked a knowledge of diplomatic history as it taken shape in past years; and this was one field that had belonged to the presidency ever since Washington had taken it by default. There was no question here of trespassing on congressional prerogatives. Cleveland had the opportunity to have redefined the relations of the United States to neighbors and dependencies. But, again, he failed.

We may well begin with Hawaii. The simplistic attitudes of a virtuous man, who was also ignorant and prejudiced, are quite evident in what happened when Cleveland had to deal with the question of annexation. The demand that Hawaii be annexed by the United States came to him tainted; he saw the taint and reacted by rejecting the proposal. What he did not grasp was the evident fact that the destiny of the islands was to be American and that some way of arranging the transition from primitive independence to partnership was needed. What he determined on, with very little study, was rejection of what seemed to him a dishonorable act.

It has to be said that during the eighties and nineties, the question of further American expansion had not yet been decided. Most Republicans—and this included Blaine and Harrison—were outright imperialists; they felt that the nation's proper boundaries had not been reached. Most Democrats held the opposite view.

The Caribbean had begun to seem an inescapable responsibility and its islands would have a special relationship to the proposed isthmian canal. Hawaii was in a strategic position off the California coast—a long way off then, but still a danger in the possession of an unfriendly power. It was not certain that the nation had found its ultimate boundaries to north or south, either; Theodore Roosevelt would still be suggesting the annexation of Canada years in the future, and the Mexican boundaries were not really fixed in American minds. The war with Spain, to come in the presidency of Cleveland's immediate successor, would be only partly for Cuban liberation, if the truth were told; it would also have the intention of expelling a foreign power from so close a neighborhood. Ever since the Civil War, there had been controversy about the policy involved in all this. The parties were just beginning to take sides.

As for Cleveland, his mind was quite clear about expansion. He was against it. He was also against foreign influence in the areas around the United States; but he felt that it was only necessary to be firm in warning off all attempts at aggression. He had said frankly that he was not sure what the Monroe Doctrine meant; but he was sure that it involved keeping the Americas for Americans. He was even more strongly against European than American expansion.

It has to be recalled that at this time Britain was in the full tide of her imperial growth. Her Navy ruled the seas, and it was an era of naval power. Admiral Alfred T. Mahan and his school were beginning to advance the theory that sea power was necessary to American survival. But the existing Navy could not be compared with that of Britain. It was the beginning of a long period when the United States would be sheltered by British sea power, a relationship that was unacknowledged and could not have been recognized by any politician, considering the strength of the Irish influence in the United States with its hatred of the British.

Cleveland had learned antipathy toward the British from Tim Mahoney and his other Irish friends and supporters; and his isolationism came from his inland breeding. All his attitudes toward other nations were consistent with his attitudes about the United States itself. The government had only to do honestly and competently the work immediately before it. So far as he was concerned he would not take on any more; and he judged British imperialism with a natively hostile mind. He had no view of a nation extending its influence, much less its territory, into the far places. True, it must take care that foreign influences did not encroach on close-by territory and become a threat. Those, however, were consistent attitudes.

At any rate, those were the attitudes he held, and he held them with the stubborn simplicity that was at once his virtue and his limitation. He would not have denied that the United States was becoming a world power, but he would have interpreted this in a different sense than the imperialists. If he had gone on being President, he might have gone to war with Spain as his successor McKinley did; but he would not have consented to the acquisition of the Philippines and Puerto Rico, or the establishment of a virtual protectorate over Cuba.

So when he seemed to be presented by a *fait accompli* about Hawaii as he was approaching inauguration in 1893, he was indignant; and one of his first actions in office was to repudiate it. An independent nation was to be taken over, and by fraud. It was intolerable. All he needed was a look at actions in themselves so indefensible that no explanation could justify their results. He did not ask himself whether, even if the behavior of American officials and armed services had been reprehensible, Hawaii still ought to be brought under the flag. All he realized was that a wrong had been done and a remedy needed to be applied.

He rested on indignation over the outrage that seemed to have been perpetrated on Queen Liliuokalani. It was a nasty piece of business, and no government could honorably accept its outcome. In the back of his mind was objection to expansion; but in the forefront was concern about a tricky maneuver.

Hawaii was a curious place by now, at a center of Pacific traffic lanes, with a mixed population of Hawaiians, Chinese, Portuguese and a small minority of Americans. Hawaiians by now were much less than half the whole number; but their Queen was in theory an absolute monarch. She was a primitive creature faced with the temptations of civilization; she was dissolute and incompetent. The commercial elite found her rule a constant threat to their interests. It was her prerogative, she felt, to cut off heads if it pleased her, and certainly to regulate commerce according to whim. Hers was not a government, it was a tribal court.

The traders and planters who now carried on the commerce and operated the plantations were mostly American, the descendants of missionaries who had gone out from New England to convert the natives. They had kept their Yankee shrewdness in business affairs, but their puritanical inheritance by now notably failed to govern their commercial customs.

They had two ambitions for the islands: the first was to

monopolize its economic life; the other was to consolidate their power by setting up a government run by themselves. The first called for the exclusion of other nationals, notably the British, and, lately, the Germans, who were showing ambitious interest in the strategic Pacific center. The second called for annexation to the United States. They went about it without reference to the moral standards they professed, and the result was in process of consummation when Cleveland took over from Harrison.

It was a somewhat complicated conspiracy, but it clearly involved displacing the Queen, setting up a provisional government and ostensibly legitimizing it by calling in United States Marines. A provisional government had occupied the palace and the Queen was in custody when appeal for annexation was made to Washington. Harrison had given his hurried consent, and the deal was already made when Cleveland was inaugurated. He refused to accept it and sent an investigator who reported that there had been a conspiracy against the Queen and that the American consul and the Navy had been involved. The illegality of all that had been done was obvious. There was no doubt, either, of the intention to use annexation as a way of establishing an economic dictatorship by the merchants and landowners.

In Cleveland's book this was enough. He repudiated recognition, ordered the Navy to desist, opted for the restoration of the bizarre Queen and, when there was a furor of protest, referred the whole matter to the Congress in a long message reciting the facts and his conclusions. There was much subsequent argument, but the provisional government, wholly illegitimate, did stay in power and, after a Senate investigation, was recognized by the United States.

In this as in so much else, Cleveland had been both right and wrong. He had acted in a way called for by the honor of the nation but a way that would have closed to it a national necessity. If he had prevailed, the British would have taken over the islands and an indispensable outpost would have been lost. A destined state of the Union and an essential shield would have remained in a sort of limbo until a later generation somehow arranged matters as they must be arranged. What he might have done was to set up a self-governing protectorate.

To consider the other notable incident involving foreign relations—that of the Venezuela-British boundary dispute—is to see Cleveland in a somewhat different role, but operating from the same base of principle. A wrong was being done; it was being done in an area that was a responsibility of the United States; a just arrangement must therefore be worked out. The United States wanted nothing except the settlement of a bothersome dispute in such a way that the national interest would be protected from encroachment.

The dispute involved a disagreement between British Guiana and Venezuela going back to the British takeover of Guiana from the Dutch in 1814. A long stretch of jungle between the two countries had been defined in such a way that later claims to it by both sides could hardly be adjudicated with any precision. This gave the aggressive British an excuse for expanding their interests in South America, but their designs had been resisted by Venezuela. There had been several attempts to arrive at a settlement, but neither side would compromise.

Now that the British were without question the paramount sea power they had no intention of relinquishing their interest in the area. Some time before, they had landed forces in Central America to collect debts the governments there would not pay. There had been no effective opposition to this by the United States; it was evidently concluded that the Monroe Doctrine, guaranteeing protection to any country in the hemisphere, did not extend to protecting the exasperating Central American governments. Venezuela had been exasperating, too. The successive regimes were unstable; they were corrupt and elusive; dealing with them was quite impossible. Besides, the quarrel with the British had become a political issue which a succession of Venezuelan dictators seemed not to want to settle, preferring to use it to detract attention from their erratic behavior in other areas.

Recurrent bouts of negotiation had become routine. But in the early 1890s the British had indicated an intention to extend their claims to the jungle at the mouth of the Orinoco River, an extension which, if successfully carried out, would give them control over a huge region on the shoulder of the continent.

The United States had never been indifferent to the conclusion of this issue. In Cleveland's first administration an offer of arbitration had been made. It had been renewed by Harrison. Now that Cleveland was again President, he indicated to the British that their delay in submitting to arbitration had become inexcusable. He suspected a scheme to wait until American attention was concentrated elsewhere and then to move in. The more he thought about it, the more annoyed he became.

He pushed the matter. In the midst of his attempt to get British attention, Walter Q. Gresham, the Secretary of State, died, and Cleveland appointed Olney to succeed him. Olney was not one to accept excuses or to tolerate dilatory tactics. When the British continued to evade and delay, his temper rose. In June 1894, the American government sent the following message to the British:

By the frequent interposition of its good offices at the instance of Venezuela . . . by pressing for arbitration of the disputed boundary . . . by expressing its grave concern whenever new instances of British aggression upon Venezuelan territory have been brought to its notice, the Government of the United States has made it clear to Great Britain and the world that the controversy is one in which both its honor and its interests are involved. . . .

● ● ●

. . . today, the United States is practically sovereign on this continent, and its fiat is law upon the subjects to which it confines its interposition.

An answer was demanded before the Congress met in December. When none came, Cleveland and Olney were convinced that their suspicion of British intentions was correct, but in his December message to Congress, Cleveland only reiterated that the dispute urgently needed settlement:

When such report [concerning the boundary] is made and accepted, it will, in my opinion, be the duty of the United States to resist by every means in its power, as a wilful aggression upon its rights and interests, the appropriation by Great Britain of any lands or the exercise of governmental jurisdiction over any territory which after investigation we have determined of right belongs to Venezuela.

In making these recommendations, I am fully alive to the responsibility incurred, and keenly realize all the consequences that may follow.

. . . there is no calamity which a great nation can invite which equals that which follows from a supine submission to wrong and injustice, and the consequent loss of national self-respect and honor, beneath which are shielded and defended a people's safety and greatness.

A week later the British answer came. It had two parts. The first discussed the Monroe Doctrine, the other concentrated on the dispute. The doctrine, the British said, did not extend, as Cleveland had contended, to compelling arbitration whenever a dispute over boundaries arose; and, with respect to the immediate dispute, British claims were reasonable and Venezuela had repeatedly evaded a settlement. There could be no submission of legitimate claims to the judgment of a foreign tribunal, especially when the Venezuelan contentions were obviously extravagant and put forward for political purposes with no expectation of their acceptance.

Neither Cleveland nor Olney was in a mood to accept instruction from the British about the meaning of the doctrine. Nor would they admit that impartial arbitration was beyond the concern of the United States. There followed a confrontation that displayed a belligerence beyond the necessities of the case and can only be explained as arising from the irascibility of Olney added to the annoyance of Cleveland at being treated to a lesson in elementary diplomacy.

Between them, they composed a message to the Congress that might well have led to war. That it did not was owed to British reasonableness—and perhaps to British preoccupation with problems elsewhere. What the message proposed was that the United States should determine what the boundary ought to be and, having determined it, should enforce its acceptance.

The Congress immediately authorized a commission for the purpose of determining the boundary. There were a few to say, aghast, that the President had gone too far. He had actually spoken as though the enforcement he had spoken of meant enforcement by arms. But most of the nation rose to his support. He had asserted a principle of the kind that held them together. It was what a President should do.

In the end there was no war and there was an arbitration. The decision was not handed down until 1899, years after Cleveland's final retirement; but almost at once there was a noticeable change in the British attitude. Before long their statesmen were insisting that between the English-speaking nations there could never again be hostilities. Their interests were mutual; they had only to find reasonable accommodations.

The strong words had that effect. They also had the immediate effect of lifting American spirits at a time of terrible distress. The uplift could not last; misery was too general. But, for the moment, troubles were forgotten and a wave of prideful exhilaration swept over the whole country. Cleveland had handled the affair well—it was one of the few triumphs of his second administration—and the country recognized it.

30

THERE had been Presidents before Cleveland who had gone through difficult years. There had even been some who, in the later years of their administrations, had lost the confidence of many former supporters—to the extent, a few times, of not being renominated. This had happened to both Adamses, to Pierce, to Buchanan and to Hayes.

Usually there had been a partisan reason, as when Jackson deliberately undermined the younger Adams; less frequently, there had been circumstances to overcome that had proved too difficult. American circumstances changed with disconcerting rapidity and Presidents were apt to be unprepared. Americans would have to look a good way back to find a President who had been able to see what the times called for and to furnish the leadership expected of him. Only Lincoln of the line as far back as Polk in 1845 had satisfied that requirement.

In fairness it has to be said that what needed to be done was often impossible. It was prohibited either by the custom of the country and its government or by the ingrained limitations of mind imposed by training. Incompetence was not a usual reason.

The bewilderment of this good man, as, one after another, his efforts failed and as, one after another, his supporters defected, is reflected only in his private correspondence. There was no show of despair in his public appearance. Nor did he admit to himself that he was finishing his presidency a failure. He continued to consider that others were mistaken and that he was right. He would go on clinging to this belief all his life.

We have seen the stubborn policies that would be responsible for the Democratic debacle in the mid-term elections in 1894. The attempt at tariff reform was coming to a humiliating end. Repeated attempts to bolster the gold standard for money had alienated the West and much of the South; worse, it had marked the President as an ally of Wall Street. Meeting violence, or imagined violence, with force in the numerous labor troubles caused by the depression had marked him as an enemy of labor. This left him few friends.

What remained to him was a small core of sound-money men, mostly financiers and their satellites, and a few of the mugwumps who had formerly been so enthusiastic. What compromises he had made, at the urging of his political advisers, had dismayed the good-government people. They would no longer cleave to him as the embodiment of the integrity they had longed for in public service. These people, moreover, usually belonged in the Republican party. A conservative Democrat was something unnatural. To retain leadership of his party, he had to find accommodation with wild Westerners and alien Southerners, and Cleveland would prefer a relationship less strained.

Cleveland may have been right to judge that a majority of the people wanted sound money. After the election of 1896 it would seem so. But most of those who felt this way were Republicans. The Democrats were now a soft-money party. They had elected him, it is true; but every month of his presidency had made more of them regret it. They would have been happier if Harrison had won again; if he had, they would at least have been fighting a Republican and not a Democrat.

The result of his alienation from so many legislators and the excoriation he was daily subjected to in the newspapers (the approval he got because of his suppression of disorder in Chicago lasted no more than a week or two) was a withdrawal from as many unpleasant contacts as possible. Until October of 1894 he stayed most of the time with his family at Gray Gables. So far as he was concerned, the congressional election did not require his participation. He had never believed in active campaigning on the part of presidential candidates, and he believed in it even less for incumbents. He said no word for any congressional candidate or about any policy the candidates presumably had to defend.

Most of them abandoned the policies he stood for, especially

Caricature of President Cleveland (*Courtesy of The New-York Historical Society, New York City*)

sound money and discipline for labor, and nothing they could say would make the tariff record more respectable. If Cleveland had said anything, it would have contradicted what others were saying. It was perfectly clear to everyone with political sensitivity that the party was in for a beating such as had seldom before been administered. And the universal feeling was that the blame was Cleveland's and his alone. Privately he blamed the agrarian radicals. And his dislike for them deepened into hatred.

It was a truly terrible beating. In the House of Representatives in 1892–94, there had been 219 Democrats and 127 Republicans. In that elected in November for 1894-96, there were 104 Democrats and 244 Republicans—an almost complete reversal. Also there had arisen a third party that might well supersede the Democrats altogether as the Republicans had once superseded the Whigs. The Populists had polled one and a half million votes. They now had six senators and seven members of the House.

It is fairly expected that mid-term elections may go against the party in power; but this may not at all indicate that the party's President has lost the country's confidence. More often it is the result of the party's reluctance to follow his leadership or, under the whip of lobbyists, to neglect the national interest for that of private ones. In this case, however, Cleveland was involved. The leadership he had given was in the unpopular direction. Moreover, he was obviously overwhelmed by the economic disaster that was still deepening with every passing month. It was not generally held that Presidents ought to take any drastic measures for recovery; according to the prevalent theory of free enterprise, they could not. Still it had always been true, however inconsistent, that Presidents were blamed for national disasters. Cleveland was being blamed now.

In another system of government, an administration repudiated as this had been would have been replaced at once by another. The American arrangement was different. The President, like other elected federal officials, had a fixed term. He had to go on even if he seemed to have lost the confidence of the country and even if he had a hostile majority in the Congress to contend with. This was now what Cleveland had to look forward to—two years of

President Cleveland (*Courtesy of The Buffalo and Erie County Historical Society*)

congressional hostility, as well, it appeared, as two years of public disapproval. It was not a pleasant prospect.

The outlook was made more sinister by the worsening depression. For unemployment was growing worse; prices were continuing to fall; and the miseries of many families were reaching the level of absolute deprivation. There was actual starvation, and the winter would bring to a situation already terrible even worse trials. How could people without jobs, without protection from landlords and with charities exhausted—how could they even survive? It would seem incredible to later generations, but it was accepted then, that public resources would not be made available for relief, that no work would be organized by government and that no kind of protection against the repeated strokes of fate would be provided.

It seems equally incredible, but is the fact, that Cleveland's most strenuous efforts during that time of terror were given to the issuance of bonds needed to pay the government's running expenses, now that its usual revenues were so depleted. Dependence on customs revenues proved to be risky; when there were few imports, the yield could not be large. Three times during this year of tensions and crises, bond issues had to be floated. They had to be bought by syndicates of bankers, since sale to the public failed— people were poor. This led to further confirmation, his enemies thought, that Cleveland was the banker's man in the government. The financiers took the bonds, then sold them to investors at a profit easily interpreted as excessive.

This method of financing was made necessary by another consideration besides that of having funds to pay governmental debts. It served also to protect the gold reserve. This was considered to be dangerously low if it fell below one hundred million. Because there was other currency marked as legal tender (silver and greenbacks), the business of exchanging it for gold at the Treasury grew month by month. The gold was then hoarded by those who received it from the Treasury as being the only really valuable medium of exchange. Gold also disappeared abroad. It went to pay for the American securities foreigners were selling because they no longer had confidence in the American economy.

It was found that when bond issues were sold to the public they paid for them in legal tender other than gold. This did not serve to protect the reserve. But when sold to syndicates of financiers, it could be specified that they should be paid for in gold; and this did increase the reserve.

Throughout this year Cleveland and his Secretary of the Treasury, Carlisle, spent an inordinate amount of time in devising ways to protect the reserve. It was a constant worry. It clearly seems to have been their view that if the ability of the government to meet its obligations in this way was impaired, there would have been something like a debacle. Their efforts to protect the gold reserve were constantly thwarted by the Congress. That body refused to change a law so that protection would be made easier, returning the advice that the sooner the nation went "off gold" the better. Also, there was mounting agitation for the infusion of *more* cheap currency into the system. Legislators who had been sound-money men until now began to defect as they saw how strong the silverites were becoming, and the defections became wholesale as the elections approached and it became obvious how immense the Democratic losses were going to be.

Cleveland was left with few political friends and with no effective allies. He could only go on acting with such authority as he had. When the gold reserves fell to half what the experts thought they ought to be, and there was a prospect that the government would soon not be able to meet its obligations, he and the Secretary offered one bond issue after another.

These did not build up the gold reserve, although they made it possible to meet expenses, so a later issue was offered on the condition that it be paid for in gold. But there was nothing to stop those who had cheaper money from exchanging it for the gold in this increased reserve. And within days or weeks there was still another crisis.

One of these was so serious, and was met in so questionable a way, that Cleveland's remaining friends were alienated in considerable numbers. There were even momentary rumors that he profited personally from the arrangement. That this suspicion was completely unjustified, and that the transaction had really been made inevitable by those who were subsequently loudest in their denunciations of him, seemed to Cleveland the last irony.

The method adopted to meet the financial crisis came to be known as the affair of the "Morgan Bonds." It was given the name because J. P. Morgan, the most powerful of all the world's financiers, devised and carried through the scheme, which in the end netted him a substantial profit and branded Cleveland once again as the friend of the financiers. Morgan's plan was that the government should issue one hundred million dollars' worth of bonds, to be paid for, not through open bidding, but by a syndicate organized by him. Once the financial world knew of the transaction, Morgan argued, the "dollar would be saved" and confidence in the American economy would be restored throughout the financial world.

The necessity for the sale of bonds to a private syndicate arose early in February of that terrible winter of 1895. It was associated with the failure of a bill—called the Springer bill after its congressional sponsor—which would have enabled the government to issue bonds redeemable only in gold from public sale, and would have authorized the government to *stop* recirculating greenbacks and silver certificates when they came into the Treasury. It would also have required that in the future, customs duties should be paid only in gold.

Cleveland had asked twice for the passage of such legislation as the crisis loomed, the last time by special message. He was encouraged by a small section of the Eastern press; but he was excoriated by papers in Atlanta and in Western centers. Omaha papers spoke of "bonds, bankruptcy, and disaster," and the Atlanta *Constitution* spoke of the act as originating in "hotbeds of gold-buggery and Shylockism." It was predicted that if it should pass, prices would fall even further, perhaps another 25 per cent. The ruin already spreading would become irretrievable.

In this atmosphere, the Springer bill proved to have no chance whatever. On an early February day, it was defeated in the House. In anticipation of defeat, the Assistant Secretary of the Treasury, W. E. Curtis, was sent to New York to counsel with financiers there. Cleveland, after weeks of constant worry and endless meetings with Carlisle and others in the Cabinet, had reached the limit of his resources. No one could think of anything that would save the situation. The only hope was that the bankers, who after all had much at stake, might make some suggestion.

2 5 7

Curtis met with Morgan and with August Belmont, who was the second most powerful of the financiers. The bankers agreed to see whether they could take one hundred million in bonds and bring the gold from Europe. This was the scheme that Curtis brought back to Washington. Both Carlisle and Cleveland were well enough aware of the consequences any such private deal would have. It might give the financial community confidence, but it would so enrage the silverites that almost any reprisal might be looked for. They rejected the scheme.

A week later they were confronted with the certainty that all the gold in the Treasury would be gone within a week. On the evening of the Springer bill's defeat, Morgan, Belmont and their lawyers (including Cleveland's former partner, Francis Lynde Stetson) journeyed to Washington in Morgan's private car. They knew that Cleveland overnight would have to make the decision he had been hoping so long to avoid. If he decided the new issue of bonds should be opened for public sale under the old conditions, it would not only be too late, but would not serve to restore the Treasury's gold supply. Automatically the country would be "off gold."

Panic was spreading in the financial community, and the withdrawal of bullion to ship abroad was massive. Within days there would be none left, and the inability to meet its obligations would have to be admitted by the government. But still Cleveland hesitated, and at first he refused to see Morgan and Belmont. He brooded all night long over his dilemma. Next morning he agreed to a meeting and, together with Carlisle, he met the bankers in his study. He was by now desperate. But he still had a faint hope that a public sale might be possible.

Morgan assured him that this could not be arranged in time. They argued for several hours. But when Cleveland was told in a telephone message that only nine million in gold remained in the Treasury and when Morgan told him that he knew of one check for twelve million that was outstanding, a fact confirmed by Carlisle, he knew that he must accept the private offer.

Morgan's syndicate, under the contract drawn up by Stetson, would furnish sixty-two million in gold to be brought from Europe in exchange for bonds; and the bankers would do their best to protect the Treasury from gold withdrawals in the future. Since they controlled the exchange market, Cleveland knew they could make good this promise.

The deal saved the dollar. When the contract became public, withdrawals stopped and gold began to come back from abroad. When the syndicate offered the bonds for sale a little later, the price was considerably above the rate of payment to the government, and this gain infuriated the opposition. Much was said about this that seemed to Cleveland most unfair. It was true that he had consented to a deal that was profitable to the bankers; but saving the gold standard was surely a praiseworthy action.

Bryan and his colleagues among the Populists denounced the deal in repeated speeches and the entire press beyond the Alleghenies let itself go without restraint. It spoke of a "bunco game," of "Jews and aliens" and of the "Shylocks in Wall Street."

The winter was hard; the suffering both in city and country was the most terrible within the memory of men; and the blame lay upon the President. If he had saved the gold standard, he had not saved the country. But he never regretted his action. Years after his retirement, he said so. By that time, no one was likely to accuse him of profiting from the deal himself, but he was still not forgiven for allowing the financiers to profit or for holding to gold when easy money was about to be achieved.

It never occurred to Cleveland, all during his long struggle for sound money, that the nation might be allowed to depart from the gold standard without disaster. It seemed to him elementary that its protection was worth all the trouble he went to and even the hints that he had been dishonest. That it prolonged the depression, favored the creditor class and was the cause of immense hardship for millions of people was something that seemed to him the allegation of crackpots.

Why? Later governments, including that of the United States, felt forced to suspend gold payments and to raise the price level by deliberate inflation, thus allowing debts to be paid and a new start of economic activity to be made. Also, they refused to tolerate unemployment and all its attendant ills. If government funds had to be used to prevent cold and hunger, they were used even if they had no gold backing. So why did Cleveland fight so hard for gold?

The explanation is that he followed a simple formula: it was honest to redeem currency as the contract called for. Above all, he was honest. That there was a higher honesty for governments and their Presidents he never comprehended.

3 1

CLEVELAND is the statesman in the public life of the United States who best represents the classic tragedy defined by Aristotle: he was destroyed—or his power and influence were— by his own strength and virtue. To recapitulate, what had gained him the presidency and regained it for him after an interval was the conviction among the voters that he was a man of immovable integrity in a time of sleazy morality. This extended to all his judgments. He would do nothing and would allow nothing to be done that he or any other might profit from. He would give no favor and accept none, except in the public interest. In the sense understood by all Americans, he was a man of conscience.

But it was his impeccable honesty that set him first against the tariffs and then against inflation; and both objectives were of doubtful use in economic crisis. It set him also against taking measures necessary to the leadership of his party that required consultation, compromise, and yielding to the demands of patronage and privilege. And he could not make those appeals and urgings that would have brought public opinion to his support. With that opinion upholding him, he might have stayed the decline of his influence. But he thought people should follow without urging, and if they were indifferent, there was little he could do.

To make everything as bad as it could be, his conviction that inflation was dishonest became an obsession. He would grant his opponents nothing. They seemed to him, more and more, to be men of bad faith, using demogogic appeals to make worse and worse a popular fallacy that in the end would ruin the country. This was the more dangerous for him because they belonged to his own party and, before his eyes, in spite of all he could do, were capturing it.

His last years in office were truly tragic. One disaster piled on another. The underlying weakness was that a depression had occurred while he was in power. If in the belief of the time there was nothing to be done but hope for the best, it was still true that the President and his policies were blamed. Blame centered in his clinging to sound money, his refusal on every occasion to yield to the silverites or to others who had monetary schemes to offer. If only he would give way, it was widely believed, something magical would occur. This became so deep a conviction that, after the defeat of 1894, the politicians of the party began conspicuously to disengage themselves from the administration. And presently they attacked the President himself.

As the Democratic convention approached in 1896, it was evident that the Democratic party was about to disappear into the maw of the Populists. The gold Democrats of the East were fewer and fewer. But a long time before that the signs had been unmistakable. Cleveland had lost contact with his party's politicians almost altogether. He no longer had many friends and supporters and those he did have were quiet. Those who were loud and conspicuous in the party competed to see who could be the most extreme in denunciation. The fanatics descended gradually to vulgarisms intended as appeals to the enraged farmers in the backwoods. When "Pitchfork Ben" Tillman of South Carolina began campaigning for the Senate in the back country of his state he shouted—and was delighted with the invention—"Send me back to Washington, and I'll tickle Cleveland's fat ribs with my pitchfork!"

A President whose power has leaked away still has to go on somehow. But there comes a time when everyone knows how weak he is. He gets little pity, curiously enough, considering the glamour he is invested with at his inauguration. No outrage is too extreme. And there begins that terrible round of derogatory stories, sometimes obscene, that seems to delight people as the twilight of a career sets in.

The loss of prestige was bound to affect the President's behavior. It affected that of his family as well. In his last year there was

Cleveland in his later years (*Courtesy of The Firestone Library, Princeton University, Princeton, New Jersey*)

little gaiety in Frances Cleveland's White House. Hardly any entertaining was done. And as a family they escaped whenever they could to Gray Gables. Even in Washington they lived most of the time at Woodley and Cleveland used the Executive Mansion only for office duties and the most necessary entertaining. He seemed to be repelled by the place where he had failed.

There was still the priceless compensation of his marriage and of a still-increasing family (a third girl was born on July 7, 1895). Frances had her children; and if official social life had slowed, she still cultivated the circle of friends who came to Woodley. It was enough for her. It would have been enough for Cleveland, too, if he could have escaped the conviction of his incompetence that somehow joined itself with the continuing conviction that he was right. As things were, he was a dogged but miserable man, and he showed it.

Throughout 1895 and on into 1896, the country went on struggling with the economic paralysis that still held it in rigid clamps. Businesses continued to fail, no bank was safe, unemployment crept higher. There were ragged soup lines in the cities and empty cupboards in the villages. Farm families lived on what they could store from their fields for the winter. And Cleveland was blamed for it all.

He was blamed for more than the depression. He was held responsible for a series of the most reactionary decisions ever reached by the Supreme Court, each calculated to further enrage an already furious section of the electorate. One of these judgments invalidated the income tax provided for, it will be recalled, as an added title in the Wilson Tariff Act. Another, just a week later, upheld the injunction against Eugene V. Debs issued during the Chicago strike (in re Debs 158 U.S. 566). And still others notably the E. C. Knight case (156 U.S. 1) made almost impossible further attempts to check the monopolies that were strangling so many small enterprisers and exploiting their consumers.

All these were judgments that would in time, and in one way or another, be reversed: the income tax decision by constitutional amendment, the trust opinion by reversal of the court itself and the use of injunctions in labor disputes by legislation.

It was Cleveland's ill luck to have been President not only

during prolonged economic distresses and to have been bound either to do nothing or to do the wrong things for recovery, but, as well, to have been in office when the court made these provocative efforts to stem the movement for change and control. It was, of course, another kind of ill luck that made him incapable of meeting the social and economic crises he was confronted with. There is a temptation to ascribe it to his having acquired the liberal part of his education mostly in Buffalo saloons. But he belonged to a whole group of reactionaries who had excellent educations in the academic sense—Justice Brewer of the Supreme Court, for instance, who upheld the Debs conviction, who felt that an income tax did not accord with the Constitution and who saw no way to bring the offending trusts within federal jurisdiction.

In a sense, all these social disasters—the Debs decision, the rejection of the income tax, the failure to find the trusts illegal—were part of the same Aristotelian tragedy. All were the result of virtue—or at least the pursuit of it. Debs was the victim of Richard Olney's persecution; and Olney was Cleveland's choice for Attorney General. The reason for choosing him, it must be noted, was because he promised, in Cleveland's kind of judgment, to be the best possible Attorney General. He was honest, aggressive and resourceful. That he was also looking for trouble and determined to punish railwaymen if he could get at them Cleveland ought to have known if he did not. And if he allowed Olney to get at them, and if Debs and the whole labor movement suffered and were alienated, that followed from his picking, with no political advantage in mind and solely because of ability, a man who corresponded with his own definition of excellence.

Even after Olney had led him into the trap that made organized labor his enemy, Cleveland had allowed him to prepare and prosecute the antitrust cases. The prosecution was done in slipshod fashion and the cases were lost. Olney afterward seemed rather pleased than otherwise, and no wonder. He had hoped he would not win. The trusts were controlled by his friends and former clients. He had no wish to see them restricted. Cleveland's good man was thus good only for the exploiters of the people, and Cleveland was inevitably involved.

It was the same with the income tax. Only indirectly, but still actually, Cleveland was involved in the result. He did not appoint Justice Brewer, but he and the justice were of the same breed of corporation lawyer. As President, he had spoken harshly of the trusts when they had so boldly penetrated the Senate and written tariffs to suit themselves. But he had nothing to say about the income tax decision, and he might very well have reached the Court's conclusion for himself. Olney did.

In these last years and months of his presidency we have a man to deal with who was being punished by his own intractability. If we judge from his private correspondence, he still stiffly held to his views even though his party was succumbing to opposing ones. What he did not understand was *why* he was being punished. If reason and virtue were on his side, it was surely hard to be deserted and condemned. There is no other way to say it: he whined. He felt so sorry for himself that he anticipated the end of his term with a relief that was almost joy. The inauguration of his successor would be the signal for his release from the burden he could no longer carry with his old energy and determination. His mood is reflected in the following letters, typical of many:

To Richard Watson Gilder, December 1894:
I am so depressed during these days . . . I am sure I never was more completely in the right path of duty than I am now; but it is depressing enough to have no encouragement from any quarter. I believe I shall hold out, but I doubt if I shall ever advise anyone to lose the support of party in the hope of finding support among those who beyond partisanship profess a patriotic desire for good government.

To Ambassador Bayard, February 1895:
. . . I want to thank you from the bottom of my heart for several very kind and very comforting letters . . . I have been dreadfully forlorn these many months, and sorely perplexed and tried.

To Don M. Dickinson, February 1895:
Somehow the kindly congratulations and remembrances of friends were peculiarly gratifying to me on my latest birthday. I suppose it is accounted for partly by the fact that as we grow older, kindness touches us more nearly, and perhaps another reason in my particular case, is found in the fact that I have had some occasion to feel unusually forlorn during the last year. Troubles in official duty follow each other thick and fast, and we are out of one perplexity to immediately face another.

To E. C. Benedict, February 1895:
I am thankful to you for the encouraging words you write me in regard to my course in financial matters. Such expressions are my only comfort, except my wife and babies, in these troublous perplexing days . . .

Before his release was final, he had one last ordeal to survive, very nearly the worst of all. This was the capture of the Democratic party by the Populists with his despised enemy Bryan as its candidate to be his successor. In the last election, the Populists had formed their own party. Now they determined to campaign as Democrats, to *be* Democrats and to rid the party of men like Cleveland who were so opposed to their views.

32

AS the year 1895 came to its last months and winter set in, the now familiar lines of ragged men could be seen in every city, waiting for a bowl of soup and a piece of bread from charity centers. The storms blew down upon farm homes with empty cupboards and with children hardly clothed well enough to make their way through the snow to school. The smell of poverty and the despair of idleness had penetrated everywhere.

Cleveland, presiding over a nation thus paralyzed, seems to have done his best to ignore what he could not change. His letters during the winter and his official communications were mostly devoted to two issues—the Venezuelan-British border dispute and the success of the bond issues that paid the government's way and secured the maintenance of an adequate gold reserve. He could count on party support for his stand against Britain. Presidents nearly always could expect support for a strongly nationalistic foreign policy. But on the question of the gold reserve there were many party members who had passed now from simple doubt to infuriated attacks. His unmoved holding to principle gave them at least something to roar about. Cleveland recognized the dangers and wrote to Governor Stone of Mississippi about them in May 1895:

[Democrats] should deceive themselves no longer, nor longer refuse to look in the face the results that will follow the defeat, if not the disintegration, of the Democratic party upon the issue which tempts them from their allegiance. If we should be forced away from our traditional doctrine of sound and safe money, our old antagonist will take the field on the platform which we abandon, and neither the votes of reckless Democrats nor reckless Republicans will avail to stay their easy march to power.

The Congress met in December 1895. He asked it, as he had the last one, for legislation to make bond issues more certain to protect the gold reserve. The remaining Democrats were obstreperously obstructive; they were largely silverites. The Republicans, with an election year impending, had no thought of making things easier for a Democratic administration. They were inclined to insist that if the President needed more revenue, the tariffs ought to furnish it; higher tariffs, not bond issues, were the answer to the Treasury's problem.

There was a question whether a new bond issue that became necessary at the opening of 1896 should be privately disposed of to another syndicate got together by Morgan, or whether it should be sold by subscription. Cleveland and Carlisle had no intention of bringing upon themselves another deluge of abuse, and they were intensely gratified to have the public sale succeed. The bankers had said it would fail, and this had added to Cleveland's worry. Actually it raised the gold reserve to a level believed sufficient to secure it for the rest of his term—this in addition to providing revenue. It had been a long struggle. Four times he had had to go through these financing crises with every effort being made by his enemies to make certain that he would fail. Four times the country had been on the verge of going off gold, and since he was more and more convinced that this would be the ultimate disaster, each crisis had been more agonizing than the one before.

These bonds had hardly been disposed of when the signs began to be unmistakable that the party at its convention would declare for soft money and everything Cleveland had fought for would be repudiated. He made such efforts as he could to stop the degeneration. He had already entered on a correspondence with political leaders in the West and South who, he believed, were still "sound," reassuring them to the extent that he could. He caused the members of his Cabinet to speak of the gold standard wherever the opportunity offered; but he was still, himself, bound by his conception of Presidential decorum, and he kept out of the open fight.

A controversy arose about the city where the convention should be held in July. The Democratic National Committee met in January and, as a compromise between St. Louis, wanted by the silverites, and New York, wanted by the sound-money members, Chicago was determined on. This was not much of a compromise; it practically resigned the galleries to Populist sympathy and invited the attacks of a hostile press.

There were large meetings of silverites in various places, beginning in winter, and, actually, in early February, the Senate passed a free-coinage bill. Twenty-four Democrats voted for it and only fifteen against. When it got to the House it was killed by a refusal to concur; but it was Republicans who furnished the votes. From then, Cleveland was a despairing man. The party situation had escaped from his control and it was futile to hope that it might be retrieved. What could he do? Cleveland at least pretended to believe that sanity would prevail at the convention and that a sound money plank would be adopted. He still hoped a candidate from his wing of the party might be nominated. Perhaps, he hoped, Carlisle.

But all during April and May, as state conventions met to select delegates for Chicago and to adopt resolutions, the soft-money trend was apparent. Some delegates actually denounced the administration. In such conventions as those in Kentucky and Virginia, Cleveland's name was booed and hissed. The Kentucky performance ended any hope that Carlisle might be the nominee. With his home state against him, he stood no chance. By the middle of June, the silverites had captured more than a majority of the delegates but not yet the two-thirds necessary for nomination. They could now adopt the platform they wanted (by simple majority), but it still remained to be seen whether they could force the acceptance of their candidate, whoever he might be.

Cleveland, in June, finally made the following public statement, printed in the New York *Herald*, June 17, 1896, expressing hope for a sound-money plank in the platform:

I have made no figures as to the probable action of delegates . . . to the National Convention, but I refuse to believe that when the time arrives for deliberate action there will be engrafted upon our Democratic creed a demand for a free, unlimited, and independent coinage of silver. I cannot believe this, because I know the Democratic party is neither unpatriotic nor foolish, and because it seems so clear to me that such a course will inflict a very great injury upon every interest of our country . . .

He must really have known that all was lost, but his statement did serve to rally the conservatives. There were editorials in the supporting newspapers, and William C. Whitney, Cleveland's onetime campaign manager, cancelled a trip to Europe and announced that he would head a campaign for a sound-money declaration by the party. He was joined by Governor William E. Russell of Massachusetts, who might under other circumstances have been the presidential nominee; he was one of the most personable politicians in the party.

Just at this time the Republican convention met. It was under the firm control of Mark Hanna, a new phenomenon in politics. He was a successful businessman who had turned to politics with the same energy and competence that had made him rich in a Cleveland, Ohio, iron business. He had become a power in Ohio politics and had made William McKinley governor. He now intended to make him President. It could be seen that he was well on his way. During the winter and spring he had corraled enough delegates to nominate McKinley—had "bought" them, his enemies said. And he was certain that the election would be won on the issue of sound money, which both he and McKinley favored. He and his delegates had not only nominated their favorite, but had conspicuously defeated the few silverites in the party. These had marched out of the convention when the gold plank was adopted and were speeded by shouts from the floor of "Go! Go! Go to Chicago!"

Throughout the West and much of the border as well as the South there was such a furor as the country had hardly ever known. Bryan, among others—but there were many others— traveled from one silverite convention to another, speaking, as well, in every meeting he could persuade to hear him. The gatherings of outraged Democrats could be roused to frenzies by the Boy Orator of the Platte. He was a remarkable speaker. His full and carrying voice was only part of his attraction. His argument was persuasive. He had a wealth of illustrative material. He knew the people to whom he spoke and they knew his style. His illusions were out of their experience. He called to their minds the anguish of the years just past. And he had a panacea. He was pushing with the arts of a political genius.

Cleveland left Washington late in June for Gray Gables. The convention in Chicago was due to meet the next week. When Whitney arrived with his small delegation of "goldbugs" they found so few friends that they knew their cause to be lost. The silverites were smelling victory, in their efforts to control the Democratic party. There was celebration in the streets, and the barrooms were jammed to the doors. The delegations from various cities and states carried their banners in impromptu parades and shouted to one another as they passed. The Bland club from St. Louis hoped to nominate the senator who was among the oldest of the silverites. There were others; but among the most enthusiastic was the Bryan club of Nebraska. If he had not been ineligible because of his foreign birth, Governor Altgeld of Illinois might well have been the favorite; but as it was, Bland seemed to be the man. There was a senatorial clique whose members had used diabolical ingenuity in knifing Cleveland. They met; and they, too, decided on Bland.

As a first victory for the Bland followers, Hill was rejected as temporary chairman and Senator Booth was elected. On Thursday the crisis came. Senator Jones read the platform offered by the committee. It not only repudiated Cleveland but referred to "trafficking with banking syndicates" and went on to condemn the use of injunctions in labor disputes. More generally, it condemned federal interference in local affairs. After Tillman had used the occasion to abuse the President in a way unknown in any former convention ("You ask us to endorse Cleveland's fidelity. In reply, I say he has been faithful unto death, the death of the Democratic party") and Governor Russell had made a plea for moderation and harmony, Bryan took the podium.

He was young and handsome, a vigorous figure, known to many of those present. As he began to speak, the twenty thousand present in the hall fell quiet. His clear and bell-like voice reached every corner. He launched into one of the most famous of all political orations, ever since known as "The Cross of Gold Speech." This, for Bryan, was the planned culmination of a campaign. He was a professional who meant to be carried into the presidency on the high tide of a movement for political dominance coming out of the West and South. He meant to speak for all those who owed debts and could not pay, for those who produced and could not sell, for the small folk exploited by the powerful ones.

Before Bryan rose to speak on that July day, the leadership of the new Democracy had not settled definitely on one man. Senator Bland was the oldest and most revered of the silverites. There were notorious agitators, many of them; but to nominate one of them would be to alienate all the moderates necessary to a successful movement. Bryan had calculated the conditions with an expert intelligence.

The Cross of Gold speech was not inflammatory. It was moving without being belligerent. It recited wrongs without bitterness. It offered an alternative now accepted widely as a panacea—the coinage of silver to supplement gold, thus increasing the supply of money and making the debtors' lot easier. There were millions now who believed this to be the way out of depression. There were millions who also believed that Cleveland was the representative of the "gold men," the bankers, the monopolists. When in his closing paragraph Bryan referred to the gold standard as an English rule, he spoke to the hearts particularly of the Irish but also of all those who had been conditioned by years of oratory to belief in an international conspiracy. It seemed to his hearers—most of them—that when he spoke for silver, he spoke for them:

They ask us why we say more about money than the tariff . . . We reply that protection has slain its thousands, the gold standard its tens of thousands. It is the issue of 1776 all over again. If they say we cannot have bi-metalism until some other nation assists, we reply that we will restore bi-metallism and let England adopt it because we have led the way. We shall answer their demand for the gold standard by saying to them, "You shall not press down upon the brow of labor this crown of thorns. You shall not sacrifice mankind upon a cross of gold!"

The speech was addressed to the amendment of the conservatives to the plank offered by the Resolutions Committee. When the applause had died down, the amendment was voted down by two to one. The party headed by Cleveland for twelve years, and by Tilden for twelve years before him, was now dead. The next day, on the fifth ballot, young Bryan was nominated for the presidency. The defeat was so complete that Cleveland had no defense. He was still President, but if he was a leader, he was one without a following. The conservatives could see no point in making a further effort within the party. Their recourse was quite obvious. They must assist in electing McKinley. The question in Cleveland's mind was whether this was indicated for him as well, and he wrote of his concern to Lamont:

I am perplexed concerning the course I should pursue. My inclination is to join the chorus of denunciation, but I am doubtful as to the wisdom of such action . . . it might do more harm than good . . . I am President of all the people, good, bad, or indifferent, and as long as my opinions are known, ought perhaps to keep myself out of their squabbles . . . In addition . . . no one of weight or judgment in political matters has advised me to speak out . . .

It was a delicate decision. He regarded Bryan as no Democrat at all; he was an interloper who had made a successful raid. His tenure would be temporary, It might be Cleveland's own duty as the legitimate leader of the party to repudiate the convention's choice, holding to a principle higher than that of loyalty to such a majority. He considered such a course carefully, discussing it with his Cabinet and with the friends he trusted most.

In the end he decided that the only course he could pursue with the dignity he must preserve was one of silence. This was not exactly neutrality, since everyone knew where he stood on the central issue and what he thought of Bryan. It was more a withdrawal. He was retreating into the shadows anyway. He would attend faithfully to his routine duties as President, but he would not intervene in the people's choice.

It may have been that this decision was made easier by the almost certain knowledge that Bryan would lose the election anyway. The campaign had hardly progressed into its second month before it was evident that although the Populists were practiced demagogues who knew how to make loud noises, they were far from commanding the votes of a national majority. The nomination of

Bryan and the adoption of an extreme platform had violated the first rule of politics—that no large body of voters should be excluded from their old affiliations. From the time of convention an effort to draw every possible voter into the fold is simple sense, but the silverites could not, and did not try to, draw in those who opposed them. Besides, the people would not support a sectional candidate. Bryan belonged to the prairies more than to the underprivileged he now said he meant to champion.

It was not until September, after a long retreat at Gray Gables, that Cleveland said anything at all. Then he sent a message to the convention in Louisville of the *National* Democratic party, a group that was the rather feeble effort of the conservatives to emphasize their belief that Bryan was no Democrat. In part, Cleveland's message read:

As a Democrat devoted to the principles and integrity of my party, I should be delighted to mingle with those who are determined that the voice of true Democracy shall not be smothered, and who insist that its glorious standard shall be borne aloft as of yore in faithful hands.

The most the Gold Democrats could hope for was to take a few votes away from Bryan and help to elect McKinley. Actually, even this was not necessary; Bryan was decisively defeated. Not until 1912, when the Republicans would be as badly split as the Democrats were in 1896—and on much the same sort of issue—would a Democrat be elected again. Was this long exclusion from power Cleveland's fault? Ought he to have held the party together on a moderate course? To have done so, if it would have been possible at all, he would have had to compromise with the Populists. The question whether it is better to give a little to gain much is one for a leader to judge. Another President might have done it that way. It would not have been in character for Cleveland. He had his principles and he stood on them.

33

S O far as Cleveland personally was concerned, the election was something of a vindication. Sound money had won even if the party had lost. Since early youth he had worked in and for the the party and had been honored by it, but it was his view that the Populists had stolen it; Bryan was a renegade and it would have been a disaster if he had won. When supporters and even members of the administration decided to support Bryan, as many did—including Hoke Smith, Cleveland's Secretary of the Interior—he regarded it as treachery.

But for a man of Cleveland's devotion to constitutional principle, this was a painful situation, and one he was never quite able to justify. Bryan had *not* stolen the nomination and the party had *not* abandoned customary processes. It had made the decisions of that year—written the platform and made the nominations—with the full use of the devices provided for that purpose. If he had kept to his lifelong custom of regularity, Cleveland should have taken part even after the conventions had gone for soft money. He should have bowed to the majority. In effect, he had walked out. That was not the action of a true Democrat. It was certain that the rest of his life would be made uneasy by this refusal to accept a decision legitimately made simply because he could not agree with it.

True, he did not make himself obstreperous. He did not rage up and down the states denouncing his former party colleagues. When once or twice, in his bitterness, he spoke out, the division in his mind could be detected. He had concluded once for all that honesty and integrity, the guides of his conduct, were involved with the gold standard. He was driven to a sort of civil disobedience by the silverites. But this defection was equally a violation of principle. What does a man do who must choose between two markers of his conscience?

We know what Cleveland did, even if we cannot know what agonies of the spirit he suffered. He continued to do his duty as President for the remaining months of his incumbency. Perhaps he tried to convince himself that McKinley would make a better President than Bryan would have made. But the Republican party had not changed from the time of Harrison, or, for that matter, had not departed from the attitudes of Blaine, Conkling and Arthur; and all of these had demeaned the high offices they had held. On everything but the money issue, the Republicans were as bad as ever in his eyes.

As the time for handing over the presidency approached, he may have wondered about the evident weakness of McKinley. The President-to-be seemed little more than a puppet for the more powerful men of his party. Mark Hanna had organized a tremendous businessmen's push, using Bryan's radicalism to scare them into making up a huge campaign fund. What would they get in return for their big contributions? Cleveland must have known that, even if the gold standard was kept, they would demand a tariff written even more closely to their specifications than the act he had refused to sign. This he cannot have liked, since lowered tariffs rated in his mind just below sound money as a measure of national honesty.

But there was another issue that had boiled up, one that would not wait for his retirement. He had to deal with it summarily, although it was complex and really needed more consideration. It did have some relation to issues he had dealt with before— Hawaii, for instance—but it was far more complex and there were far stronger pressures to be resisted. It was the quarrel, growing up early in 1895 and now rapidly becoming acute, over Cuba, where rebellion against Spanish rule was growing stronger. There were those who, for their own purposes, intended to thrust the nation into war.

From the presidential point of view, one trouble about the question was that, although the chief executive and commander in chief could see clearly what those who were agitating for war with

Spain were up to, the war's promoters were able to make the American people see the situation in quite another way. They dwelt on the horrors of the Spanish occupation in Cuba, reporting in detail the sufferings of the rebels, neglecting to say that the same cruelties were perpetrated by both sides. They played on the traditional American revulsion against colonialism and support for independence. But what they were after was the chance to replace the Spanish colonialists and themselves exploit Cuba and the Cubans.

It was even worse than this; the competition between two press magnates, Hearst and Pulitzer, was rapidly becoming a contest for credit in the opportunity closest at hand. Would Hearst, or would Pulitzer, push the nation into war? And which would benefit most from its sensations? Both were "yellow journalists," neither had the least scruple about exploiting the excitement they were able to create. It was a dangerous business, and although Cleveland's time was running out and the issue would last beyond his term, he set himself as he had before, to resist a force he regarded as evil.

There was nothing he could do to influence matters beyond his retirement. At least he could think of nothing, nor could Olney. At one time they considered the possibility of proposing to purchase the island from Spain. But if they then made a present of their purchase to the Cuban rebels, the United States would have spent something like a hundred million dollars with nothing to show for it except the removal of the Spanish overlordship. There was not the slightest chance that the Congress would approve such an expenditure.

The belligerence of the press and of other interests wanting war had infected the Congress. What they wanted, too, was intervention on the side of the Cuban rebels. There was a fever in both Houses that expressed itself in fiery denunciations of Spain and irrational praise of the Cuban demagogues who were clearly trying to substitute themselves for the Spanish administrators. Actually, the rebels would not suit the American interests unless the new men were ones they could control. But this attitude was offensive to those who were excited about the wrongs of the rebels and thought of intervention as leading to independence. They spoke grandly of liberty and self-determination; but they avoided mentioning the probability that the Cuban people, themselves, would have less liberty with dictators of their own than they had with the Spanish bureaucrats.

The situation in the island had degenerated rapidly during the winter of 1895-96. The rebels, made frantic by the repressions of the army sent to subdue them, adopted a policy of destruction. They would make the island worthless so that the Spanish would no longer want it. This brought every Cuban into the area of misery. The sugar crop of some million tons was reduced to one fifth that. Tobacco production was cut an equal percentage. The rich countryside was made worthless by sabotage. All Cuba was a shambles.

Cleveland and Olney felt that their best chance of bringing about conciliation lay in efforts to influence Spain. They could argue that insurrection had become immensely costly; it was bringing the nation into disrepute with others; and the struggle was quite obviously going against the occupying troops. But the Spanish were less willing to listen than they otherwise might have been because they knew, as everyone else did, that the rebellion could not have gone on if it had not had support from the United States. This, they said, was what Cleveland should do something about.

Olney used his best efforts to get some concession from the Spanish. All he got were delays and evasions that amounted to refusal. Meanwhile the administration did make a more vigorous attempt to stop the numerous Spanish expeditions, fitted out in American harbors, from reaching Cuba; and increased American patrols had more success. After Cleveland issued a proclamation of neutrality, the Navy had the authority it needed for interception.

It had the authority, but neither the Navy nor the commander in chief, Cleveland, could feel that there was adequate support for such a policy. There was a rising bellicosity in the Congress. It was added to by the chance Cleveland's enemies saw of embarrassing him once more. These enemies were not only Republicans who were conscious that they were entering on an election year; they were also those Democrats in the South and West who, every month, were allowing their frustrations more freedom. They did not hesitate now to attack their own President in the most immoderate terms. Nor did they hesitate to push for war if it would further their determination to discredit Cleveland. They meant to take possession of the party at convention time. They would beat down the Clevelandites in advance.

That this would contribute to the split of the party and make its defeat certain they refused to consider. Their long struggle against the ogres of Wall Street had destroyed all their customary political loyalties. They would expel the goldbugs, drive them into the Republican party and have a straight-out battle over the issue.

This made a strange and unnatural coalition between Western and Southern radicals and Eastern businessmen anxious for war. The debtors and creditors had come together in a common hatred. If the one group talked of freedom and Spanish cruelties and the other of the need for order and discipline in the Caribbean, the policy came to the same thing—intervention.

In April both Houses of the Congress passed a concurrent resolution recognizing Cuban belligerency. It went on to propose that Cleveland should offer Spain assistance in bringing about peace with an independent Cuba. Cleveland ignored the action (if it had been a *joint* resolution, he would have had to recognize it; a *concurrent* resolution did not require presidential notice). There followed even more heated speeches, some of them so provocative that they might well have forced the hand of a weak President. When there was no response from the White House, there was talk of recognizing Cuba. This would have meant war with Spain; and even the excited senators did not go quite that far, even if it had been possible for the Congress to bring the war about without the President's concurrence.

This issue survived the nominating conventions, the campaign and the defeat of the Democratic party in November. Cleveland would still be in the White House until March 4, and being the sort of man he was he did not stop trying to find some solution. He continued to counsel the Spanish that if they would offer the Cubans home rule, they might have peace. But as time passed and he got no response he warned them that the United States was losing patience with bloody but ineffective suppression. There was, he said, a higher obligation than that owed to a friendly Spanish government. He knew that when the Congress met in December he would at once be faced with worse pressures than those of the preceding winter. He was really warning Spain of this probability and at the same time was asking the Congress to allow more time for negotiation.

He got no response. When the Congress met, the Foreign Relations Committee at once took up a resolution to recognize Cuban independence. Senator Sherman, the chairman, told Olney that the committee was determined to approve it. This infuriated Olney after his long and patient struggle for conciliation; and he met the senators on their own ground by making a public statement. He said that such a resolution as was proposed would be only an expression of opinion by the eminent gentlemen who voted for it. The power to recognize Cuba rested solely with the executive.

There were furious responses by the senators, and for a few days the constitutional issue was debated in the press. But the resolution was not passed. After that, until their terms in office ran out, Cleveland and Olney merely temporized with a situation they were unable to improve. But it is possible to guess that if they had stayed in office, with a renewal of power, they would have been able to prevail on Spain to modify its Cuban policy; and if the rebel leaders had been deprived of their American subsidies they might have lost their ability to keep their people in a self-sacrificing mood. Some better arrangement might have been reached than the useless and futile conflict that reached none of the objectives reasonable men could support.

It is arguable, of course, that Cuba would have had a happier future, and the United States far less exasperating trouble, if the ultimate solution had brought Cuba into some close relation to its larger northern neighbor—perhaps like that of Puerto Rico, whose people were destined to prosper and find satisfaction in a free association. But Cleveland did not think of that.

PRINCETON'S NEW BOY.

GROVER (FREE AND HAPPY): "HOORAY, HOORAY, HOORAY, TIGER—SIS—BOOM—AH! PRINCETON!"

Cleveland enters Princeton (*Courtesy of The Firestone Library, Princeton University, Princeton, New Jersey*)

34

THE Clevelands, leaving the White House permanently on March 4, 1897, decided to establish themselves in Princeton. Going back to Buffalo seemed as unpleasant a prospect as it had in 1888. That city had never been forgiven by Cleveland for the exposure and exaggeration of his relationship with the Widow Halpin; he had once said, it will be recalled, that "my home is no longer home." This sad separation from the place where the most active years of his career had been spent deprived him of a satisfaction that means much in the later years of life.

Actually only fifteen years, an amazingly short time for all they contained, had passed since he had become mayor of the city, and his friends there had tried to make him forget the malicious attacks of the clergy abetted by the Buffalo *Telegraph*. They knew, however, that his other grievance was also still alive. When he had become President, largely because he had promised to consider only the public interest and, specifically, to end the era of spoils and favors, they had harassed him unmercifully for jobs and had called him unkind names for forgetting his friends. This had hurt; he could not resume the old relationships.

Return to New York was considered but rejected. Any one of a dozen prominent law firms would have been glad to have him, including the one he had joined in 1887. But he was now nearly sixty years old and an old sixty. For eight years he had labored at his presidential duties; and during the four years between his terms he had worked almost as hard at his practice and at the maneuvering necessary to reelection. Then, too, he had had the serious operation for cancer and a slow recovery. His weight had gone off by a hundred pounds and left him flabby and wrinkled. He was no longer the mountain of vigor he had been some years before.

Princeton drew the family by its attractiveness as a village; it seemed a suitable place for the children to grow up. Perhaps, also, the campus of the university, the friendly members of the faculty and the lively students had something to do with the decision.

It is true that in late years Cleveland had found comfort in the family life Frances had provided. Many vacations had been spent at Gray Gables. Fishing there and occasional hunting excursions up and down the coast provided the recreations he enjoyed most.

It was true also that, although he had left office in a fog of popular disapproval amounting to hatred among the more fanatic Populists, he still had numerous affluent friends. Of these, Commodore Benedict, on whose yacht his operation had been performed, was the most devoted. Because of the approval of these friends, he could have the assurance that he had been right all along. They saw nothing in his career that he ought to regret. At Princeton and at Gray Gables he would be near most of them.

Still, there could be no escaping the lingering shadows of failure, or the sadness of separation from his oldest friends in Buffalo. Another man, Cleveland felt, would not have lost control of the party and allowed it to be stolen by the Populists. True, he could claim to have defended the policies best for the country; and at least one of them—sound money—had been maintained. But about the others no more than temporary successes could be claimed. Especially he had had to leave the Cuban question to a successor who had none of his own stubborn resistance to pressures.

On McKinley's inauguration day, after going with the new President to the ceremony at the Capitol, Cleveland went off on another fishing trip with Captain Robley D. Evans. They had arranged for two weeks on a lighthouse tender in the waters behind Cape Hatteras. He boarded the small ship, lowered himself gratefully into a deck chair and remarked how lucky McKinley was to have had his mother present at his swearing-in. Evans was touched by his evident weariness. The concerns of office had not yet dropped away either; he spoke earnestly about a conversation he had had the day before with McKinley. He had warned the new President about the difficulties he would have in defending the gold standard.

The Family (*Courtesy of The Firestone Library, Princeton University, Princeton, New Jersey*)

Also he had spoken seriously to him about the danger of an unnecessary war with Spain. Evans could see that he would for a long time be ridden by a conscience that would not accept even the stoutest protestations from friends that he had done all any man could do.

Cleveland came back to Princeton after the fishing trip to find the family installed in the new home there and extensive alterations already under way. The house was a large and dignified stone mansion on a quiet street. It had been found for him by Andrew West of the Princeton faculty, whose acquaintance he had made when he had spoken there at the time the old college had celebrated its becoming a university.

West was one of those big men Cleveland liked, perhaps because of their physical resemblance to himself—Daniel Manning and Shan Bissell had been heavyweights too. At any rate the friendship with West and through him his introduction to the community helped enormously in the difficult transition to placid private life from his years at the exciting center of affairs. Presently he accepted an honorary degree, something he had refused twice during his presidency—once from Harvard and once from Princeton. He had said, simply, that he had no qualifications for such an honor. Now in retirement he thought acceptance more seemly—a recognition of service bravely completed.

Before long he had fallen into the routine of the new existence quite comfortably. He was kept busy in the preparation of articles for magazines and speeches to be made before Union League Clubs or other such conservative groups. He wrote painfully, as always, and what he wrote was no more lucid or sparkling than it had ever been. Going over and over it as he did, he seemed only to make it more turgid. But he felt a continuing responsibility to the public. He must write and speak of the nation's problems.

Gradually his unpopularity diminished. He was held in such obvious esteem by eminent members of the bar and leaders of the business community that his failures faded from his mind. He assumed the role of a respected elder statesman and he protected his dignity as he had always done when he had been President.

He accepted some engagements he felt to be seemly. He acted as counselor, and even as an official of an insurance company—

insurance companies were at the moment under investigation for misusing the funds entrusted to them. He was well paid for such work, and, although Presidents still left office with no pension and no assistance, there were no serious financial problems. He had already accumulated a small fortune. Some of it had come from the sale of Oak View (or Red Top) after leaving Washington in 1887; and he had saved something from the prosperity of his later Buffalo years and also from his practice in New York. With some three hundred and fifty thousand dollars entrusted to Commodore Benedict for management, and with the income from articles and counseling, an appropriate establishment could be kept up.

The family was still growing. After his retirement, the three small girls acquired two brothers. There was, however, a devastating loss—that of the oldest girl, Ruth, to a quick infection. The grief was much more painful than it would have been if she had not been so much the center of his long-frustrated affections. Because of it, he could not bear to visit Gray Gables again where the small girl had had her happiest times. It was sold, and after that the family's summers were spent elsewhere in New England.

It is of some interest that he had no desire to go abroad, or even to visit other regions of the United States. He remained, as he had always been, a citizen of the Northeast.

Such public responsibility as he felt still was not drawn off into interference in public affairs except in the most reserved and cautious way. Even the Spanish War and the reelection of the Republicans in 1900 hardly drew any comment from the aging ex-President.

He did, however, develop a most unlikely interest in Princeton's academic management, and the deference of the undergraduates seemed to give him a curious satisfaction. On occasion they respectfully surrounded his porch and asked a few words of recognition. He always obliged.

His closest friend in the academic community, West, was soon made dean of the graduate school. Before long Cleveland himself became a trustee of the university. He attended meetings, read reports and participated in decisions with his customary industrious care. Some time later he helped to select Woodrow Wilson as

Last photograph taken of Grover Cleveland, March 5, 1908 (*Courtesy of The Firestone Library, Princeton University, Princeton, New Jersey*)

President; and then when Wilson offered a somewhat radical program of academic reform and it was opposed by a faction headed by his friend West, he came down hard on the side of traditionalism.

He had no more foresight about Wilson's future than anyone else. That he, a former Democratic President of the United States, was making life as difficult as possible for the next Democratic President was something he never for an instant imagined. What he did know was that Wilson was making trouble for his preferred friends, and it was a simple matter to judge that his own weight ought to be lent to the opposition. The weight was considerable. And Wilson escaped from Princeton into the governorship of New Jersey barely in time to avoid removal from his university office.

When Wilson became governor, however, Cleveland would have been dead for two years. From about 1906, he had been a man whose time in this world was obviously limited. He had a combination of diseases, traceable partly to age, partly to the immoderate strains he had put on his constitution through most of his life. The long spells of intense sedentary work and the heavy weight he had carried around for so long now had the inevitable result.

His last years, when he was confined to bed through the long winters, seem, from his correspondence and from his conversations with friends, to have been ones of contentment with his own contribution to his country. Especially he was more than ever certain that he had acted as the national conscience. He had kept the debtors from cheating their creditors. He had held to the constitutional injunction of maintaining domestic tranquillity, or at least, of restoring it when unruly agitators had threatened the public peace. He had faced other nations in the mantle of national courage and had won their respect. Above all, he had shown how a man whose deepest commitment was to an inner honesty could rise to the highest posts in the people's gift with no other appeal than the externalization of that virtue.

It could be said of him that in this respect he had renovated the national integrity. His limitations lay in the simplicity of that approach. He had not been one of those who had advanced the plans and ideas needed for the age being entered on. He had been merely a good and faithful servant as he had understood the meaning of goodness and faithfulness. He had looked backward to the ministry of the village parsonage, not forward to the wider ministry of national well-being.

What had been on his mind during his last years was made quite plain by his dying words: "I have tried so hard to do right." That was on June 24, 1908.

Index

2 9 2